Florida Keys
Paddling Atlas

Bill and Mary Burnham

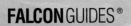

GUILFORD, CONNECTICUT
HELENA, MONTANA

AN IMPRINT OF THE GLOBE PEQUOT PRESS

Benthic Habitat

Hard bottom

Hard bottom with sea grass

Continuous sea grass

Discontinuous sea grass

Tidal flats

Land Cover

Mangrove

Mangrove swamp

Water Depth

| 0 ft | 5 ft | 10 ft | 15 ft | 20 ft | 25 ft | 30 ft | 35 ft | > 40 ft |

———— Major road

———— Minor road

– – – Water channel

1 US highway

5 State highway

905 County road

– – – County boundary

–·–·– Park boundary

〜〜〜 Submerged cable

⊥⊥⊥〜〜 Submerged cable area

Beacon

Bird viewing

Bridge

Campground (primitive)

Campground (commercial)

Campground (public, fee)

Campground (public, no fee)

Can/cylindrical buoy

Caution

Conical buoy

Creek entrance/exit

Day marker

Diving area

End navigation

Fishing hole

General obstruction

Go-to point

Hiking trail

Light

Lighthouse

Lodging

Offshore platform

Off-chart destination

Outfitter

Patch coral

Pile

Point of interest

Put-in (public, fee)

Put-in (public, no fee)

Put-in (kayak only, public, fee)

Put-in (kayak only, public, no fee)

Ranger station

Rest spot

Restrooms

Rock, awash

Rock, covers & uncovers

Shoaling

Snorkeling

Sounding in feet

Swimming area

Tower

Wreck, exposed

Wreck, submerged dangerous

Wreck, submerged non dangerous

Dry Tortugas

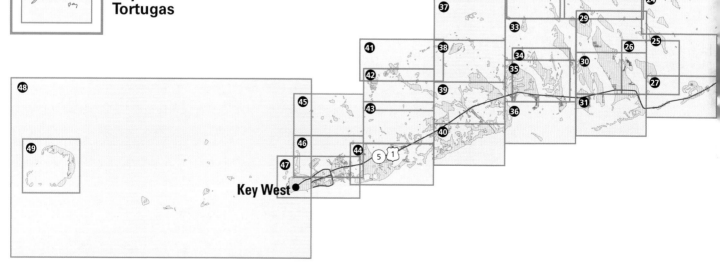

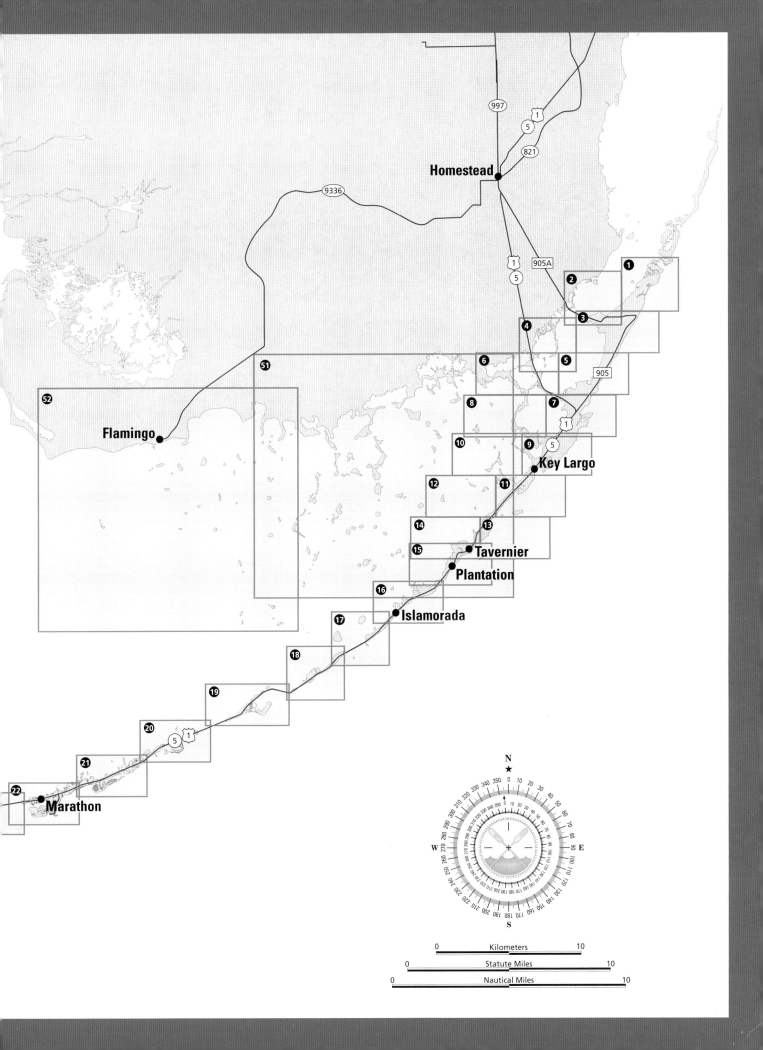

For Sasha

FALCONGUIDES®

Copyright © 2007 Morris Book Publishing, LLC

Photos by Bill and Mary Burnham unless otherwise indicated

Charts by Mapping Specialists © Morris Book Publishing, LLC

Text design by Nancy Freeborn

Library of Congress Cataloging-in-Publication Data is available.
ISBN 978-0-7627-3857-1

Printed in Canada
First Edition/First Printing

Contents

Acknowledgments

Over the course of years spent outdoors, we've learned it's not always about where you go, but who goes with you. There's no greater bonding experience than delving into nature with friends.

We thank Frank Woll, owner of Florida Bay Outfitters (FBO), and his wife, Monica, who helped us in the formative stages of this project. The Florida Keys paddling community owes much to the Wolls' promotion of kayaking and for their work in pioneering the Florida Keys Overseas Paddling Trail.

The FBO crew and entourage paddled with us, critiqued map drafts, provided shelter, and gave advice—solicited and otherwise—over many a pitcher of beer at Upper Crust Pizza. With heartfelt thanks, we recognize Cynthia Boerner, Dave and Lynda Williams, Josh Gregory, Greg Byrd, Colleen Boyle, Robert Findley, Steve Snyder, Melissa Cyr, Sarah Scaruto, Greg Hagbery, Micah Gardner, Joel Beckwith, Jamie Jackson, Rick Bartoli, Christine Clarke, and last, but not least, Mr. Forward Stroke, aka Richie Prado. Other local paddlers provided advice about new routes, in particular Paradise Paddlers' Sharon Alvarado and Dee Bowers, and Lower Keys kayak guide Rob Marrow. Jason Dreuenak of Conch Republic Kayaks took us on our very first Keys paddling trip—an awesome experience from which we clearly have never recovered.

Debra Stucki of Florida Greenway and Trails, and Doug Alderson of Florida Fish and Wildlife Conservation Commission, assisted with numerous technical details relating to the Florida Keys Overseas Paddling Trail. Officials with Florida State Parks, Florida Keys National Marine Sanctuary, Everglades National Park, and the national wildlife refuges of the Lower Keys were always helpful with our questions. We thank the staff and volunteers at Bahia Honda State Park for allowing us to share their camp for several weeks of research. Anne Rice with Monroe County Library helped us with historical photographs, available through the Mile Markers program (www.mile-markers.org).

We thank everyone at Globe Pequot for their perseverance; in particular, Scott Adams, Stephen Stringall, and Jan Cronan. At Mapping Specialists, we thank Don Larson and Brad Butkovich for assisting us along the steep learning curve that is GIS mapping.

Let's go paddling!
Bill and Mary

Welcome

We are paddling offshore of Big Pine in the Lower Keys. It's a clear day, and calm water reflects back the azure sky, forming a shimmering Caribbean-like mirage. Beneath our boats a blue-green field of water frames darker shapes. The water surface ripples like some giant's taut muscular skin. With each stroke we fall inexorably into this living tapestry of sky and water.

Welcome to the Florida Keys, where the ordinary is extraordinary. From mangrove-lined creeks in Key Largo to magnificent frigatebirds soaring above the remote Dry Tortugas, the Keys and surrounding shallow tropical water possess wonders—natural and man-made—unmatched in the continental United States.

In the virtual aquarium beneath a kayak, a southern stingray the size of a car hood lies on the silty bottom off the Barracuda Keys. Beady eyes of young tarpon streak like red neon as they dart through headlamp beams on an after-dark paddle in the Taylor Creek mangroves. Sharks school on the back side of Little Pine Key. Tiny starfish cling to sponges on red mangrove roots through the Dusenbury Grottos. A skinny fish tails across nearshore flats off Dreguez Key, its prey firmly lodged in vice-grip jaws. And minutes after this display of raw nature, a small seahorse, one of the most delicate of creatures, swims past.

With these, and much more, indelibly etched in our memories, we dedicate this atlas to every paddler who seeks his or her own absolute Keys experience.

The Keys

The Florida Keys are a chain of islands that tail south and west off Florida's southeast tip. Archeological evidence of habitation dates back almost 4,000 years. During the Glades Period (500 B.C. through A.D. the 1500s), human habitation intensified and adapted to the water environment. Instead of farming, they fished, hunted turtles, trapped lobsters, and gathered wild plants for subsistence. In precolonial times, turtlers and fishermen from the Bahamas settled the islands intermittently. From the Spanish period came the term *key,* derived from the Spanish *cayo,* which means "small island." English speakers shortened the term to *cay* and pronounced it *key*. In time, the phonetic spelling became accepted usage.

In nature and character, the Keys share much with its Caribbean neighbors. Tropical hardwood hammocks harbor West Indian plants found nowhere else in the United States. In the lee of mangrove islands in the wide, shallow Florida Bay, a virtual painter's palette of bird plumage stands out in stark contrast to the red mangroves' dark foliage. The water is shallow and, under ideal conditions, gin-clear, and small coral heads, sea whips, and the orange, green, and purple sponges make snorkeling a treat.

Add to this the world-famous Keys character. What's to do in the Keys? "Dive, drink, and fish" the old saying goes—to which we modestly add "kayaking." For those who like to end their trip with a libation, it seems a tiki bar is convenient to every launch. Strains of acoustic guitars float out over the water as Keys troubadours add their voice to the island feel.

Photo by WillArts.com

> "Life is pretty good
> when you travel with friends."
>
> —Micah Gardner and Greg Hagbery, *Low on Money, High on Life*

The Atlas

Linked by roads, bridges, and railroads, the Florida Keys remain first and foremost a water world and boater's playground. Every boater needs a good chart, and the *Florida Keys Paddling Atlas* aims to provide just that for paddlers.

Our custom-made charts provide paddlers with the detail they need to find one-of-a-kind areas. Field notes gathered firsthand provide paddling highlights. For quick-glance reference, each map contains latitude and longitude, as well as a letter and number grid. In margin notes, these grid coordinates are labeled as A1, B2, C3, etc.

Other chart features include:

Go-to Points. A GPS-referenced location, shown on the charts as a red number next to a magenta circle. Important Go-to Points are referenced in margin notes. A chart in the appendix lists coordinates for each point.

Off-Chart Destination Cues (D/Cs). A reference to a critical location on adjacent or nearby charts, shown as a labeled arrow positioned near the margin. A majority of Off-Chart D/Cs reference a put-in or a Go-to Point.

Getting There. Launch options for charts where no boat launches appear. On Chart 42, for example, *Getting There* lists three launches and provides map numbers and grid coordinates for each.

Navigation. Route-finding information, including launches, distances, and suggested routes. Navigation notes may also provide straight-line compass bearings and mileage. Distances are estimates and meant for reference only; every route varies depending on ability, weather conditions, and tides.

Additional information is contained in *Cautions* (advice about safety rules, regulations, or hazards), *Alerts* (information not related to personal safety), *Public Lands* (a description of parks and refuges), as well as notes on *Rest Areas, Paddling, Landmarks, Creeks, Nature, Field Notes, Hiking, Snorkeling, Camping, History, Names, Dining, Outfitters, Services,* and miscellaneous information.

The appendix is a critical element of the atlas. In addition to raw data on Go-to Points it contains information on launches, outfitters, camping, lodging, and dining.

U.S. Fish and Wildlife Service

Getting There

U.S. Highway 1 is the main roadway through the Florida Keys. Green markers tick off each mile beginning with Mile Marker 0 in Key West at Truman Avenue (US 1) and Whitehead Street. Mile Marker 126 is just south of Florida City. People in the Keys give directions in this way: Mrs. Mac's Kitchen, MM 99.5 B/S (B/S = bayside), or, Bahia Honda State Park, MM 38.6 O/S (O/S = oceanside). In the Lower Keys, bayside is also referenced as gulfside (G/S).

From Florida City, there are two routes to the Keys. "The Stretch" is an 18-mile causeway that carries US 1 to Key Largo. At the Jewfish Creek Bridge (MM 107), travelers cross onto Key Largo and officially enter the Keys. An alternate route follows Card Sound Road from Florida City to Key Largo. (There is a toll at the Card Sound Bridge). South of the private community of Ocean Reef, Card Sound Road turns right and continues as County Road 905 to US 1 in Key Largo. All mileage cues for Card Sound Road are referred to as "C" and measured from the intersection with US 1 in Key Largo. For example, a launch at C 4.7 is 4.7 miles north of that intersection.

And the 110-mile Florida Keys Overseas Paddling Trail extends from Key Largo to Key West; www.dep.state.fl.us/gwt.

Upper Keys

What surprises await a paddler in the Upper Keys?

An overgrown mangrove tunnel that empties into a quiet lake behind Card Point.

Hundreds of upside-down jellyfish nestling in a sea grass meadow near Rattlesnake Key.

Great white and tri-colored herons stalking about grass flats and mangroves in Little Basin, their silhouettes reflected in the glassy water.

A web of creeks throughout John Pennekamp Coral Reef State Park.

A mangrove sanctuary in Dusenbury Creek.

Green-blue waters that stretch to the horizon beyond the Swash Keys.

A hidden lake inside Shell Key.

Old tombstones and cisterns on Indian Key.

When southbound traffic passes over Jewfish Creek near the south end of the 18-mile Stretch, or over high-arching Card Sound Bridge, they cross an imaginary line. Behind them, mainland United States. Ahead of them, the Florida Keys, 100-plus miles of coral rock islands linked by a highway and forty-three bridges, bounded by the shallow Caribbean-like waters of Florida Bay and the Florida reef, North America's only coral barrier reef.

Mainland or island? At first glance, it's difficult to tell in the Upper Keys. Key Largo's four-lane highway and shopping centers give it a bit of the mainland feel. A quick stop at the Caribbean Club, setting for scenes from the 1948 movie *Key Largo,* dispels such notions. Off the bar's back deck, Blackwater Sound laps up against a boat dock. Soaking in the atmosphere, listening to clattering wild parrots that flock from one palm to the next, you might spy a small boat on the water moving slowly toward the far line of trees. It is a kayaker, heading out to explore Dusenbury Creek.

Within an hour of parking, you've slipped into a quiet creek. A red mangrove canopy overhead creates a winding tunnel. Sunlight dapples a leaf here, a spot of water there. Down into the clear water, you see sponges, and fish swim away from your boat.

Mainland? What mainland? Welcome to the Keys.

Geologists will tell you that Soldier Key, offshore of Miami, is the northernmost island in the Florida Keys chain. Our atlas coverage for the Upper Keys begins a few miles south, at Key Largo, the first of the inhabited keys. From here to Bahia Honda Key, the principal islands are underlain with Key Largo limestone—essentially the dead skeletons of ancient coral formations—covered with a thin layer of soil. In the Marvin D. Adams Cut between Blackwater Sound and Largo Sound, millennia of dead coral skeletons are visible in

hewn-out walls. Farther offshore, divers and snorkelers throng to swim among the living version of these marine animals. The famous coral reef is a major tourism draw for the Keys, but they are beyond the reach of recreational kayakers.

If divers come to the Upper Keys for the offshore coral reef tract, kayakers come for clear, shallow nearshore waters. Florida Bay and its countless mangrove islands cover nearly 1,000 acres between the Everglades and the Keys. In this large estuary, freshwater from the Everglades mixes with ocean water pushed in by the tide. Water depth averages 5 to 7 feet, and long sandy mud banks criss-cross this shallow pool, forming a patchwork of tiny lakes or lagoons. The hundreds of mangrove islands are critical bird foraging and nesting grounds. Except for two specially designated islands, landing or wading within 100 feet of any mangrove island in Florida Bay is prohibited within Everglades National Park, which encompasses all of the bay north of the Intracoastal Waterway.

Backcountry anglers rave about the quality sight-fishing in Florida Bay, but it's the grass beds that hold the key to this fragile ecosystem's continued viability. Florida Bay contains one of the largest concentrated masses of this subaquatic vegetation in the United States. The thick meadows of turtle, shoal, and manatee grass shelter and sustain young shrimp and fish. They also provide wading birds and manatees with habitat and foraging grounds. The grass beds are highly threatened, affected by man-induced changes in the flow of freshwater from the Everglades (i.e., flood control) and damage by boat propellers. Paddlers who want a more comprehensive description of the grass meadows of Florida Bay are encouraged to read *The Florida Keys Environmental Story,* available at local outfitters and bookstores.

Sheltered paddling on the oceanside is a distinguishing feature of the Upper Keys, one kayakers will find less frequently as they head into the Middle and Lower Keys regions. The Upper Keys' string of oceanside islands begins with Rattlesnake and El Radabob Keys, replete with small mangrove creeks and tunnels. Farther south, Rodriguez, Dove, and Tavernier Keys stand alone, surrounded by sea grass meadows and a white sand bottom that, on clear days, reflect the cloudless blue sky.

The dangerous business of salvaging ships that wrecked on the reef—known as "wrecking"—and an Indian massacre are two hallmarks in the history of Indian Key. This small lump of coral rock has figured prominently in Upper Keys history and lore. A one-time seat of Dade County, it is now a state park, as is nearby Lignum-vitae Key, where there's evidence of an Indian burial ground. Landing is permitted on both islands (use kayak landing/launch areas, not the government docks), and rangers provide tours twice daily, Thursday through Monday. On Lignumvitae there's a grassy area for picnicking, a composting toilet, the 1919 Matheson historic house museum, and a nature trail through the virgin forest. Beware the mosquitoes.

With viable paddle spots on both sides of the Upper Keys, kayakers have options. If winds are stiff from the north and west, there is likely a sheltered spot on oceanside. Likewise, a strong southeast wind can make bayside paddling a breeze. Channels between bay and oceanside are found on Key Largo at MM 103.4 (Marvin D. Adams Cut); in Islamorada at MM 91 (Tavernier Creek); MM 85.5 (Snake Creek); MM 84 (Whale Harbor Bridge); and MM 79, MM 78, and MM 77 (Teatable Relief, Indian Key Channel, and Lignumvitae Channel).

The Upper Keys is the region of North American crocodiles and roseate spoonbills. North Key Largo, known predominantly for the Ocean Reef Club, contains two of the Upper Keys' most significant nature and wildlife preserves. Within Crocodile Lake National Wildlife Refuge, more than one hundred of this ancient reptilian live and breed. The Upper Keys and the southern Everglades are their only habitat in North America. Like the bald eagle, the crocodile has rebounded from near extinction and is now being studied for delisting as an endangered species. Steamboat Creek, off Card Sound Road, is one spot paddlers can put in within the refuge, although chances of seeing a crocodile are slim. Despite their public perception as man-eating monsters, North American crocodiles are a shy bunch. Sightings in the wild are rare; more likely, a paddler will notice tail drags where the animal climbs up and down muddy banks.

North Key Largo also features the largest West Indian hardwood hammock in the continental United States, within Dagney Johnson Key Largo Hammock Botanical State Park. Trees like the Bahama strongbark and gumbo-limbo (the "tourist tree") are among a host of hardwoods that recall the forests of the Caribbean. White-crowned pigeons rely on the milky juice of the poisonwood fruit to survive, especially during breeding season. The wild lime and torchwood are host trees for the federally endangered Schaus swallowtail butterfly, a brown-black specimen with yellow markings, whose range is restricted to this park and a few other islands of Biscayne Bay. This park is all the more special considering it was once the target of development on the scale of Ocean Reef.

Remember that imaginary line? It's been a few hours since we crossed it and slipped into the quiet of a mangrove creek. Perhaps a manatee has gently bumped the underside of your kayak or poked its gray snout and rough whiskers out of the water. Maybe you've been startled by the sudden "whoosh" of a stingray or shark swimming away.

What's certain is you've never paddled in a place quite like the Keys.

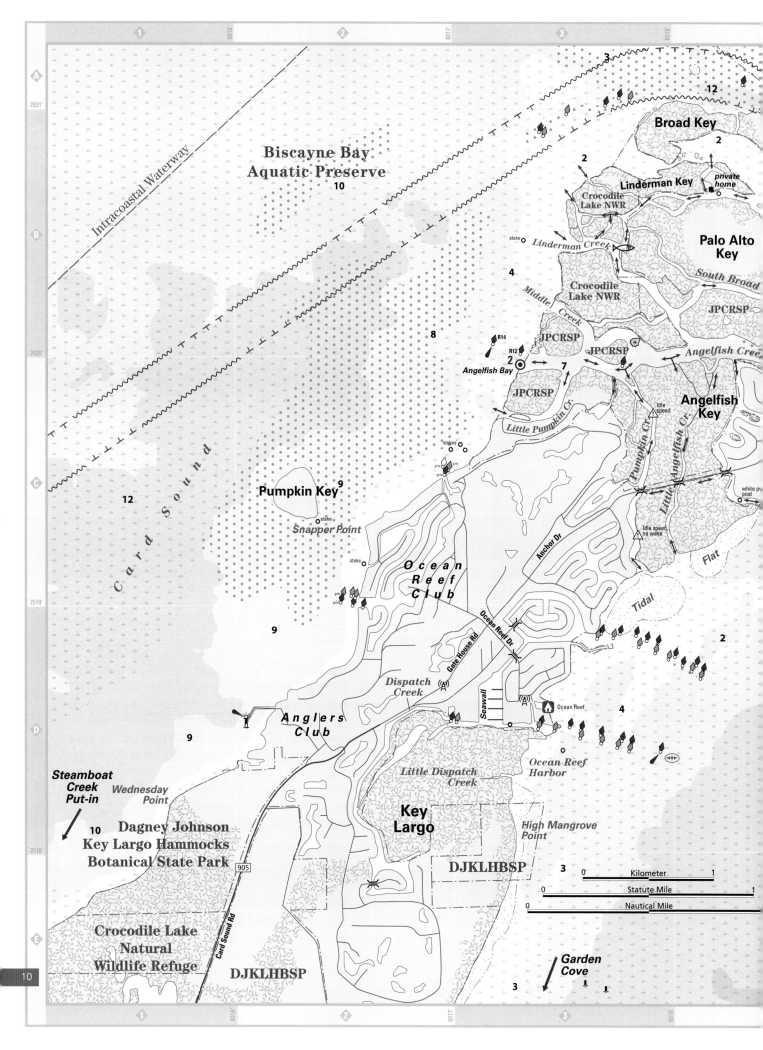

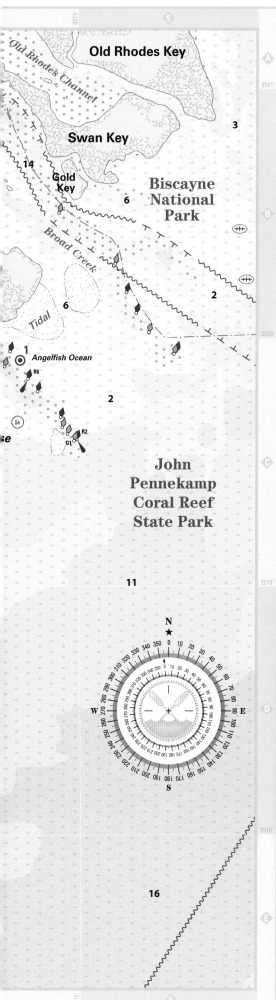

01 Angelfish Creek

Go-to Points: 1 (Angelfish Ocean);
2 (Angelfish Bay)
Off-Chart D/Cs: Steamboat Creek Put-in;
Garden Cove
Caution: The Ocean Reef Club enforces a members-only policy on all home canals within its community. Respect their rules.

During crocodile nesting season, March through October, there is a no-access shoreline buffer of 100 feet around the entire Crocodile Lake National Wildlife Refuge. The rest of the year anything above mean high water is off-limits. In addition, all canals within the refuge are off-limits at all times.

Getting There: Angelfish Creek is a 5-mile paddle north from the Steamboat Creek put-in, Chart 2, D5.

Public Land: Angelfish Key, Palo Alto Key, and a few of the smaller islands north of Ocean Reef fall within John Pennekamp State Park and Crocodile Lake National Wildlife Refuge.

Paddling: Angelfish Creek (C3, C4) links the Atlantic Ocean and Card Sound (the next pass-through between ocean and bay is 17 miles south at the Marvin D. Adams Cut). Expect heavy motorboat activity on weekends and holidays.

Kayakers can avoid motorboats by using Little Pumpkin Creek (C3). A tight mangrove tunnel branches south off Little Pumpkin and empties into a private boat basin. Do not paddle through the basin; turn around and retrace your path.

A canal (C3) runs under the bridge from Ocean Reef to Sunrise Cay. Threading the bridge pilings offers shade on hot, sunny days. This canal also makes possible shorter loops on Little Angelfish and Pumpkin Creeks.

Small mangrove creeks, some no wider than a kayak, branch off Pumpkin and Little Angelfish Creeks. Most dead-end, but adventurous explorers will find a barely passable creek beginning at coordinates N25°19.950' W80°16.150' that moves south and rejoins Pumpkin Creek.

Grass flats bayside of Linderman Key and the small islands adjacent attract anglers (B3).

Landmark: The wealthy and exclusive Ocean Reef Club (C2) has anchored Key Largo's northern tip since Minnesota developer Morris Baker bought a fish camp and surrounding land on Dispatch Creek in 1945. Within 11 years there were home canals and docks, an inn, a gas station, and an airport. Private homes soon followed. In 1993 its members bought the development from then-owner/developer Carl Linder and the American Financial Corporation.

History: Incorporated in 1955, the city of North Key Largo was proposed on 1,500 acres south of the Anglers Club, but the land was never cleared nor buildings raised. In the early 1970s, developers proposed single family homes, marinas, hotels, and health spas. Again, nothing materialized. In 1975, the state of Florida assumed control of growth in Monroe County as a way of checking rampant development. In 2003, the incorporated North Key Largo was voided, officially ending a municipality that only existed on paper.

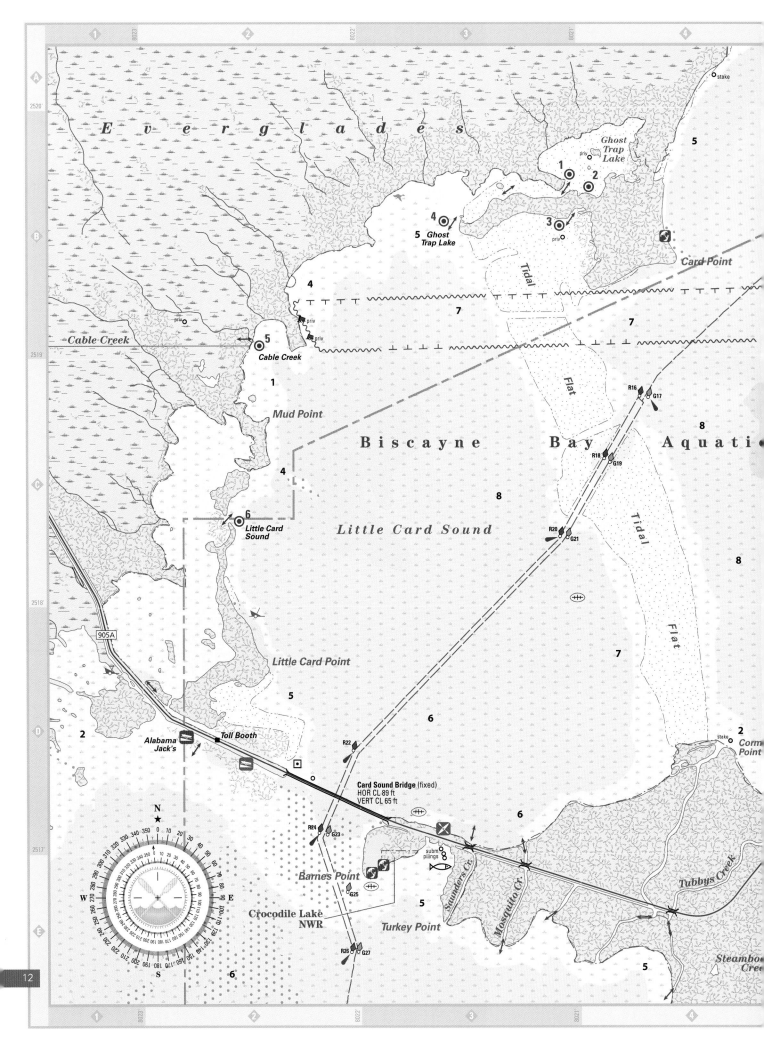

E v e r g l a d e s

Ghost Trap Lake

1

2

priv

4

3

priv

5 *Ghost Trap Lake*

Card Point

4

priv
priv

Tidal

7

7

Cable Creek

priv

5

Cable Creek

1

Mud Point

Flat

R16
G17

8

B i s c a y n e   B a y   A q u a t i c

R18
G19

4

5

8

6

Little Card Sound

R20
G21

8

L i t t l e   C a r d   S o u n d

Tidal

Little Card Point

5

7

905A

Flat

6

2

R22

Alabama Jack's

Toll Booth

2 Corm
Point

stake

Card Sound Bridge (fixed)
HOR CL 89 ft
VERT CL 65 ft

6

N
★

350 0 10
340 20
330 30
320 40
310 50
300 60
290 70
280 80
270 W   E 90
260 100
250 110
240 120
230 130
220 140
210 150
200 160
190 180 170

R24
G23

subm
pilings

Barnes Point

G25

5

Saunders Cr.

Mosquito Cr.

Tubbys Creek

W   E

*Crocodile Lake
NWR*

5

Turkey Point

S

R26 G27

6

Steamboat
Creek

5

Go-to Points: 1–3; 4 (Ghost Trap Lake);
5 (Cable Creek); 6 (Little Card Sound);
7 (Steamboat North)

Off-Chart D/Cs: Angelfish Creek

Caution: During crocodile nesting season, March through October, a no-access buffer extends 100 feet off the shoreline of Crocodile Lake NWR. The rest of the year, anything above mean high water, as well as the canals within the refuge, are off-limits at all times.

Paddling: A sand beach marks high ground on the north side of Card Point (B4). A fire ring, trash pail, and platforms in the Australian pines indicate camping activity; however, it is

Ryan Hagerty, U.S. Fish & Wildlife Service

not known if this is legally permitted. Look for juvenile sharks in shallow water off the point.

A set of stakes in the water just south of Card Point mark where commercial spongers anchor their fresh catch. Paddlers may see large net bags laden with sponges tied to each stake.

Nicknamed for the abandoned crab traps,

Ghost Trap Lake (B3, B4) is an Upper Keys paddling secret. Most charts indicate a wide entrance from the south, but this is now overgrown with red mangroves. Go-to 4 (Ghost Trap Lake) is a prop channel barely deep enough for a skiff. Go-to 3 marks a rewarding kayak-only route through a mangrove swamp and canopied mangrove tunnel. The lake's shallow water and remote location—4 miles from the put-in on Card Sound Road—makes this a high-value bird-viewing spot.

Explore the man-made 1.3-mile (2.6 round-trip) Cable Creek (B2) around high tide only. The entrance, Go-to 5 (Cable Creek), is hidden by a large mangrove island. The creek's east-west path seems to have been created when a utility laid an underwater cable. By the time the creek runs out of water, Card Sound Road is within earshot, but not accessible.

Go-to 6 (Little Card Sound) (C2) is within easy distance of the Card Sound Boat Ramp. Roseate spoonbills and manatees have been spotted in the shallow, sheltered pockets of water and nearshore mangrove islands.

Landmarks: The original Card Sound Bridge, built in 1927, was a wooden span with a swing bridge for passing boat traffic. It burned in 1944, and for the next 25 years, residents of the north shore of Card Sound lived an unfettered, isolated existence. A few fish camps and houseboats operated there, along with the funky watering hole Alabama Jack's. In 1969 the current 65-foot-tall toll bridge opened and became a landmark for miles around. A bridge of similar scope is being constructed on US 1 over Jewfish Creek (Chart 7, A2).

Alabama Jack's (D2) open-air restaurant and canal-side bar was established by Jack Stratham. This is a popular "first-stop" for tourists heading to the Keys, as well as bikers and boaters and manatees (the latter are in the water, not at the bar!).

Go-to Points: 1 (Steamboat North);
2 (Steamboat South)
Off-chart D/Cs: Pumpkin Creek; Garden Cove;
Jewfish Creek
Paddling: Six creeks run through the
mangroves east of Card Sound Bridge. The
largest, Steamboat Creek, links Card Sound and
Barnes Sound and is used by motorboats. A
half-mile south of the Steamboat Creek Bridge
put-in (A4), boaters encounter relic bridge

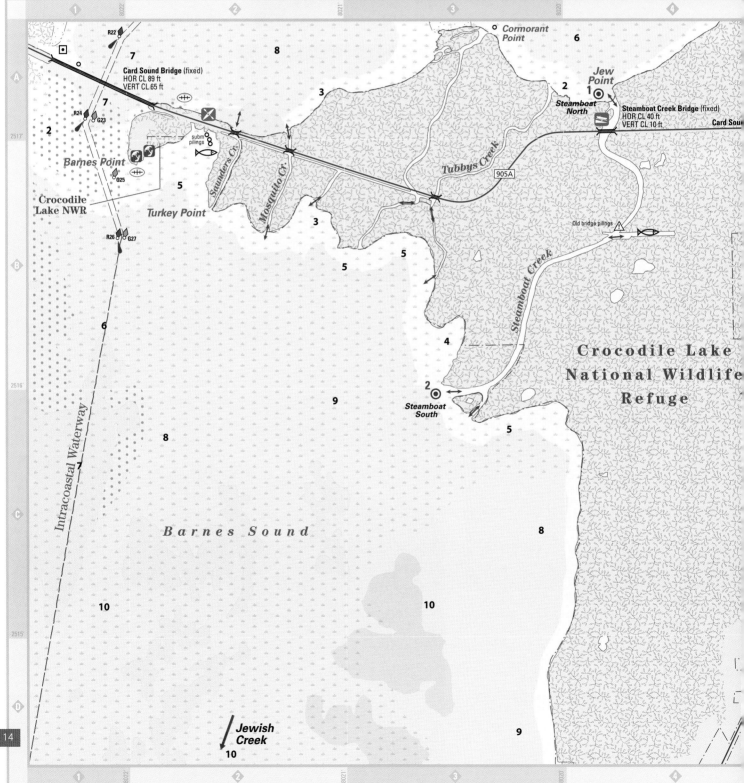

pilings from old Card Sound Road; the adjacent roadbed was torn up and made into habitat for the American crocodile.

Off Tubbys Creek south of where it flows beneath Card Sound Road (B3) a narrow mangrove tunnel runs west beneath full canopy of tall mangroves. Look for schooling mullet at its west end.

At low tide, wading birds work shallow grass beds between Turkey Point and Barnes Point (B2) for their diet of small fish and crustaceans.

Landmarks: Miami's booming growth, the Cuban missile crisis, drug smuggling: A small island—just a pile of rocks, really—lays claim to having a small role in each. The island (B6) was built by the military as a place to off-load dynamite, which was then transported to the mainland via Card Sound Road. The U.S. military built a Nike Missile Radar Tracking Station nearby during the Cuban missile crisis, and that base remained active until 1979. In the 1980s the island's remote location made it a

convenient dumping point for drugs being smuggled into south Florida. The state park service has removed a jetty that linked the island to the mainland, restoring natural water flow.

Nature: Least terns, the smallest North American tern and a threatened species in Florida, may nest on Dynamite Island (B6) May through September. Monitoring is hindered by the island's remote location and disturbances by people who land on it.

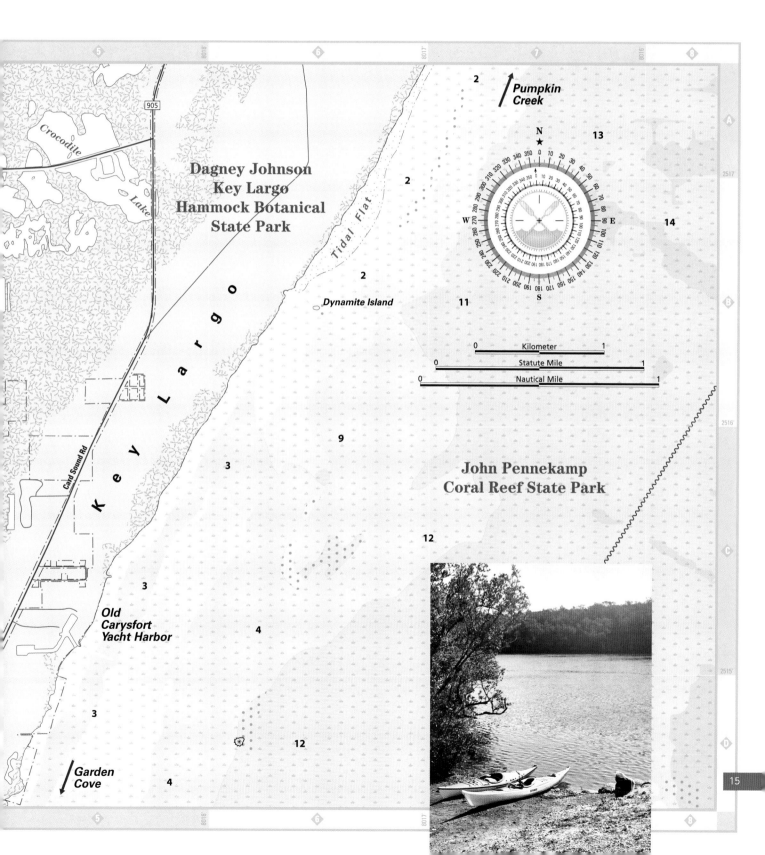

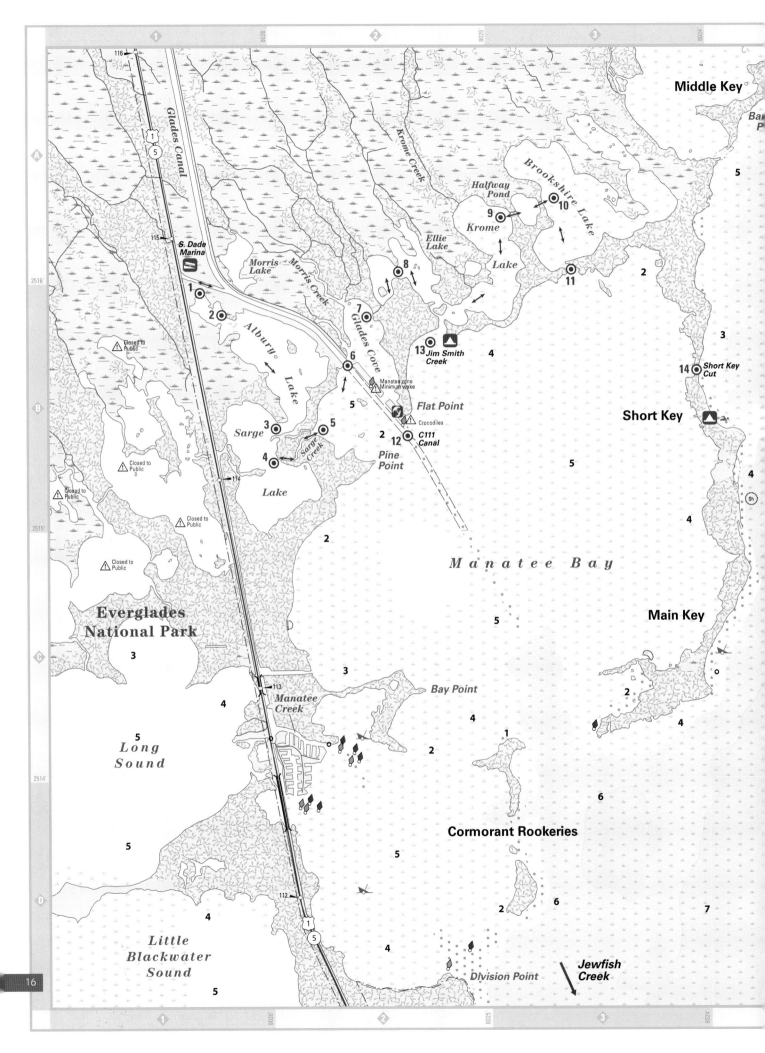

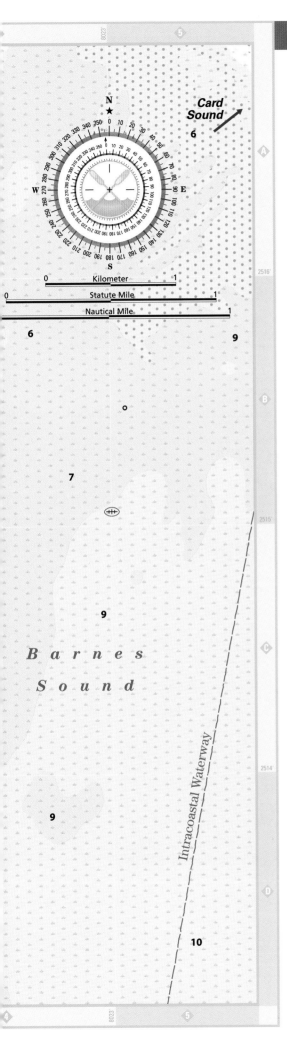

Card Sound

Kilometer
0   1

Statute Mile
0   1

Nautical Mile
0   1

Barnes Sound

Intracoastal Waterway

Go-to Points: 1–11; 12 (C111 Canal); 13 (Jim Smith Creek); 14 (Short Key Cut)

Off-Chart D/Cs: Jewfish Creek; Card Sound

Caution: South Dade Marina is a private marina, with a launch fee. Closed Tuesday and Wednesday; call (305) 247–8730. Alert staff if you would like to leave a car overnight.

Paddling: Morris Creek (B2) leads north from Glades Cove into Morris Lake, a swampy backwater. It is easy to lose your bearings in these conditions, so bring some means of marking your passage.

When a north wind kicks up, look for shelter in small bays and creeks along the Manatee Bay Trail (B2, B3). White PVC pipes mark key turns along a 5.5-mile trail, as do our Go-tos 6–11. After a heavy storm, trail markers may be missing or moved. Also, marker 8 at the east end of Halfway Pond is overgrown by small clump of red mangroves, and is not visible from marker 9.

The 2.5-mile Windy Day Trail (B1, B2) works mangroves and lakes southwest of the Glades Canal. The highlight, Sarge Creek, offers pretty paddling under canopied mangroves. The trail begins at a cut in the red mangroves, 300 feet south of the South Dade Marina put-in. Emerging from this cut, bear southeast 120 degrees, paddle around a point, and scan the water ahead for a white PVC post, marker 3 (Go-to 2). For additional guidance, use Go-tos 3–5.

The aptly named Lost Trail (B1) begins at the same break in the mangrove as the Windy Day Trail. Where the latter takes a southeast bearing from the break, Lost Trail heads due south into a mangrove swamp. Old PVC pipe markers lure you farther and farther into a maze of red mangrove sprouts, clumps, and islands. When you've had enough, take a due-north heading and return to the marina.

Landmark: The 18-mile US 1 causeway from Florida City to Key Largo is known locally as "The Stretch." It follows the abandoned Florida East Coast Railway right-of-way. A major construction project will widen the road and accommodate road shoulders and a concrete median to prevent head-on collisions. The costly and controversial project is scheduled for completion in 2009. In the short term, travel on the Stretch will remain problematic. For updates, visit www.fla-keys.com.

Camping: A primitive campsite is on Short Key (B4) 3 miles from the South Dade Marina put-in. Also, a small clearing on the shoreline at the entrance of Jim Smith Creek (B2) can accommodate two tents.

Go-to Point: 1 (Jewfish Creek)
Off-Chart D/Cs: Garden Cove; Steamboat Creek; Pumpkin Creek
Caution: A no-access shoreline buffer of 100 feet in the Crocodile Lake NWR protects nesting crocodiles March through October. *This boundary is strictly enforced along inland canals north of Cove Point.* Throughout the refuge, land above mean high water is off-limits all year. All canals within the refuge are off-limits at all times.

Public Land: The 6,700-acre Crocodile Lake National Wildlife Refuge protects habitat for the American crocodile along Barnes Sound and lower Card Sound. Nearly decimated by hide-seeking hunters, the reptile was placed on the endangered list in 1975, when numbers declined to a few hundred. Today there are perhaps up to 1,000 throughout the Keys. Everglades National Park marks their northernmost habitat, and fully half of the breeding population is found in the lakes and bays north of Long Sound. The refuge's tropical hardwood hammocks also harbor the Key Largo

woodrat, the Key Largo cotton mouse, and the only federally endangered insect in Florida, the Schaus swallowtail butterfly. There is a chance of seeing the latter at the butterfly garden at the refuge headquarters on Card Sound Road (CR 905), 1.8 miles from US 1 in Key Largo (D3).

Nature: White-crowned pigeons live and nest on mangrove islands in Florida Bay, but their primary diet is fruit from poisonwood and other tropical hardwood trees. Dagney Johnson Key Largo Hammock (DJKLH) Botanical State Park, which protects land oceanside of Card Sound Road, contains the largest stand of tropical

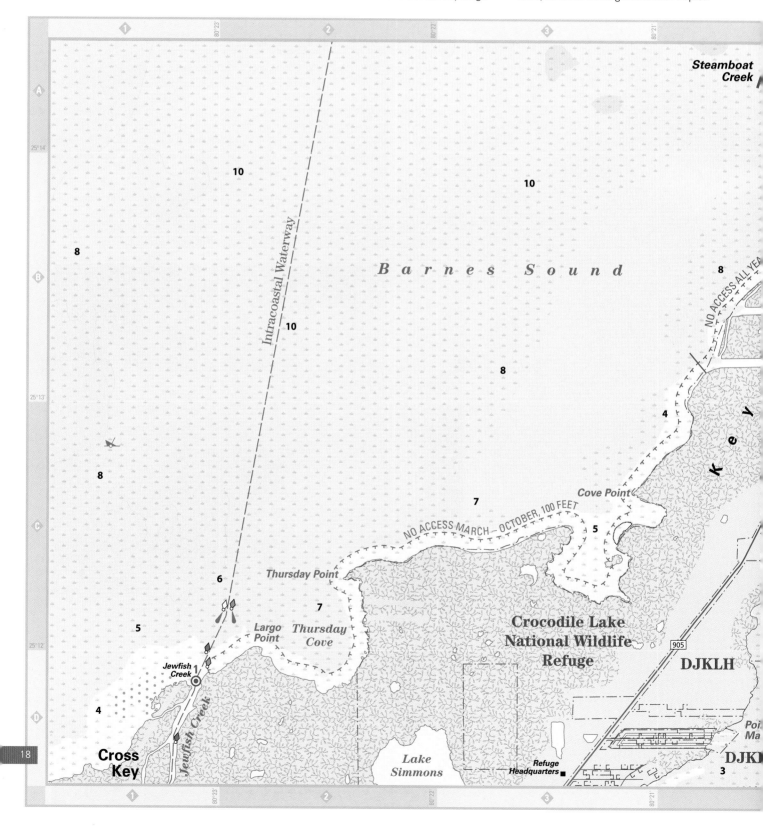

hardwoods in the continental United States, making it a critical link to preserving this Florida threatened species.

The American crocodile is not the man-eating monster known to other parts of the world, like Africa. In fact, the American croc is less aggressive than the alligator, which is common throughout Florida (except in the Keys). The croc has a more tapered snout, and the fourth tooth of the lower jaw shows when its mouth is closed. It's unlikely you'll get close enough to notice this, however. These reptiles are so shy, females have been known to abandon nests after just one disturbance.

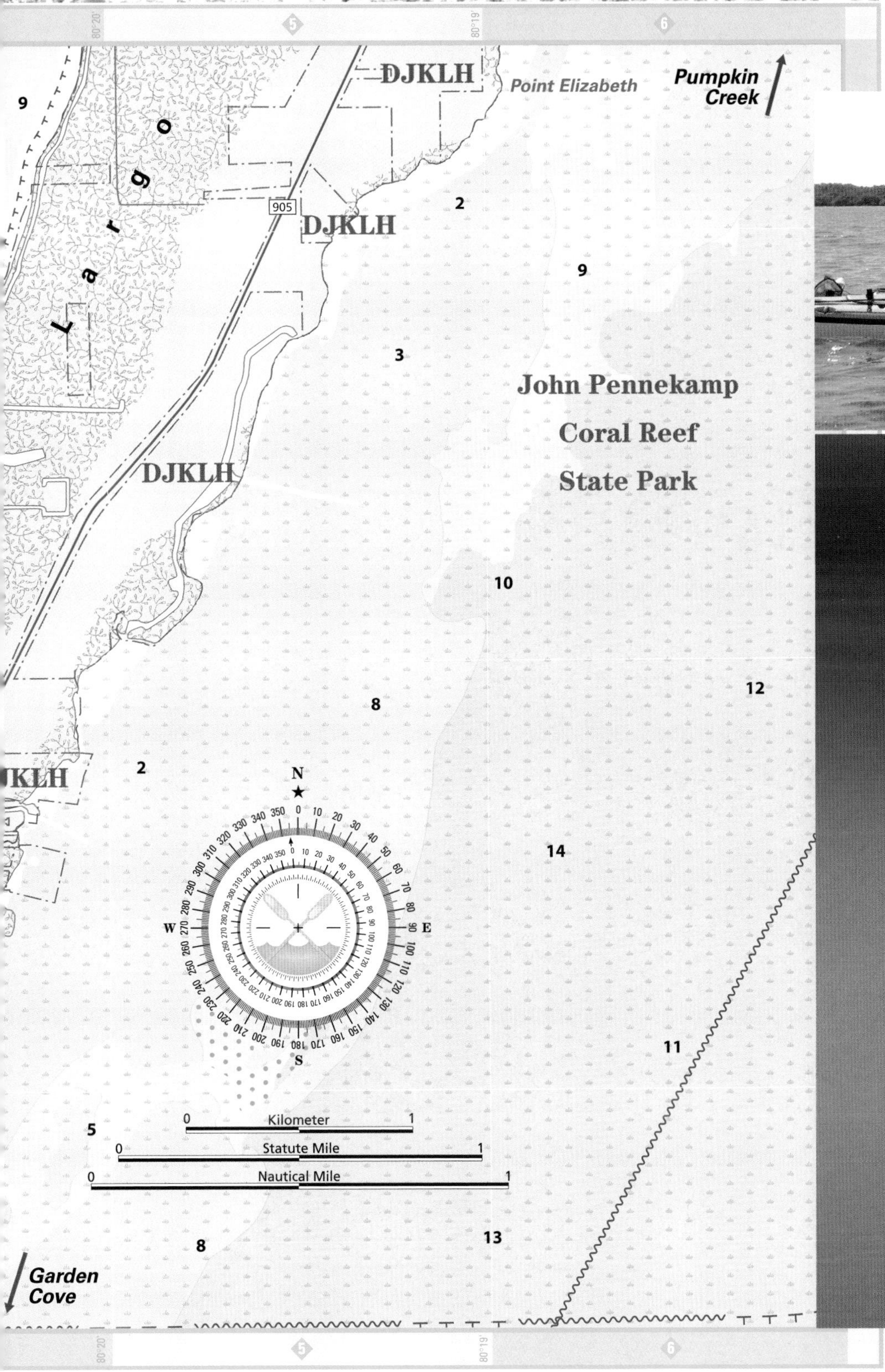

DJKLH
Point Elizabeth
Pumpkin Creek

9

905 DJKLH
2

9

DJKLH
3

John Pennekamp
Coral Reef
State Park

DJKLH

10

12

8

KLH 2

14

N

W E

S

11

5

	0	Kilometer	1
	0	Statute Mile	1
	0	Nautical Mile	1

8 13

Garden Cove

Go-to Points: 1–3; 4 (Blackwater Pass); 5 (Long Sound Pass)

Off-Chart D/Cs: Boggies North; Boggies South; Jewfish Creek

Public Land: Little Blackwater and Long Sounds fall within Everglades National Park. There is no public access into streams or bays on the mainland for protection of crocodiles and manatees.

Paddling: Shell Creek (C2) is a key pass-through between Long Sound and Florida Bay. Portions flow beneath a shady mangrove tunnel. A 16-mile loop from Jewfish Creek is possible using Shell Creek and the Boggies.

We nicknamed Railroad Creek (C6) for the old wooden pilings, some still visible, that once supported Henry Flagler's Overseas Railroad. Notice where single mangrove shoots grow from the center of a piling. If successful, these

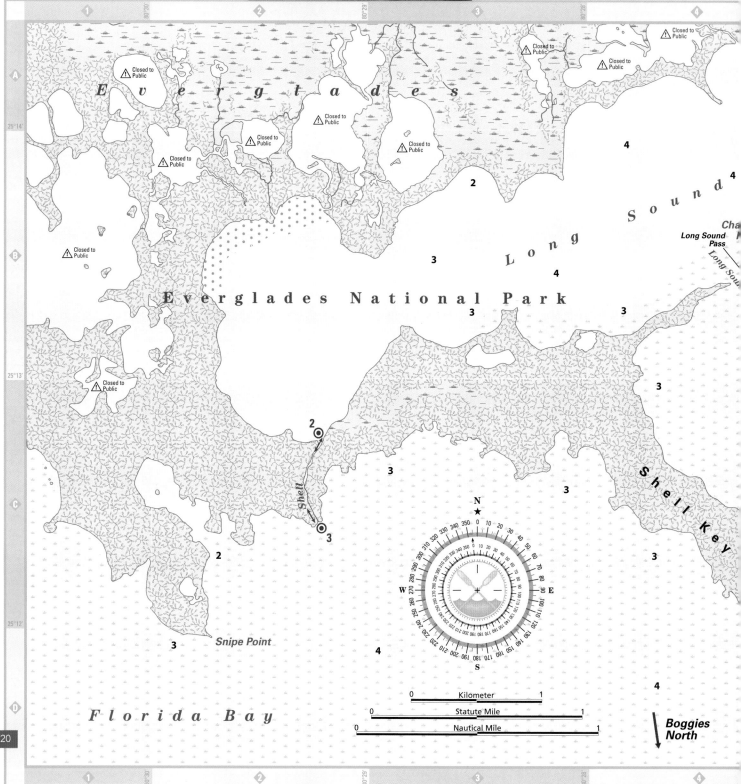

pioneers will form a clump, then a small island. In time, the tree will swallow nearby pilings—much like the islands that now separate sets of pilings.

Despite difficult passage, an unnamed mangrove creek northeast of Blackwater Pass (C6) is more than worth the effort. Prepare for pushing your boat over downed logs and ducking under low branches. Some branches show signs of cutting, but it's been a while since anyone has pruned.

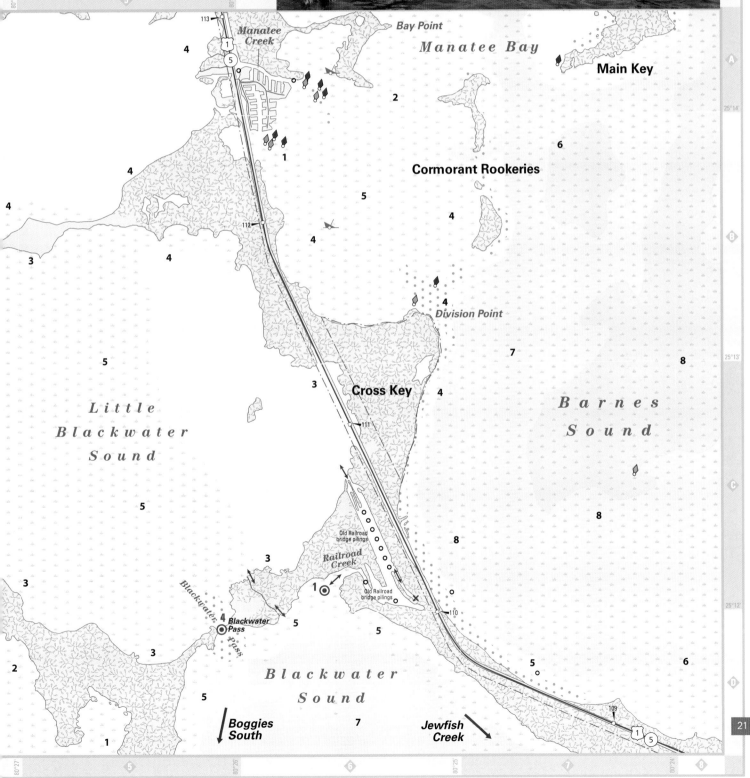

Manatee Creek

Bay Point

Manatee Bay

Main Key

Cormorant Rookeries

Division Point

Little Blackwater Sound

Cross Key

Barnes Sound

Old Railroad bridge pilings

Railroad Creek

Old Railroad bridge pilings

Blackwater Pass

Blackwater Pass

Blackwater Pass

Blackwater Sound

Boggies South

Jewfish Creek

Go-to Points: 1–8; 9 (Jewfish Creek); 10 (Rattlesnake)

Off-Chart D/Cs: Boggies South; Adams Cut; South Sound Creek; Dusenbury Creek

Caution: Garden Cove and The Meadow may be impassable at low tide. Astute paddlers may discern a low-tide channel between the Garden Cove put-in to Rattlesnake Key (B4, C4). Otherwise, use the boat channel to reach Rattlesnake Key.

Public Land: John Pennekamp Coral Reef State Park landholdings include El Radabob Key and mangrove swamps adjacent to Taylor Creek. Rattlesnake Key is a private inholding of the park. Dagney Johnson Key Largo Hammocks (DJKLH) Botanical State Park extends north of the Garden Cove put-in. Paddlers may enter the Port Bougenville Canal, which is marked by pilings across the entrance.

Paddling: Use Taylor Creek (C3) to avoid full-speed motorboat traffic between Largo Sound and Garden Cove. The creek clocks in just shy of 2 miles long, but myriad mangrove creek options can lengthen this journey into a full day's paddle. Of note, at the north end, are two narrow creeks that intertwine and form the Figure Eights (C3).

Near Largo Sound, the Taylor Creek mangroves (D2) form a variety of small creek options for paddlers who don't mind tight squeezes, overhanging branches, and the back paddling that comes from an occasional wrong turn. Go-tos 5 and 8 provide entrance and exit guidance.

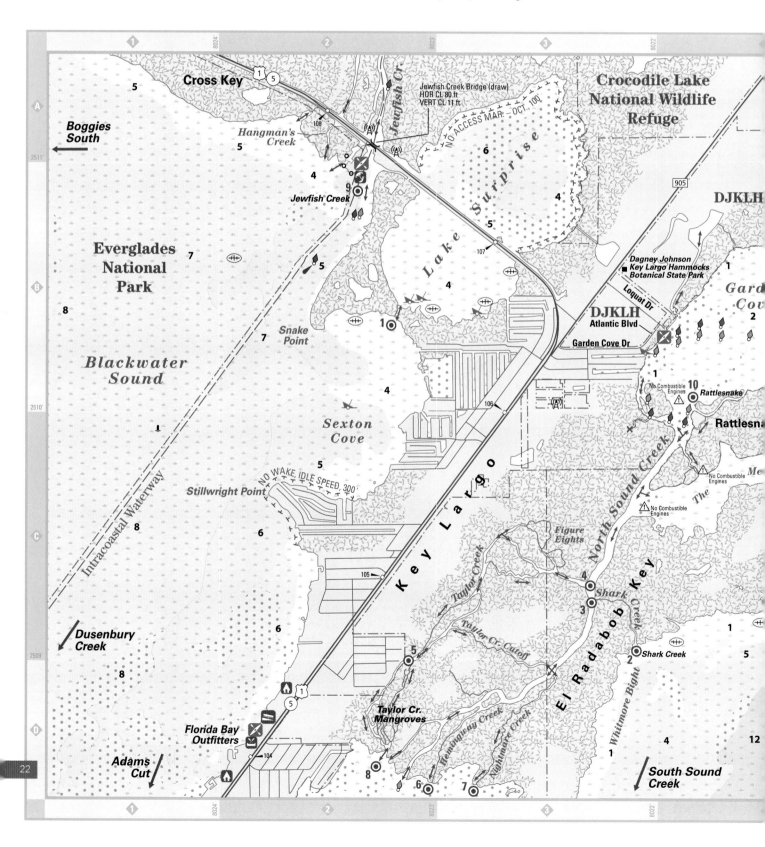

Hemingway and Nightmare Creeks thread long, windy routes through El Radabob. Fish shelter in the undercut mangrove banks on Hemingway; through Nightmare, the webs of spiny orb weavers stretch about head-high across the creek.

Landmarks: The Caribbean Club (D2) next door to FBO is a great place to end a trip with a sunset toast. A few scenes of the 1948 Humphrey Bogart/Lauren Bacall film *Key Largo* were filmed at the hotel, which subsequently burned and morphed into this bar adored by locals. It has been operated by the same family since 1961, and the walls are covered with memorabilia from the film.

Lake Surprise (B2) got its name during the rerouting of US 1 in the 1940s. The half-mile-wide inland lake hadn't shown up on previous land surveys. Workers hacking their way through mangroves discovered the body of water—hence the name. The soft bottom wouldn't support a trestle bridge, so it took 15 months to build a causeway across.

Snorkeling: A partially submerged concrete barge (B5), 1.7 miles east of the Garden Cove put-in, attracts large, colorful fish. The nearshore bottom habitat off Upper Sound Point (B4, B5) contains red calcareous algae. This underwater plant secretes calcium carbonate into its tissue. When it dies, the

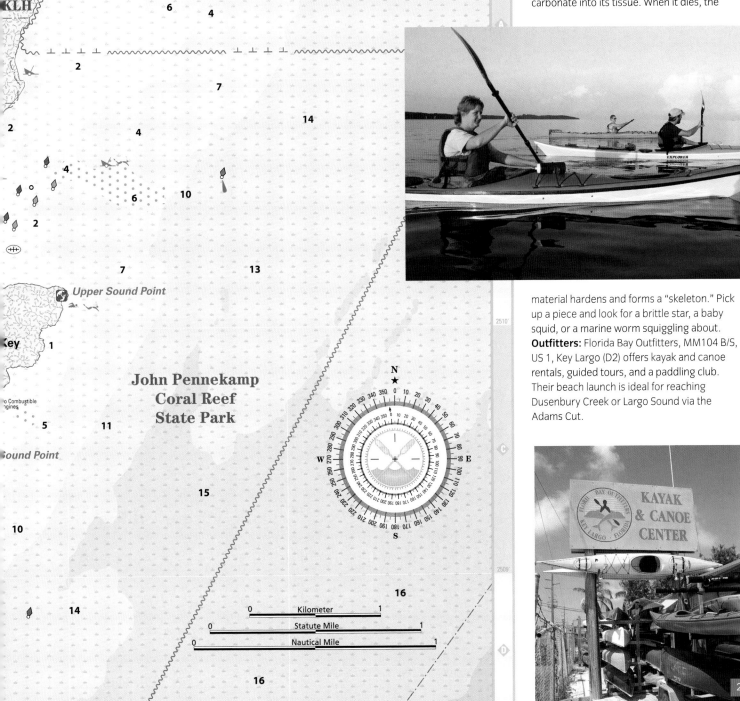

material hardens and forms a "skeleton." Pick up a piece and look for a brittle star, a baby squid, or a marine worm squiggling about.

Outfitters: Florida Bay Outfitters, MM104 B/S, US 1, Key Largo (D2) offers kayak and canoe rentals, guided tours, and a paddling club. Their beach launch is ideal for reaching Dusenbury Creek or Largo Sound via the Adams Cut.

John Pennekamp
Coral Reef
State Park

Upper Sound Point

0   Kilometer   1
0   Statute Mile   1
0   Nautical Mile   1

Go-to Points: 1; 2 (Boggies North); 3 (Boggies South); 4 (Dusenbury Creek)

Off-Chart D/Cs: Grouper Creek; Adams Cut; Jewfish Creek

Caution: Check wind forecasts before heading offshore into Blackwater Sound. A north wind in excess of 15 knots kicks up larger waves than might be expected.

Getting There: The Boggies (B5, B6) lie 4 miles northwest of the kayak launch at Florida Bay Outfitters (FBO).

Dusenbury Creek (D7) is a 1.7-mile paddle west from Florida Bay Outfitters.

The North Nest Key campground (C2) is an 8.5-mile one-way trip from FBO via the Boggies. A return to FBO by way of Grouper and Dusenbury Creeks is an 18-mile round-trip.

Public Land: The Everglades National Park lies north of the Intracoastal Waterway. Landing on islands or wading within 100 feet of islands is prohibited for protection of birds.

Paddling: The Boggies (B5, B6) are short channels between Blackwater Sound and wider Florida Bay. Go-tos 2 (Boggies North) and 3 (Boggies South) mark a motorized boat channel. North of this, two shallow channels, overgrown with mangroves, are ideal for kayakers. Manatees have been sighted here.

WillArts.com

Everglades National Park

Duck Key

Florida Bay

North Nest Key

Grouper Creek

Kilometer

Statute Mile

Nautical Mile

Dusenbury Creek (D7) was dredged by an engineer named Dusenbury to support passage of construction boats for Flagler's railroad. See Chart 9 for paddling details.

Camping: North Nest Key (C2) is one of two islands within the Florida Bay portion of Everglades National Park where people can land and camp. Up to 25 people may stay on the island. There's a narrow beach along the northwest side of the island, with small spots for tents. A dock on the island supports an outhouse.

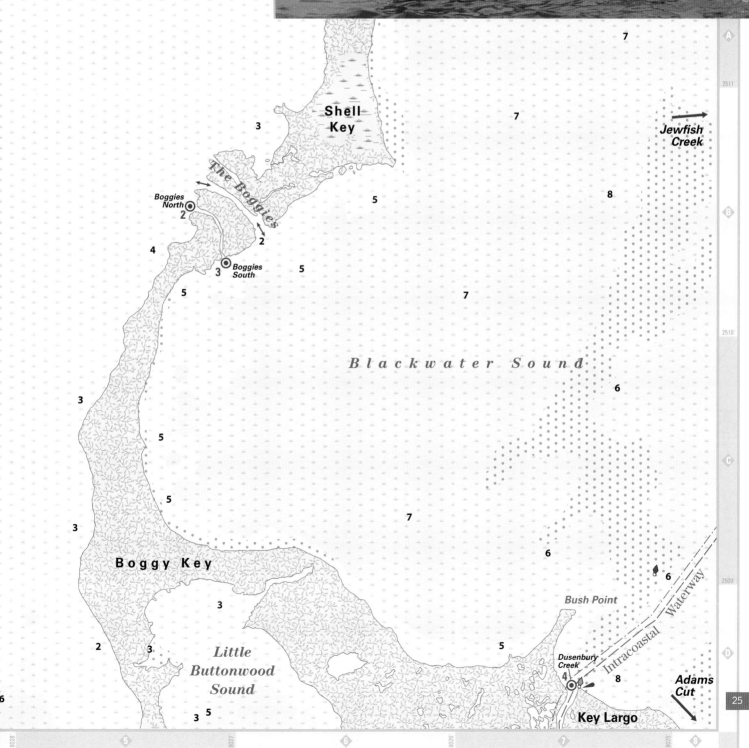

Shell Key

Jewfish Creek

The Boggies

Boggies North

Boggies South

Blackwater Sound

Boggy Key

Little Buttonwood Sound

Bush Point

Dusenbury Creek

Intracoastal Waterway

Adams Cut

Key Largo

Go-to Points: 1–14; 15 (Dusenbury Creek); 16 (South Sound Mangroves); 17 (Trail of Tears); 18 (South Sound Creek)

Off-Chart D/Cs: Garden Cove; Rodriguez Key

Caution: On weekends and holidays motorboat traffic is heavy through the Marvin D. Adams Cut (A3, A4). Pennekamp State Park put-ins provide alternate access to South Sound Creek kayak trails.

Public Land: Mostly offshore and underwater, John Pennekamp Coral Reef State Park preserves the largest living coral reef in the continental United States. There is a marked canoe trail through protected mangroves near the park headquarters (B3), ideal for windy days.

Landmarks: From Largo Sound, boaters can see the Castle (A4), just north of the Adams Cut. This coral rock home was built in the 1920s for a New Jersey dentist, Dr. George Engel. With walls 3 feet thick, it was one of the few homes to survive the 1935 hurricane and hence is one of

the oldest homes in the Upper Keys. It is privately owned and inhabited.

The Adams Cut (A3, A4) is a convenient pass-through from ocean to bayside. The high rock walls offer a fascinating eye-to-eye glimpse of dead fossils of million-year-old coral.

Creeks: Narrow passages, wrong turns, and dead ends give the Trail of Tears (C3) a reputation for reducing unsuspecting paddlers to tears. Wide at its southern end, this mangrove-lined passage reaches a point at its north end so tight that paddles can no longer be

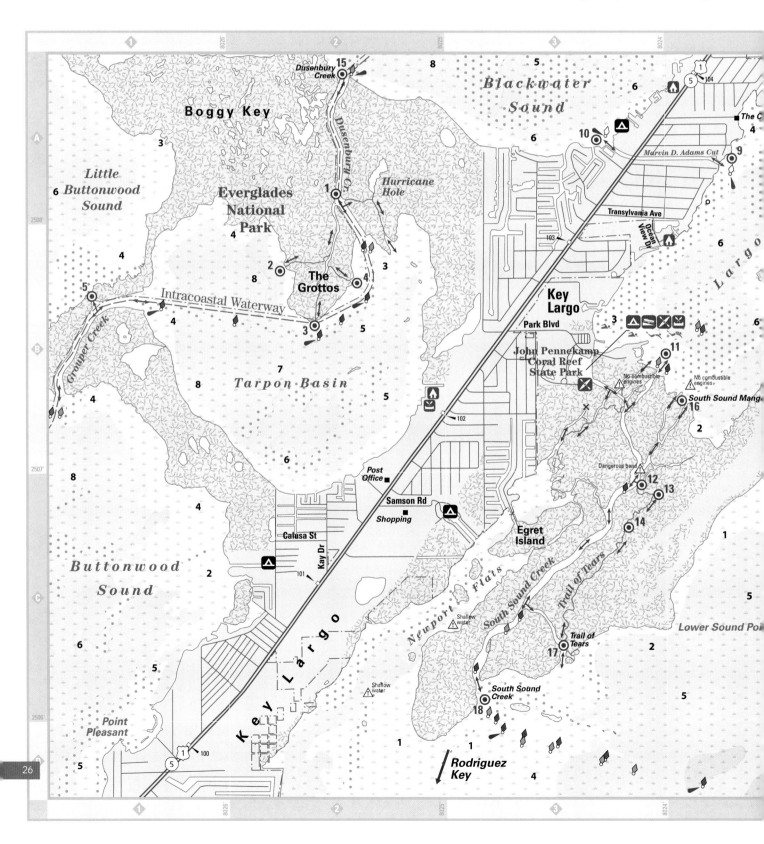

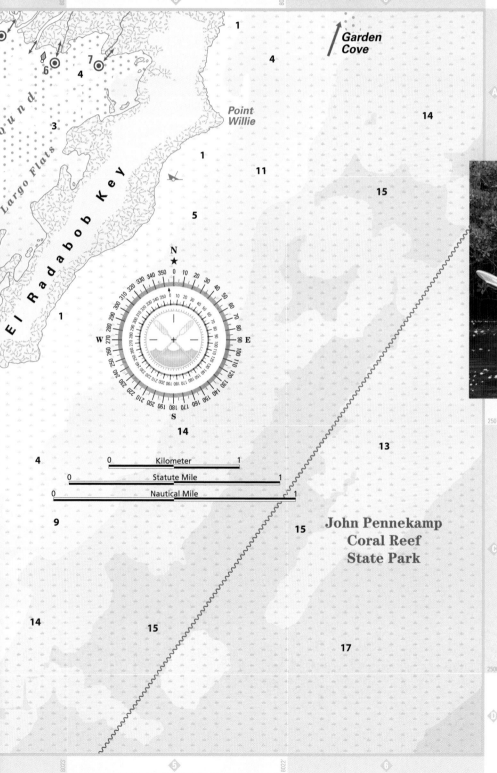

Garden
Cove

Point
Willie

El Radabob Key

Largo Flats

1
4
14
1
11
15
5

N

W
E

S

14

Kilometer
Statute Mile
Nautical Mile

9
15
14
15
17

**John Pennekamp
Coral Reef
State Park**

used. First-timers should enter the creek from the south, at Go-to 17 (Trail of Tears). At Go-to 14 turn right. At Go-to 13 turn left (a right at this T-junction dead-ends in a small lake). Exit the trail into South Sound Creek at Go-to 12.

At red channel marker 42 on Dusenbury Creek (A2, B2), a wide creek branching west leads into the Grottos. In this otherworldly and quiet mangrove forest, high mangrove branches form a cathedral-like canopy. Clear water permits viewing of varied marine life: colorful sponges, sea stars, and young mangrove snappers schooling amid submerged roots. Well-hidden entrance and exits on Tarpon Basin can be found using Go-tos 2, 3, and 4.

Grouper Creek (B1) connects Tarpon Basin to Buttonwood Sound. A small cut in the north bank (Go-to 5), 0.2 mile from the north entrance of Grouper Creek, leads into Little Buttonwood Sound. It is too shallow for powerboats and, as a result, makes a quiet place to paddle. Sightings of rays, sharks, and dolphins are common in Little Button-wood Sound.

Largo Flats (A4) and Newport Flats (C2) feature "skinny water"—depths of 6 inches or less at low tide—and are ideal for spotting small sharks, rays, and wading birds.
Outfitters: Kayak Bob runs eco-tours out of Double Tree Resort Key Largo (B2), MM 102 B/S, US 1. The Grottos and Dusenbury Creek (A2, B2) are within easy striking distance of the resort (formerly Howard Johnson). See the appendix for details.

27

10 North Swash Keys

Go-to Points: 1 (Swash Buckle); 2 (Little Buttonwood Sound); 3 (Upper Swash Pass)
Off-Chart D/Cs: Boggies North; North Nest Key; Sunset Park; Grouper Creek
Caution: Reaching the Swash Keys requires an open-water paddle of more than 2 miles. Any open-water kayak trip requires paddlers be in good physical condition, possess proper skills, and use the right equipment.

Getting There: Starting point for Swash Keys (C4): Sunset Park Put-in, Chart 12, D6. See appendix for put-in details.
Navigation: Distance to Go-to 3 (Upper Swash Pass): 4.4 miles from Sunset Park Put-in via Go-to 6 (Lower Swash Pass, Chart 11, A1); 3 miles from Key Largo Grande Resort Key Largo via Go-to 6 (Lower Swash Pass, Chart 11, A1); 2.5 miles, from Rock Reef Resort, Kona Kai Resort, Coconut Bay Resort and Bay Harbor Lodge.
Public Land: The Everglades National Park boundary runs concurrent to the Intracoastal

Waterway. Landing on islands or wading within 100 feet is prohibited for bird protection.
Paddling: Much of the Swash Keys' allure lies in the Caribbean-blue water that surrounds them. A white sandy bottom helps create this color, as opposed to darker hues in bays and sounds that support sea grass bottoms. On the north side of the Swash Keys, mainland Key Largo is out of sight and mind, noise from US 1 traffic drifts away, and the shallow depths restrict motorboats to deeper channels.

A short, but fun, kayak-only pass called the

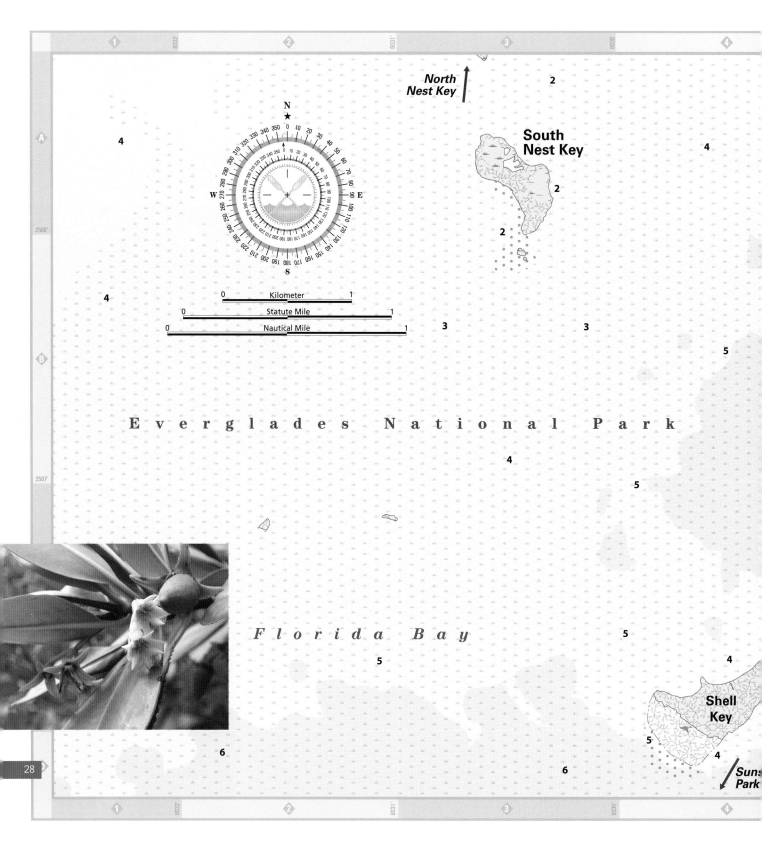

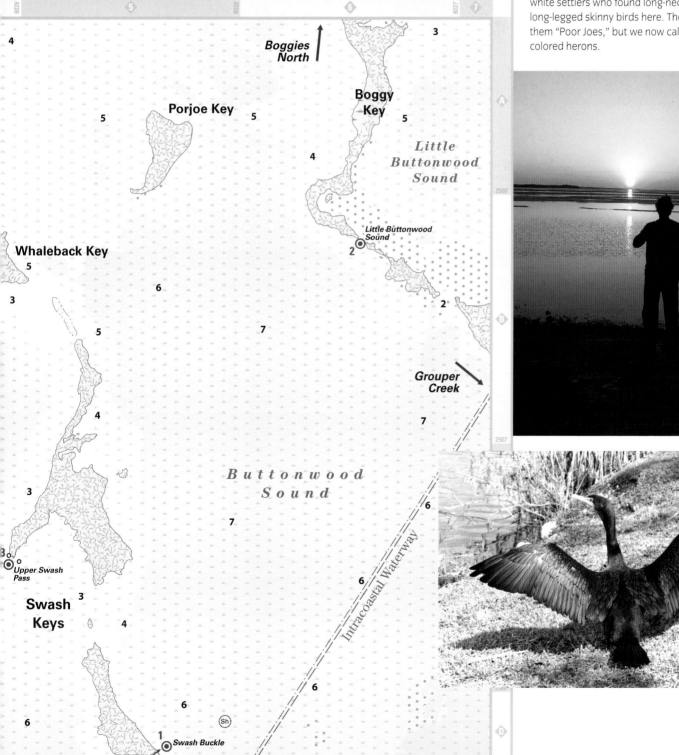

Boggies
North

4

Porjoe Key   5

Boggy
Key   5

Little
Buttonwood
Sound

5

4

Little Buttonwood
Sound
2

Whaleback Key

5

3

5

6

2

7

Grouper
Creek

7

3

4

Buttonwood
Sound

6

3

7

6

3
Upper Swash
Pass

Swash
Keys   3

6

4

Intracoastal Waterway

6

6

(Sh)

6

1
Swash Buckle

Swash Buckle (D5) leads from inside the Lower Swash Keys into wider Buttonwood Sound.
Nature: The grass flats and mangrove swamps off the west side of Shell Key (D4) are ideal bird-watching areas. American egrets, snowy egrets, and great blue herons are most often sighted. Keep an eye on the water for the darting silhouette of sharks cruising the flats in search of prey. The sea bottom within Everglades National Park is federally designated wilderness, the highest form of protection for public lands in the United States.

Porjoe Key (A5) derives its name from early white settlers who found long-necked and long-legged skinny birds here. They called them "Poor Joes," but we now call them tri-colored herons.

Go-to Points: 1–3; 4 (Rock Harbor); 5 (Home Canal); 6 (Lower Swash Pass)

Off-Chart D/Cs: South Sound Creek; Harry Harris Park; Sunset Park; Grouper Creek

Caution: A low tide will leave you stranded in the mangroves off the Harbor Drive put-in (A3). Plan your trip to coincide with high tide.

Getting There: Starting point for Swash Keys (A1): Sunset Park Put-in, Chart 12, D6. See appendix for put-in details.

Harry Harris Park (Chart 13, B3) is 4.3 miles from Go-to 4 (Rock Harbor).

Public Land: Rodriguez and Dove Keys are recent additions to John Pennekamp Coral Reef State Park, and managed as wildlife management areas by the Florida Keys National Marine Sanctuary. Landing is prohibited.

Paddling: The Lower Swash Keys (A1) are a special destination for paddlers and more accessible than adjacent Upper Swash and Butternut Keys. Set amid Caribbean-blue water, they harbor wading birds, manatees and plenty of sharks and rays that cruise the grass flats searching for a meal. Go-to 6 (Lower Swash Pass) is a paddler's portal into this special world. Search out a small passage through the mangrove swamp just west of the pass.

County-owned Varadero Beach (C1), 0.4 mile north of Sunset Park, is an official rest stop for the Florida Keys Overseas Paddling and Heritage Trails. Hungry paddlers can walk to nearby Harriette's Restaurant, famous for hearty breakfasts served daily.

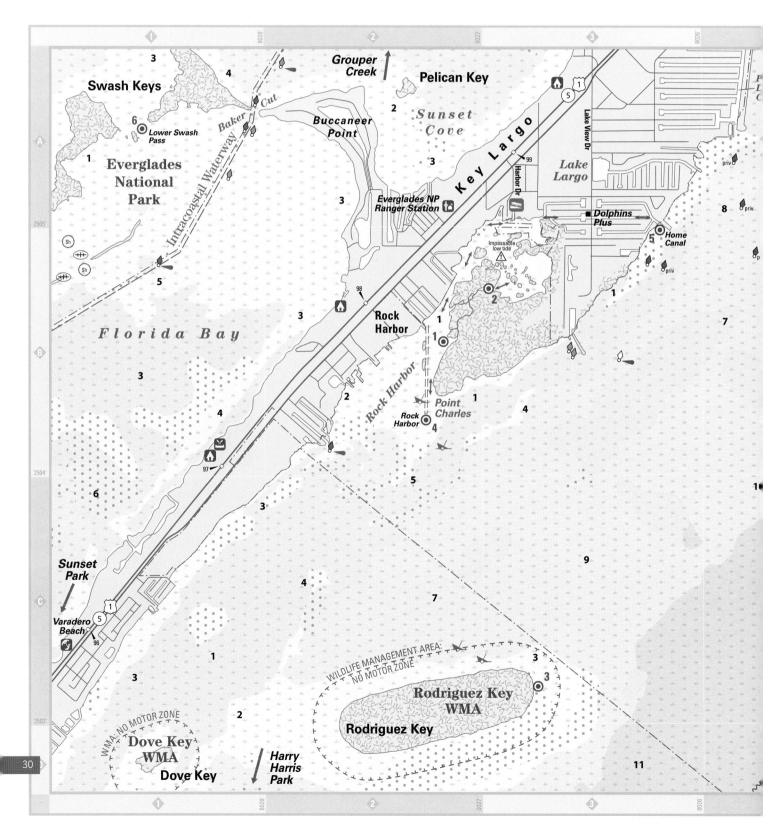

A no-motor zone surrounds Rodriguez Key (D2) and Dove Key (D1) for protection of pelicans, cormorants, and wading birds. Paddlers should maintain a distance that will not flush the birds from their perch. A hidden creek on the oceanside of Rodriguez is a reputed drop-off for Cuban refugees seeking political asylum in the United States.

Landmarks: Key Largo Grande Resort (B1) is a paddle-friendly rest stop with a sandy beach, tiki bar, and beach grill that serves a great fish sandwich. Outfitter Caribbean Watersports operates on the resort beach.

Dolphins Plus (A3), a human-dolphin encounter and education center, straddles a home canal accessed by Go-to 5 (Home Canal) and the Harbor Drive put-in. You can see the dolphins at eye level as you paddle past, but don't linger—it's distracting to the mammals.

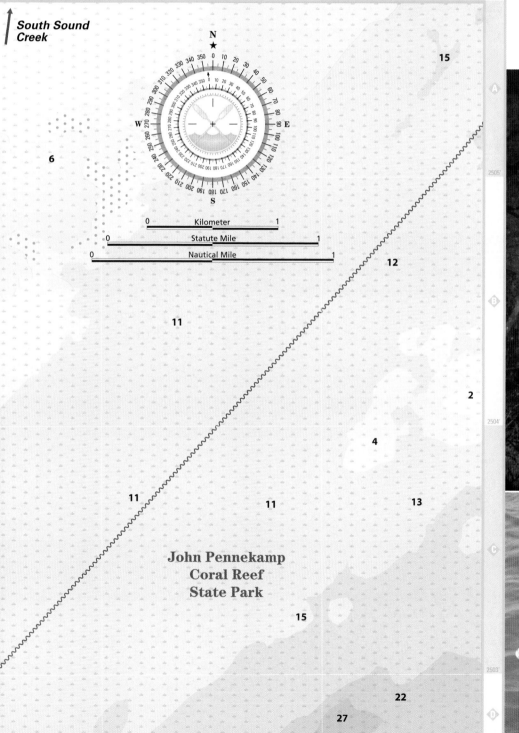

South Sound Creek

6

15

12

11

2

4

11

11

13

John Pennekamp Coral Reef State Park

15

22

27

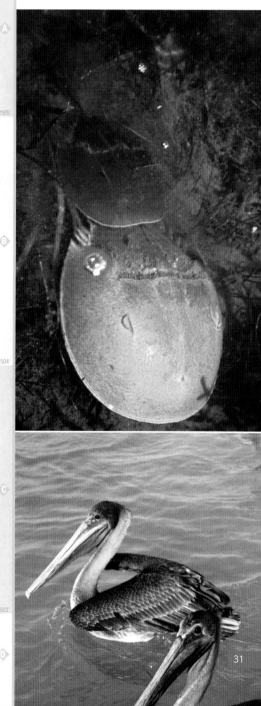

12 Bottle Key

Go-to Points: 1; 2 (Butternut Key); 3 (Bottle Key)
Off-Chart D/Cs: Baker Cut; Tavernier Creek
Caution: The trip from Sunset Park put-in to Bottle Key is a 4-mile open-water crossing. Winds in excess of 15 knots can make this trip difficult for beginners.

Upper Cross Bank is impassable at low tide.

Public Land: The Everglades National Park boundary runs concurrent with the Intracoastal Waterway. Landing on the park's islands or wading within 100 yards of the islands are prohibited.

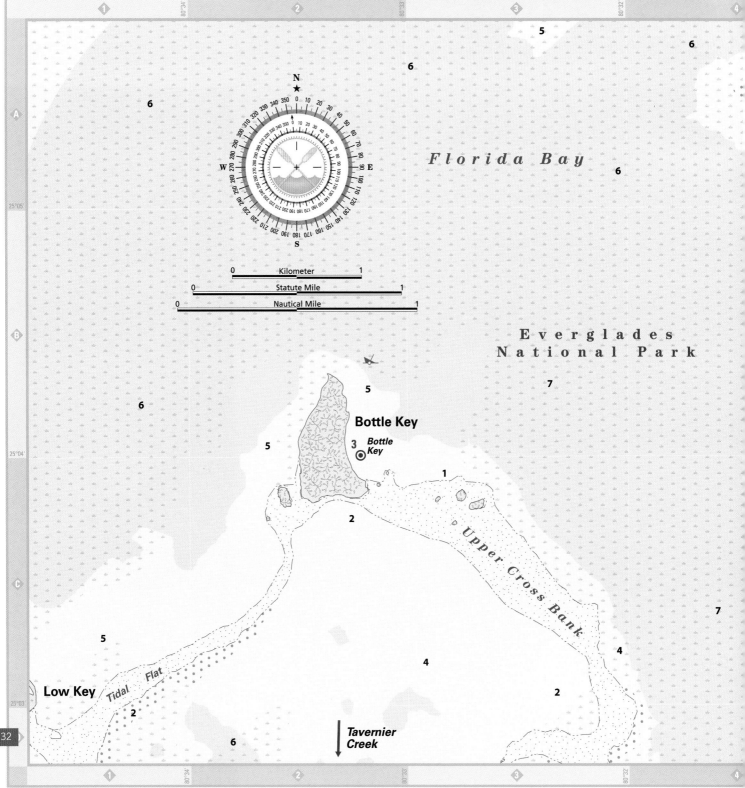

Florida Bay

Everglades National Park

Bottle Key

3 Bottle Key

Upper Cross Bank

Low Key Tidal Flat

Tavernier Creek

Paddling: Three islands form a grouping known as the Butternut Keys (A4, B5, B6). White-crowned pigeons, a threatened species in Florida, nest on Middle Butternut. Least terns have attempted nesting on the uppermost key. This seabird feeds by hovering and then plunging head-first into the water after small fish. Paddlers may see small sharks and stingrays along the sandbars that extend between the islands. Go-to 2 (Butternut Key) is a prop channel passable at low tide.

Audubon scientist Robert Porter Allen made Bottle Key (B2) and its resident bird, the roseate spoonbill, famous by his 1939 book, *The Flame Bird.* Sightings of this bird today are infrequent, but the 4-mile paddle out to Bottle Key is worthwhile for other reasons. Red mangrove are "growing" the island by spreading through shallow sandbars that extend off the southwest and southeast tips. Amid the resulting mangrove swamps, egrets, herons, and other birds rest and forage.

Landmark: The Florida Keys National Marine Sanctuary Headquarters (D6) is located at MM 95.1 B/S, Key Largo. The sanctuary encompasses 2,800 square nautical miles around the Keys to protect the fragile coral reefs and coastline. (305–292–0311, www.fknms.nos.noaa.gov)

Nature: The roseate spoonbill is the only spoonbill native to the Western Hemisphere and the only pink bird that breeds in Florida. Its striking pink-bordering-on-magenta color and an unlikely spoon-shaped bill make this a memorable sighting for birders. The Butternut Keys, Bottle Key, and Pigeon Key are recorded nesting areas. The bird's population has recovered dramatically since 1935, when Bottle Key was thought to harbor the remaining five nests of this bird anywhere in Florida. Today the Audubon Society encourages nature watchers to report sightings of banded roseate spoonbills at www.audubon.org/states/fl/fl/science/spoonbills.htm. Paddlers should use extra caution when paddling to Bottle Key during breeding season, November to April, so as not to disturb nesting birds.

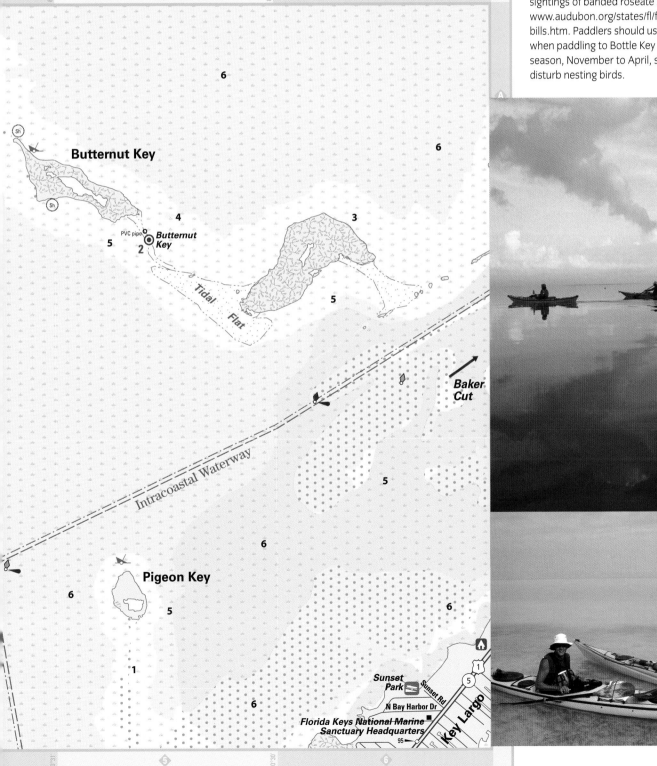

Go-to Points: 1–2; 3 (Dove Creek); 4 (Tavernier Key)

Off-Chart D/Cs: Sunset Park; Tavernier Creek Bayside; Tavernier Creek Oceanside; Rodriguez Key

Getting There: It is a 2-mile paddle one way from Harry Harris Park to Dove Sound. Low tide leaves a foot or less of water around Long Point. Plan your route accordingly.

WillArts.com

Public Land: State-owned Dove Creek Hammocks Wildlife and Environmental Area protects 226 acres of land surrounding Dove Creek and Dove Sound. Access is by foot and boat; motorized vessels are prohibited in certain areas of the creek and lake. Camping is also prohibited.

A no-motor zone surrounds Tavernier Key (D2), a wildlife management area administered by the Florida Keys National Marine Sanctuary.

Paddling: Enroute along a 0.75-mile paddle on Dove Creek (A3), from its ocean entrance to the

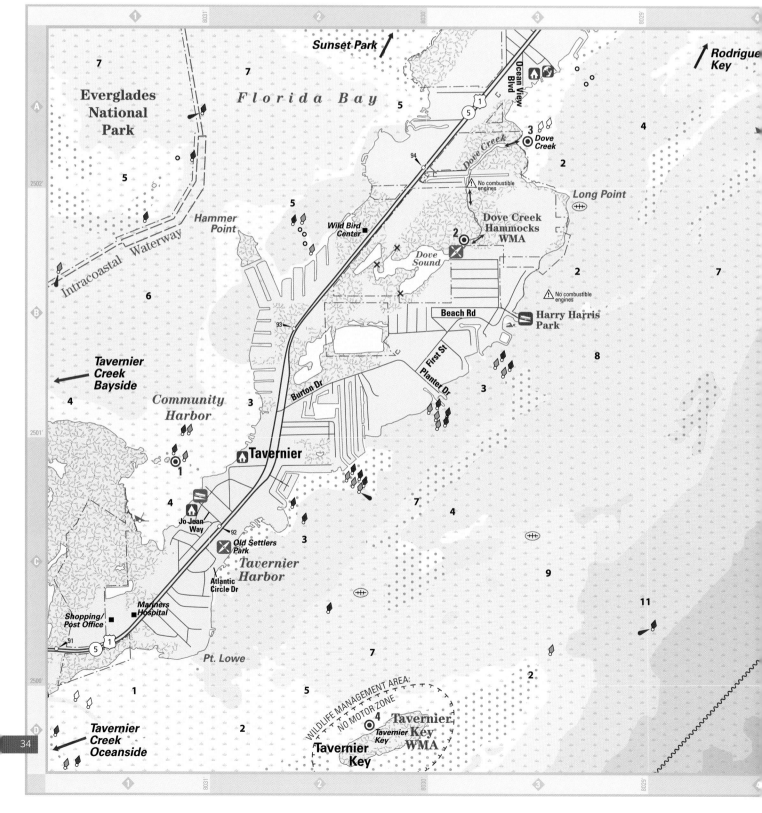

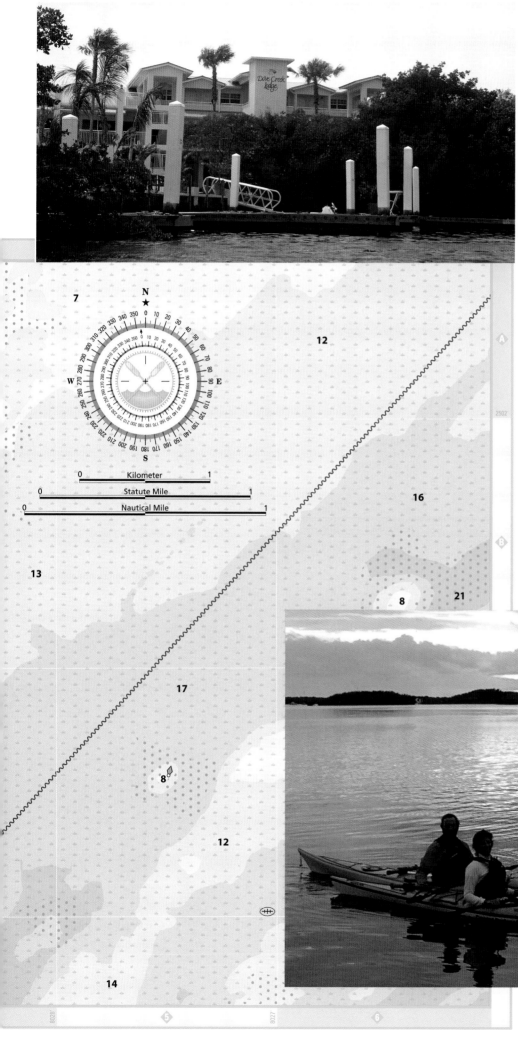

shallow interior lake, paddlers will see plenty of wading birds and schooling fish. Bottom habitat in the small creeks branching off and then rejoining Dove Creek vary from hard to soft. Orange, green, and purple sponges attached to the mangrove roots are colorfully vibrant.

Landmarks: Snapper's Restaurant (A3) is popular with visitors and locals for dinner and cocktails. Next door, Dove Creek Lodge caters to the overnight fishing crowd.

See Chart 14 for information on Old Settlers Park (C2).

Laura Quinn has devoted her retirement years and life savings to the protection of injured and orphaned pelicans, hawks, ibis, owls, egrets, and spoonbills on her private, five-acre sanctuary known as the Wild Bird Center (B2), MM 93.7 B/S, US 1. Laura welcomes kayakers to land on the center's sand beach, an ideal rest spot for Bayside paddlers. Admission is free, but a donation is appreciated. (305–852–4486, www.fkwbc.org)

History: Early Spanish reports referred to "Cayo de Tabona," the area known today as Tavernier. *Tabona* is Spanish for horsefly, something the Spaniards reportedly encountered while camping on the island to recover their shipwrecks. Keys Names, an online database of name origins from the Keys, lists Tavernier as the site of the first modern settlements on Key Largo. How *Tabona* migrated into *Tavernier* is not known; Keys Names indicates variations of the term *Tabonas* were used consistently on charts until 1775, when Cay Tavernier is first mentioned.

Services: See Chart 14 for services (C1).

WillArts.com

14 Tavernier Creek

Go-to Points: 1–5; 6 (Tavernier Creek Bay);
7 (Tavernier Creek Ocean)
Off-Chart D/Cs: Founders Park; Harry Harris Park
Caution: Exercise care when paddling Tavernier
Creek. Motorboats enter this major pass-through
between ocean and bay at full speed. In particular,
flats boats use two passes near the bayside
entrance of Tavernier Creek; the blind corners
have earned them the nickname "Suicide Cuts."

Photo courtesy of Monroe County Public Library, Mile Markers Project

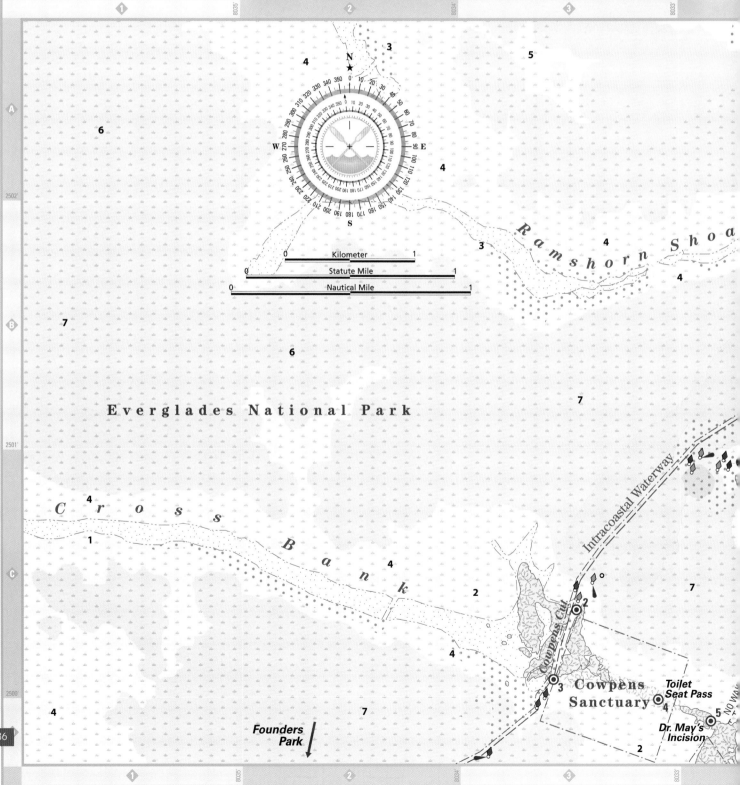

Everglades National Park

Ramshorn Shoal

Cross Bank

Intracoastal Waterway

Cowpens Cut

Cowpens Sanctuary

Toilet Seat Pass

Dr. May's Incision

Founders Park

NO WAY

Kilometer
Statute Mile
Nautical Mile

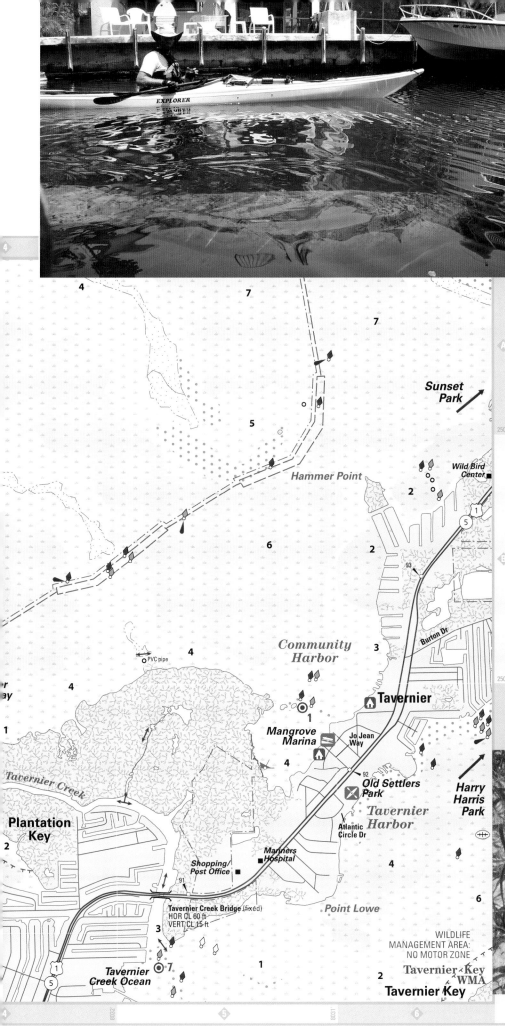

Getting There: Starting point for Tavernier Creek: Founders Park, Chart 16, A5. See appendix for put-in details. Alternate access to Tavernier Creek is possible from the south bridge abutment, oceanside. To reach this put-in, paddlers must carry their kayaks more than 100 yards and negotiate large rocks at the water's edge. Streetside parking at the dead end of the Old Highway is limited.

Navigation: Distance to Tavernier Creek (Tavernier Creek Bay Go-to 6): 4 miles from Founders Park put-in via Toilet Seat Pass.

Paddling: Three small unnamed creeks branch off into the undeveloped north shoreline of Tavernier Creek. The first creek, 0.3 mile north of the bridge, maintains a paddle's width through several tight meanders. Watch for a spot to turn around before the creek ends; there is no good turnaround at the dead end.

The second creek entrance, north of the first, is wide and inviting. After a short paddle, however, it too dead-ends. Smaller passages extend farther into dense mangroves, but ultimately these run out of steam, and paddlers must back out.

After an initial wide stretch, the third creek, 0.6 mile north of the US 1 bridge (N25°00.552′ W80°31.960′) canopies overhead, then runs a delightful 15 to 20 minutes before emptying into a sheltered wetland (N25°00.884′ W80°31.775′). Clipped branches indicate someone maintains this trail. Bring surveyor's tape as a way of marking your entrance/exit from the interior wetland.

See Chart 15 for paddling Dr. May's Incision and Toilet Seat Pass.

Old Settlers Park (C6) is a pleasant place to stop and take a walk through a quiet waterfront area, the site of an early community, homesteaded in the 1870s. There are no facilities at the park, but you can walk to a nearby Cuban restaurant.

Services: At MM 92 B/S you'll find Mariners Hospital and Tavernier Towne Shopping Center, with groceries, pharmacy, post office, and cinema.

Go-to Points: 1 (Snake Creek); 2–5; 6 (Tavernier Key); 7 (Tavernier Creek Ocean)
Off-Chart D/Cs: Harry Harris Park; Founders Park
Caution: Exercise care on Tavernier Creek. Motorboats enter this major pass-through between ocean and bay at full speed.
Getting There: Starting point for the Cowpens: Founders Park, Chart 16, A5. See appendix for put-in details.

Navigation: Distance to Cowpens Go-to 4 (Toilet Seat Pass): 3 miles from Founders Park put-in.
Public Land: A no-motor zone surrounds Tavernier Key (B7), a wildlife management area managed by the Florida Keys National Marine Sanctuary.
Paddling: See Chart 14 for details on paddling Tavernier Creek (A5, A6).

A local doctor, paddler, and WWOW (Wild Woman on the Water) is the namesake for Dr. May's Incision (B5), a mangrove creek reached at Go-to 5. At its most narrow, paddlers must break down their paddle to squeeze through.

Toilet Seat Pass (A4) is a cut through a mud bank lined with dozens of toilet seats installed by residents and painted with family and business names, anniversaries, memorials—even the name of a local Boy Scout troop. Go-to 4 is the north side of the pass.

Extensive mangrove swamps spread southeast of Cowpens Cut (A4). Numerous small creeks flow through grass beds and mangroves, and shallow water throughout makes ideal conditions for bird and marine life viewing.

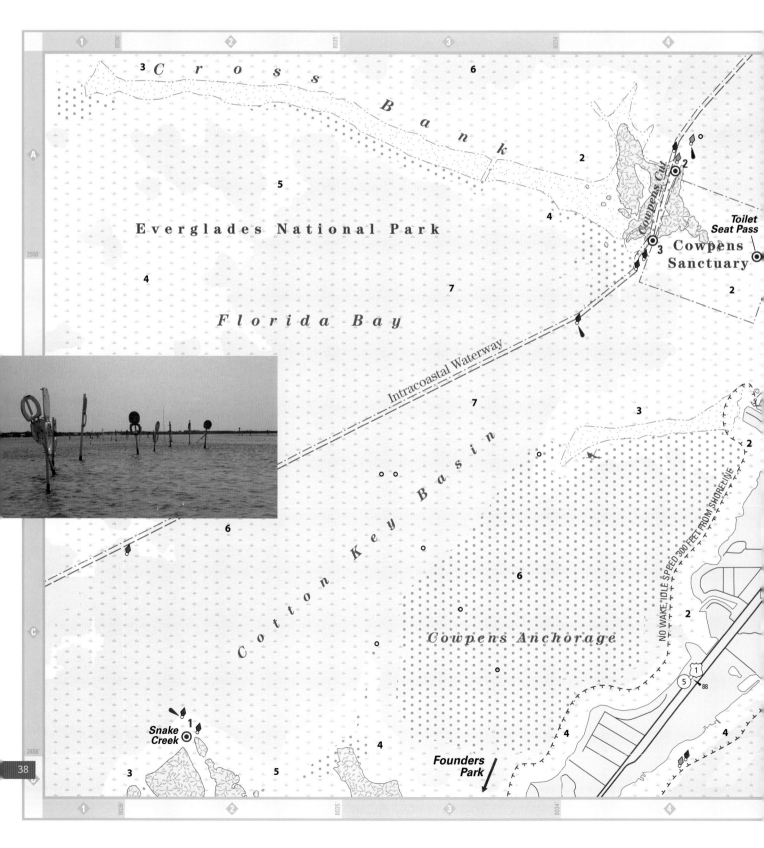

Landmark: Manatees, also known as sea cows, were once penned in the natural basin known as the Cowpens (C3) for later slaughtering.

See Chart 14 for Old Settlers Park (A7).

History: Plantation Key's human history can be traced to a large Indian community of around A.D. 500, based on evidence found in a large mound leveled for a subdivision in 1958. In the 1870s the island was homesteaded by pineapple farmers. Tomatoes, coconuts, limes, apples, and oranges were also grown on the island.

Services: See Chart 14 for services (A6).

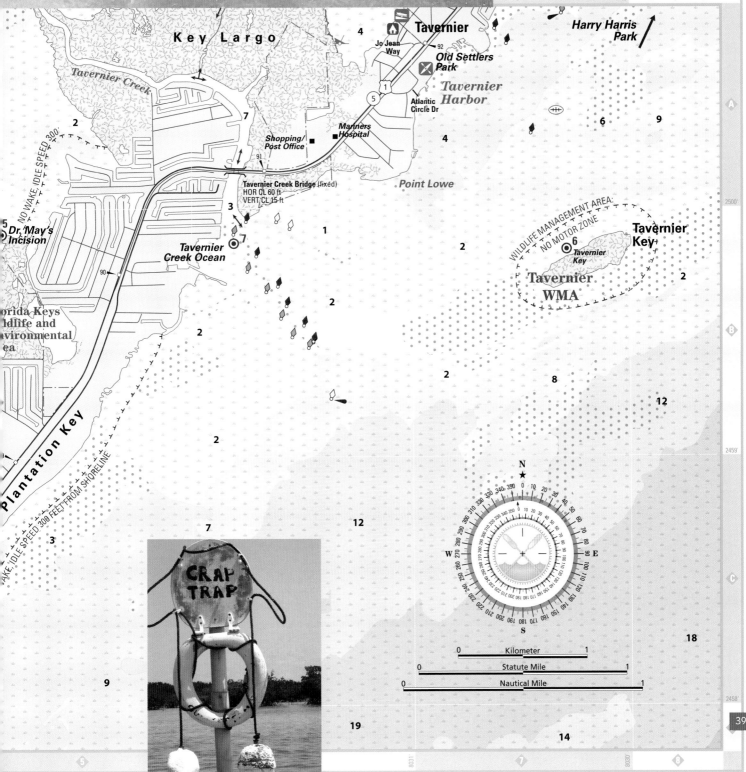

Go-to Points: 1; 2 (Little Basin North); 3 (Snake Creek Ocean)

Off-Chart D/Cs: Tavernier Creek; Indian Key; Shell Key

Caution: Only experienced paddlers should attempt the 2-mile-plus open-water trip to Hen and Chickens and Cheeca Rocks. We recommend filing a float plan with a friend, detailing your trip departure time, destination, and projected return time. Travel with a friend, carry a marine radio, and plan your trip when winds are less than 10 knots.

Getting There: Cheeca Rocks is a patch reef 2.5 miles south of the Whale Harbor Bridge put-in (MM 83.7 O/S). Take a 188-degree bearing off green day marker 9, just south of the bridge put-in. Yellow balls mark the sanctuary preservation area.

Hen and Chickens is a patch reef with star coral located 3 miles southeast of the Snake Creek Bridge put-ins. Paddle south out of Snake Creek and take a 107-degree bearing off green day marker 1. Yellow balls mark the sanctuary preservation area.

Public Land: Founders Park (A5) has a beach to rest on, restrooms, picnic tables, walking trails, and a pool.

The last 100,000 years of geologic history of the Upper Keys is captured in rock at an old quarry turned state park, Windley Key Fossil Reef Geological State Park (A4), MM 85.1 B/S, US 1 (305–664–2540, www.floridastateparks.org/windleykey)

Prohibited activities at Florida Keys National

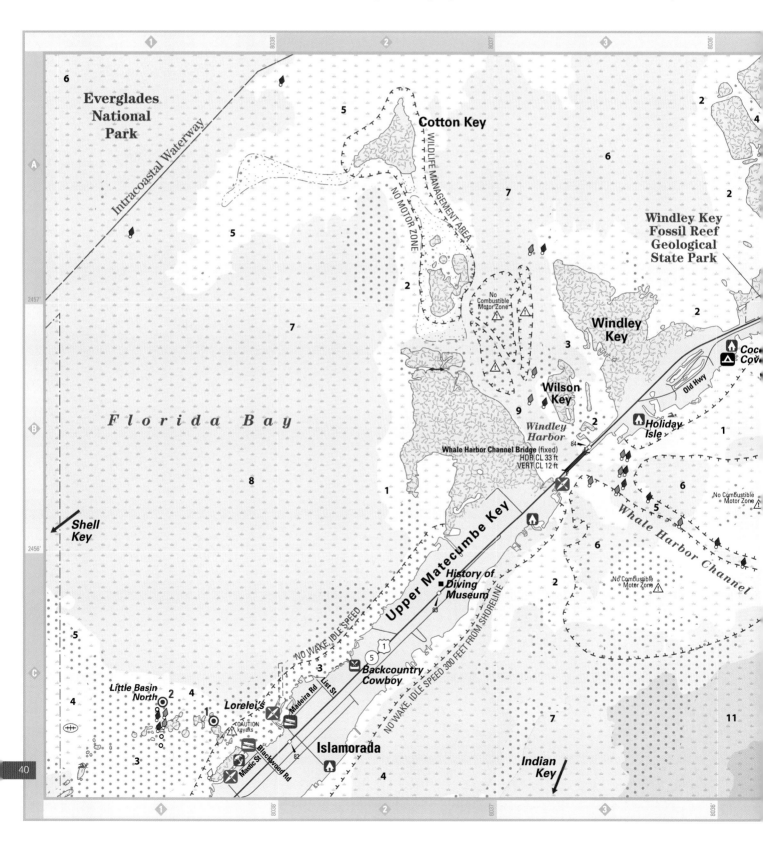

Marine Sanctuary's Hen and Chickens and Cheeca Rocks patch reefs include discharging any matter except cooling water or engine exhaust; fishing by any means; removing or harvesting marine life; catch-and-release fishing by trolling; and touching, standing on, or anchoring on living or dead coral. Bait fishing is allowed by sanctuary permit. Call (305) 852–7717 for information.

Paddling: With major offshore reefs out of reach of kayaks and canoes, patch reefs at Cheeca Rocks (N24°54.100′ W80°37.000′) and Hen and Chickens (N24°56.040′ W80°33.190′) offer Upper Keys paddlers a rare opportunity to snorkel amid brain and star corals, sea whips, and sea fans in waters 3 to 10 feet deep. Bring a tether rope to tie your kayak up to one of the white mooring balls. A diver-down flag is required.

See Chart 17 for Little Basin (C1) paddling details.

Landmarks: Treasure Village (A5) at Treasure Harbor, MM 86.7 O/S, is now a school, but it was once known as the McKee castle. Famed treasure seeker Arthur McKee Jr. built it in 1949 to house a museum for the loot—namely silver—he salvaged from the 1733 Spanish fleet of 22 ships that wrecked all along the Upper Keys in a hurricane.

The History of Diving Museum (C2), at MM 83 B/S, US 1, opened in 2006 and houses an extensive collection of artifacts from 3,000 years of diving history. (305) 664–9737; www.divingmuseum.com.

Names: It is popular belief that the name *Islamorada* is derived from the Spanish "islands of purple." Historian Irving R. Eyster, however, writes that village founder William Krome named it for the schooner *Island Home* (translated in Spanish as *Ees la morada*), which often passed by the island between Key West and Miami. His source? Krome's wife, who shared the story before she died.

Dining: A white mermaid statue marks the canal entrance to the Island Grill (A4). There's a sandbar just offshore where you can take a refreshing dip.

Land at the gravel beach to enjoy lunch or the nightly sunset party at Lorelei's Restaurant & Cabana Bar (C1).

Outfitters: Backcountry Cowboy, MM 82.2 B/S. US 1 (C2) is a full-service retail and kayak dealer in the heart of Islamorada. The shop delivers rental kayaks for vacationers.

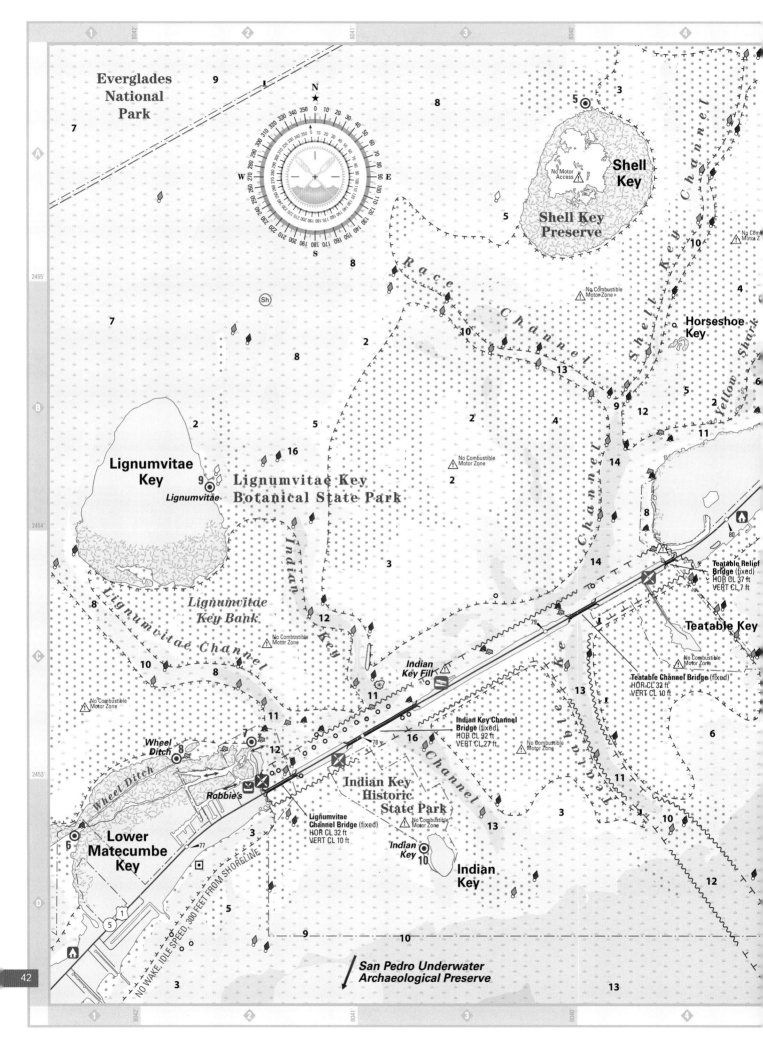

Everglades
National
Park

Shell
Key

Shell Key
Preserve

*No Motor
Access*

Horseshoe
Key

Lignumvitae
Key

Lignumvitae Key
Botanical State Park

Lignumvitae

Lignumvitae
Key Bank

Teatable Relief
Bridge (fixed)
HOR CL 37 ft
VERT CL 7 ft

Teatable Key

Teatable Channel Bridge (fixed)
HOR CL 32 ft
VERT CL 10 ft

Indian
Key
Fill

Indian Key Channel
Bridge (fixed)
HOR CL 92 ft
VERT CL 27 ft

Wheel
Ditch

Robbie's

Indian Key
Historic
State Park

Lignumvitae
Channel Bridge (fixed)
HOR CL 32 ft
VERT CL 10 ft

Indian
Key

Indian
Key

Lower
Matecumbe
Key

NO WAKE, IDLE SPEED, 300 FEET FROM SHORELINE

San Pedro Underwater
Archaeological Preserve

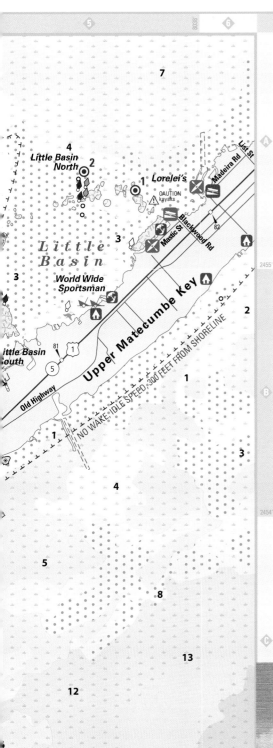

Go-to Points: 1; 2 (Little Basin North); 3; 4 (Little Basin South); 5-7; 8 (Wheel Ditch); 9 (Lignumvitae); 10 (Indian Key)

Off-Chart D/C: San Pedro Underwater Archaeological Preserve

Caution: From Indian Key Fill (MM 78.5 B/S) kayaks launch into a busy boat channel; safety is found in shallow water beyond the power lines.

Six motorboat channels criss-cross the area between Lignumvitae, Shell Key, and Little Basin, north of US 1. At low tide, exposed grass flats force paddlers to travel near or in marked motorboat channels.

Public Land: Indian Key Historic State Park, Shell Key Preserve, Lignumvitae Key Botanical State Park, and the San Pedro Underwater Archaeological Preserve are jointly managed. Call (305) 664–2540 for information.

Paddling: At the south end of Little Basin (A5, B5), birders will find exceptional viewing of egrets, herons, and other wading birds amid shallow flats that are being claimed by mangroves. There is a swimming hole at N24°55.129′ W80°38.917′.

Less than a mile south of US 1, tiny Indian Key (D3) looms large in Keys history and lore. (See Upper Keys introduction for details.) Land at Go-to 10 (Indian Key), a designated kayak/canoe landing. Walking paths criss-cross the 12-acre island, and a climb up the observation tower makes for a good leg-stretcher. There are no facilities on the island. Ranger-led tours (fee) are given Thursday through Monday, or you can tour on your own any day. (305) 664–2540, www.floridastate parks.org/indiankey.

San Pedro Underwater Archaeological Preserve State Park is 1.25 nautical miles southeast of Indian Key. In 1733, the *San Pedro* was part of a flotilla carrying Spain's New World treasure from Havanna to Europe when, a day into their voyage, a hurricane wrecked the ships on the Florida reef. There's no silver at the San Pedro today, only an authentic ballast pile and seven replica cannons marked by white mooring buoys. N24°51.802′ W80°40.795′.

Lignumvitae Key Botanical State Park (B1, B2) is 1 mile off the bayside of Indian Key Fill. Go-to 9 (Lignumvitae) is a designated kayak landing, right of the smaller of two boat docks. Guided ranger walks (fee) are given twice daily, Thursday through Monday; otherwise, visitors can self-guide the property of William J. Matheson, who built the caretaker residence. (305–664–2540)

The interior lake on Shell Key (A3, A4) makes for ideal foraging for egrets, herons, and roseate spoonbills. Be aware that its size and the many tuck-aways around the lake are disorienting. Consider surveyor's tape to mark your entry/exit point. Go-to 5 is the creek access for the lake.

Horseshoe Key (B4), named for its shape, is a popular cormorant and pelican rookery and has the accompanying smell of guano to prove it. It's a good place to rest out of the wind and boat traffic.

Landmarks: Land at Worldwide Sportsman's (B5) boat ramp for some nautical shopping and alfresco lunch at the Islamorada Fish Company.

At Robbie's Marina (C2) feed the giant tarpon, then head to their namesake eatery, the Hungry Tarpon, for great seafood.

Outfitter: Florida Keys Kayak & Ski at Robbie's Marina has rentals and ecotours to Indian and Lignumvitae Keys. Backcountry Cowboy does tours of the Little Basin and Horseshoe Key area.

M.36—Fishing is Good at Indian Key Bridge, Overseas Highway—in the Florida Keys Between Miami and Key West, Florida

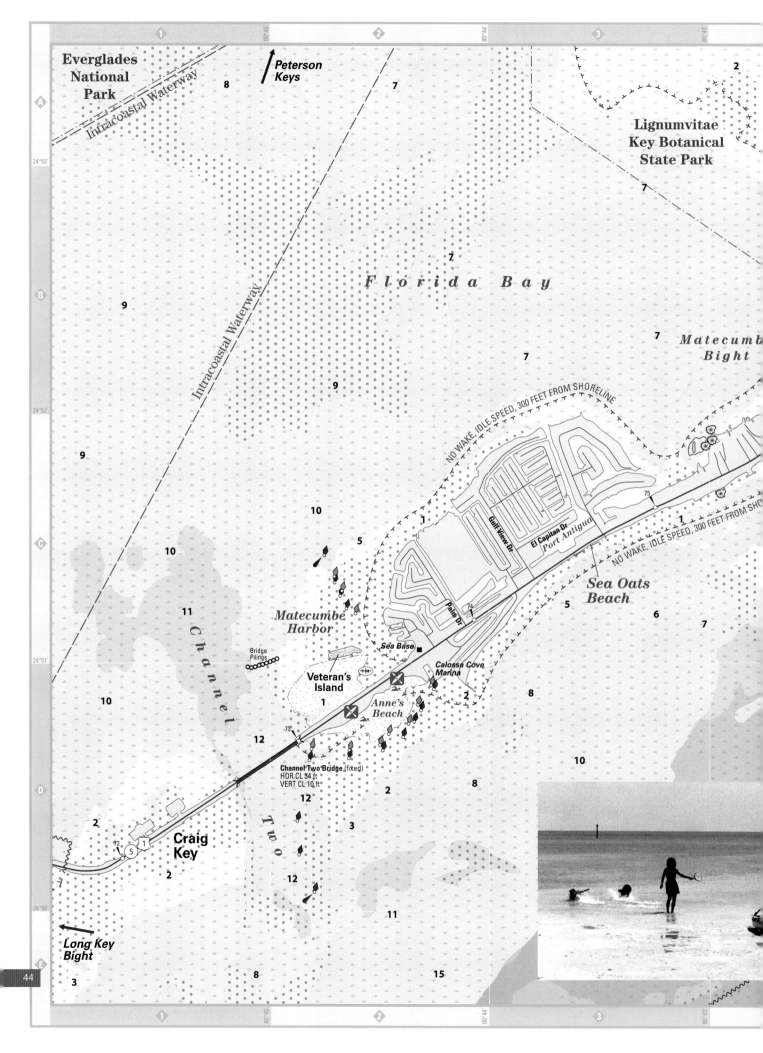

1 2 80°45' 2 80°44' 3 80°43'

Everglades National Park

Peterson Keys

Intracoastal Waterway

A

8

7

Lignumvitae Key Botanical State Park

2

7

24°53'

B

Florida Bay

7

Matecumbe Bight

9

7

7

9

24°52'

9

NO WAKE, IDLE SPEED, 300 FEET FROM SHORELINE

Intracoastal Waterway

10

75

Gulf View Dr

El Capitan Dr

Port Antigua

7

C

10

5

1

NO WAKE, IDLE SPEED, 300 FEET FROM SHO

10

Sea Oats Beach

11

5

6

Channel

Matecumbe Harbor

Palm Dr

74

7

24°51'

Bridge Pilings

Sea Base

Calossa Cove Marina

Veteran's Island

1

2

8

10

Anne's Beach

12

73

2

8

Channel Two Bridge (fixed)
HOR CL 34 ft
VERT CL 10 ft

12

2

8

10

D

Two

3

2

72

5

1

Craig Key

12

2

24°50'

7

12

11

15

Long Key Bight

E

44

3

8

1 80°45' 2 80°44' 3 80°43'

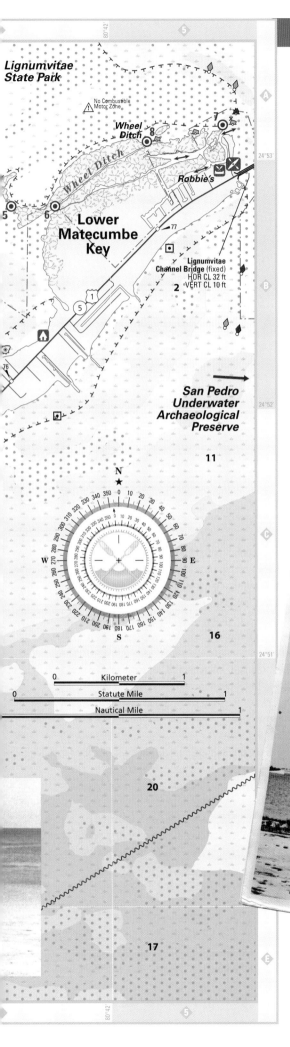

Go-to Points: 5–7; 8 (Wheel Ditch)
Off-Chart D/Cs: Peterson Keys; Lignumvitae Key State Park; San Pedro Underwater Archaeological Preserve; Long Key Bight
Caution: Paddlers risk life and limb traveling through the Wheel Ditch (Go-to 8, A5), a narrow motorboat channel between Matecumbe Bight and Lignumvitae Channel. Use adjacent smaller creeks at Go-tos 5 and 6 for safe passage.
Paddling: Behind Robbie's Marina (A5) a long mangrove forest known as the Klopp Tract stretches southwest to Matecumbe Bight. A creek accessed by Go-to 6 begins narrow, lined with dense red mangroves, but soon widens. On this same creek, just past a junction with a home canal that branches south, paddlers can explore a dead-end creek at the base of a deep V-cut in the left-hand shoreline.

Bayside off the southern tip of Lower Matecumbe, eight concrete bridge pilings (D1) stand as relics of a bridge destroyed during the infamous Labor Day Hurricane of 1935. More than 250 men working to build the bridge were killed in the storm. (See the Middle Keys introduction for the story of the 1935 hurricane.)

Anne's Beach (D2) is a rarity in the Keys, a long stretch of beach where dogs can run free. The sand is more of a marl clay, and the water is very shallow for at least 100 feet offshore, but this is still a great place to take a rest or stretch your legs on the boardwalk through the mangroves. There are restrooms and outdoor shower at the northern end. North parking area: N24°50.924′ W80°44.447′. South parking area: N24°50.795′ W80°44.651′.

Sea Oats Beach (C3) is popular with anglers sitting in kayaks or wading in the shallow water. Long-distance paddlers can stop here and pop across the street to Angelo's Country Store. There isn't much sand left at Sea Oats Beach after 2005's Hurricane Wilma, and limited roadside parking.

History: The word *Matecumbe* appears in Spanish writing as far back as 1571, when Spanish soldiers stopped to fish there and were attacked by Indians. It's believed Matecumbe may be a variation of the Spanish *mata hombre,* or "kill man."

The original community on Craig Key (D1) grew on a wide spot along the highway, and was shown in a Ripley's Believe It or Not! cartoon as "the town built on a highway—instead of a highway built through a town." Because of its deepwater access, Miami fishing charter boats stopped here to resupply in the 1920 and '30s. The island visible today has been enlarged by fill.

Photo courtesy of Monroe County Public Library, Mile Markers Project

45

Middle Keys

What surprises await a paddler in the Middle Keys?

Little blue herons foraging in quiet Long Key Lakes.

A sun-splashed swim hole in the heart of Boot Key.

A bright orange starfish framed by dazzling white sand.

Graceful spandrel arches supporting the 2.5-mile Long Key Viaduct.

The flash of a spotted eagle ray swimming through a sea grass bed behind Deer Key.

The full moon rising over Rebecca Key.

Beachcombing on Long Key Point.

Resting beneath palms on Money Key, watching traffic on the Seven Mile Bridge.

The view from the bridge high above Channel Five goes on and on. Beyond Long Key, the Atlantic Ocean stretches for distances only imagined. West of the bridge, Florida Bay's vast expanse is interrupted only by a few far-off mangrove islands. In a glance, it seems the epitome of the popular Florida Keys ideal: remote islands framed by Caribbean-blue water.

Ideals aside, this snapshot nicely captures the transition from Upper to Middle Keys. Beginning at Craig Key, the Middle Keys further taper into a narrow chain of islands. For 33 miles—across Long Key, Grassy Key, Key Vaca, and a host of smaller islands set in between—there are areas where only a few hundred yards of land separate ocean and bay. The distance from one island to the next grows wider. And, there are fewer nearshore mangrove islands of the kind that typify the Upper Keys.

In the Middle Keys, the great estuary that is Florida Bay gives way to greater influence from the Gulf of Mexico. Local terminology reflects this change. By the time you've reached Marathon and the Seven Mile Bridge, locals refer to the bayside of the Upper Keys as "gulfside" instead.

The physical layout of the Middle Keys, coupled with fewer offshore coral reef tracts, shapes the paddling experience. The Keys' first legitimate beach is found at Sombrero Beach in Marathon, a gorgeous strip of sand that was replenished (naturally) by Hurricane Georges in 1998. Extensive sea grass meadows give way to patchy grass beds, intermixed with hard-bottom communities. Patches of white sand bottom frames brightly colored sea stars and sea cucumbers. Soft corals, sea whips, and hard-bottom sponges populate these areas and are especially notable around Molasses and Money Keys.

A dearth of sheltered paddling makes those areas with such character all the more special. In Long Key Lakes, part of Long Key State Park, kayaks and canoes glide inches above a silty bottom replete with Cassiopeia jellyfish. Scores of killifish glitter like silver rainbows as they jump from the water. At Go-to 1 (Chart 19, B5), you can poke through overhanging mangroves to emerge into a second chamber of the lake. Here's where wading birds find shelter in tight-knit mangroves, out of the hot after-noon sun.

In the Whiskey Creek mangroves, narrow passages link three interior lakes. Mullet jump in frenzied fashion as you push through a break of mangrove branches into yet another shallow, sea grass–lined "room." Wading birds flush from the trees. A circuit through this wonderland clocks in at only 2 miles, but it takes a full day of paddling to soak in the beauty.

If open water distinguishes the Middle Keys, the crossing between Long Key and Conch Key is perhaps its best display. From a boat it is possible to see up close what people in cars never do: the architecture of the Long Key Viaduct. In name and appearance, this bridge conjures Romanesque grandeur. In a bygone era, its 186 "spandrel arches" across 2.5 miles of open water carried passenger railcars on a narrow track 30 feet above the water. The bridge was the "first completed triumph" of Henry Flagler's Overseas Railroad, writes Pat Parks in her book *The Railroad that Died at Sea*.

With the coming of the railroad, the Florida Keys were assuming a new identity, one far removed from that of an isolated archipelago suitable for only the toughest and hardiest pioneers.

Flagler built the railroad—officially the Florida East Coast Railroad's Key West Extension—as much to cash in on Cuba's proximity as to promote the Keys. Its impact is undeniable. Long

Key Fish Camp, built as a work camp, has been called the Florida Keys first "resort." The cabins were converted into lodging for guests of the railroad and postcard images of small seaside shacks set amid silver palms did much to boost the image of the Keys as a tropical paradise.

Zane Grey, the famed Western writer, frequented Long Key Fish Camp and popularized the area as a sportfishing destination. Today a creek on Long Key bears his name. Used primarily by Layton residents for access to the ocean, Zane Grey Creek holds two hidden delights for paddlers in the form of short, narrow mangrove passages. The twice-daily flush of tides from the ocean keep waters here clean and clear, making it easy to see the mangrove snappers that school amid submerged roots. Small sharks congregate near the mouth of the creek to feed on fish that ride the tides in and out.

Long Key bore witness to one of the seminal events in Keys history, the Labor Day Hurricane of 1935. In an era before named hurricanes, it registered the lowest barometric pressure in history, at 26.35 millibars. Not until Hurricane Gilbert in 1988 was the record supplanted. The wind and resulting "wall of water" produced by a storm surge killed an estimated 408 people. Tragically, 252 of these were World War I veterans, nicknamed the Bonus Army, who were building a highway to Key West. When evacuation efforts failed, the veterans and Keys residents alike were left at the storm's mercy. In *Florida's Hurricane History,* author Jay Barnes relates the outrage of Ernest Hemingway, who called for accountability in an article for the Marxist publication *New Masses*: "Who sent nearly a thousand war veterans, many of them husky, hard-working and simply out of luck . . . to live in frame shacks in the Florida Keys in hurricane months?" Bayside of Channel Two Bridge, just south of Lower Matecumbe Key, eight concrete bridge pilings in the water mark what's left of the Bonus Army's highway work.

The Labor Day storm ended the reign of the railroad in the Keys. Debt-ridden and facing an insurmountable rebuilding campaign, the Florida East Coast Railroad sold its right-of-way to the state in 1935 for $640,000, "less than the cost of one of its still-standing bridges," Parks writes. The right-of-way eventually became the route for the Overseas Highway from Key Largo to Key West.

These days the Seven Mile Bridge has replaced the Long Key Viaduct as the transportation symbol of the Keys. It spans 7 miles of open water between Marathon and Duck Keys, a gap that also marks a break between the Middle and Lower Keys. If the views from Channel Five Bridge seemed to capture so conveniently a segue from the Upper to Middle regions, they are matched—superseded, even—by the views from the Seven Mile Bridge. Here, again, US 1 climbs more than 60 feet above water, this time to cross Moser Channel. Tiny Molasses and Money Keys perch in shallow water oceanside, surrounded by hard-bottom sponge flats.

Beyond them await the Lower Keys.

Go-to Points: 1–2; 3 (Mangrove Creeks)
Off-Chart D/Cs: Little Rabbit Key; Anne's Beach; Toms Harbor Keys
Caution: It's skinny water inside Long Key Lake, and at low tide paddlers may have to pole through the shallowest areas.
Alert: Trail markers on the Long Key Lakes Canoe Trail may be missing or moved by storm activity.
Navigation: Radio and cell phone towers near the park ranger station are a handy navigation aid. Paddling from Long Key Point to Go-to 3 (Mangrove Creeks) (B5), keep these towers on your left. Or, from deep inside Long Key Lakes, use the towers to relocate the launching dock.

Public Land: Long Key State Park (C4) offers camping, canoe and kayak rentals, hiking trails, a picnic area, and a thin slice of ocean beach. Walk-in/paddle-in campsites are handy for travelers on the Florida Keys Overseas Paddling Trail.

Paddling: Numbered posts and a sheltered environment make the Long Key Canoe Trail (B4) an ideal outing for families. Go-to 1 is a small overgrown hole in the mangrove that leads to quiet lakes. The state park provides a brochure with natural history highlights throughout the trail.

Approximately a half mile down Zane Grey Creek from Long Key Lakes trail marker 13, two short creeks branch right. These shortcuts to Long Key Bight are a treat. Small sharks hang out where they exit into the bight, at Go-to 3 (Mangrove Creeks) (B5).

Go-to 2 (B6) marks the entrance to a mangrove swamp at Long Key Point. Although

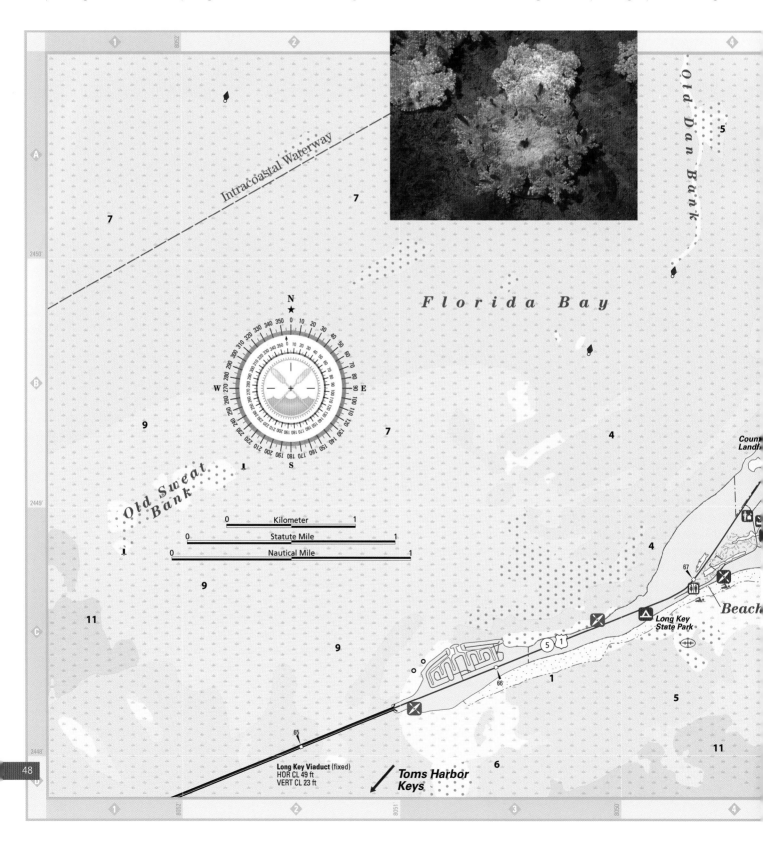

it meanders, a southwest route through the mangrove eventually empties back into Long Key Bight.

Landmarks: Pat Parks, in her book *The Railroad that Died at Sea,* described the Long Key Viaduct (D2) as the "first completed triumph" of the Overseas Railroad. Its architecture recalls Roman aqueducts, and it quickly became a trademark symbol of the railroad.

A set of narrow-gauge railroad wheels outside the Long Key State Park ranger station (C4) hearken to the Long Key Fish Camp, from which they were salvaged. Novelist Zane Grey was an avid sportfisherman and helped popularize this resort. The 1935 Labor Day Hurricane destroyed it.

Names: Fiesta Key (A6) is today the site of a KOA campground. Originally called Jewfish Bush Key, the Greyhound bus company bought it in 1947 and renamed it Greyhound Key. In 1966 KOA purchased it and renamed it Fiesta Key.

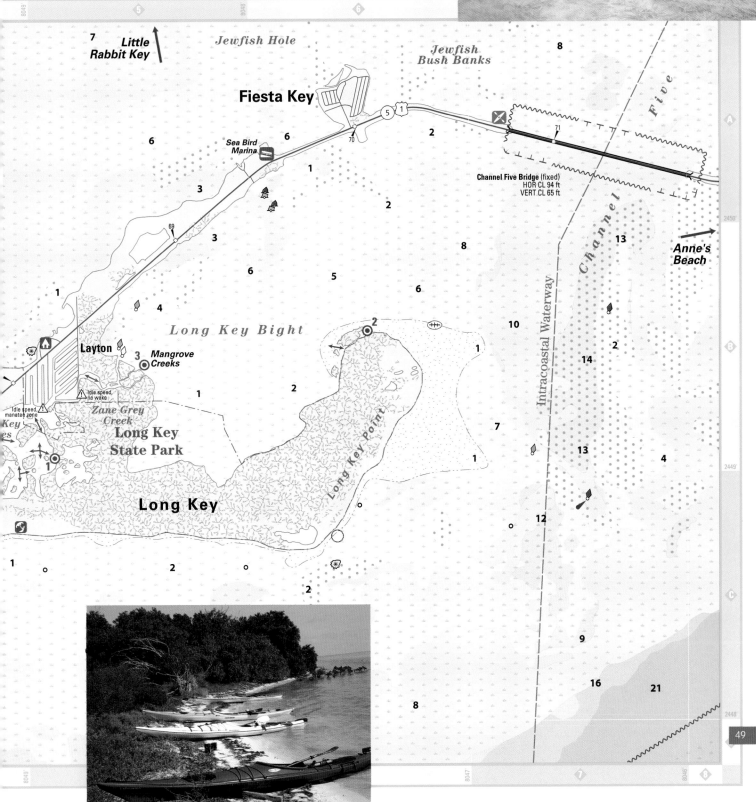

Jewfish Hole

Jewfish Bush Banks

Fiesta Key

Little Rabbit Key

Sea Bird Marina

Channel Five Bridge (fixed)
HOR CL 94 ft
VERT CL 65 ft

Anne's Beach

Long Key Bight

Layton

Mangrove Creeks

Idle speed, no wake

Idle speed, manatee zone

Zane Grey Creek

Long Key State Park

Long Key Point

Long Key

Intracoastal Waterway

Channel Five

Go-to Points: 1–4; 5 (Duck Key Channel)
Off-Chart D/Cs: Long Key State Park; Curry Hammock State Park
Caution: At low water, tidal flats emerge offshore of Toms Harbor Keys. In order to land, paddlers may have to walk a few hundred feet across these flats.
Getting There: Starting Point for Toms Harbor Keys: Curry Hammock State Park, Chart 21, B5. See appendix for details.

Photo courtesy of Monroe County Public Library, Mile Markers Project

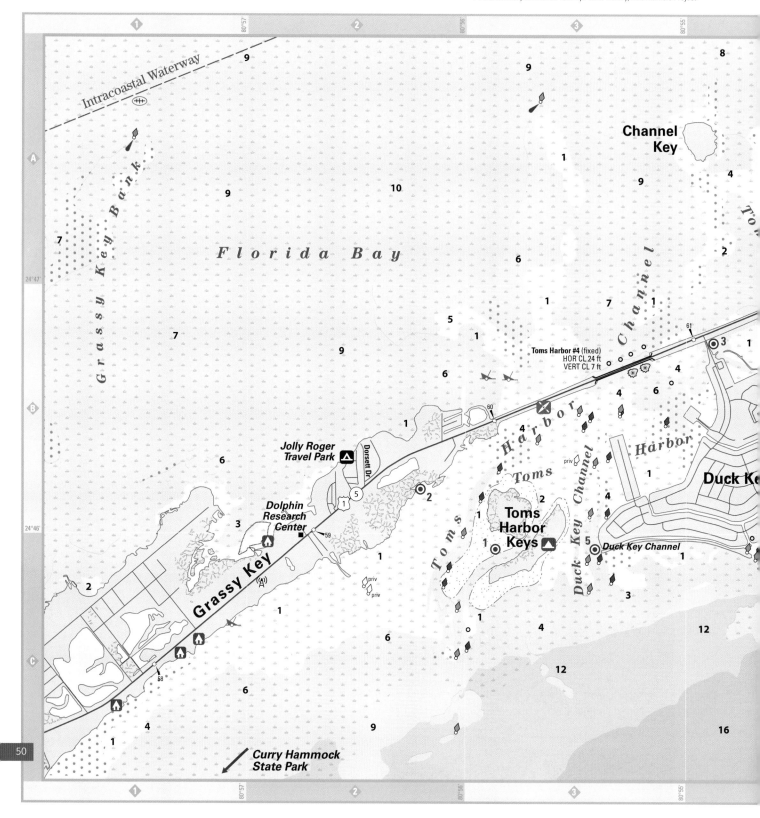

Navigation: Distance to Go-to 1 (Toms Harbor Keys): 3.5 miles from Curry Hammock State Park.
Paddling: Although put-ins on US 1 are more convenient to Toms Harbor Keys, launching from Curry Hammock State Park allows for a scenic 9-mile round-trip paddle along the oceanside of Grassy Key.

A wild beach fronts the ocean-facing side of the southernmost Toms Harbor Key (C3). Both Toms Harbor Keys are targeted for purchase by the state to protect tropical hardwood hammocks. As of publication, they were still privately owned, with a history of public use. N24°46.016′ W80°55.554′.

Small mangrove shoots and clumps are spreading through nearshore waters oceanside at Grassy Key's north end (Go-to 2, B2). Amid this soft shoreline, a kayaker can weave a boat through mangrove forest sheltered from sun and wind.

Landmarks: At the Dolphin Research Center (B2), MM 58.9 B/S, US 1, you can swim with some of Flipper's descendants—for real. Fee. (305–289–0002, www.dolphins.org)

Duck Key, also known as Hawk's Cay Resort, is a classic mid-twentieth-century Keys development. Owners had canals dredged, and resultant fill material created high ground for homes. This practice was widespread in the Keys and created miles of waterfront property out of swamps and mangrove forests. In the process, mangroves and sea grass beds were destroyed, and wetlands—essential feeding grounds for birds—were filled. Fish and bird populations dropped in historic proportions. Large-scale dredge-and-fill projects were halted in the mid-1970s, and mangroves were given protected status in 1985 by the Florida Mangrove Protection Act.

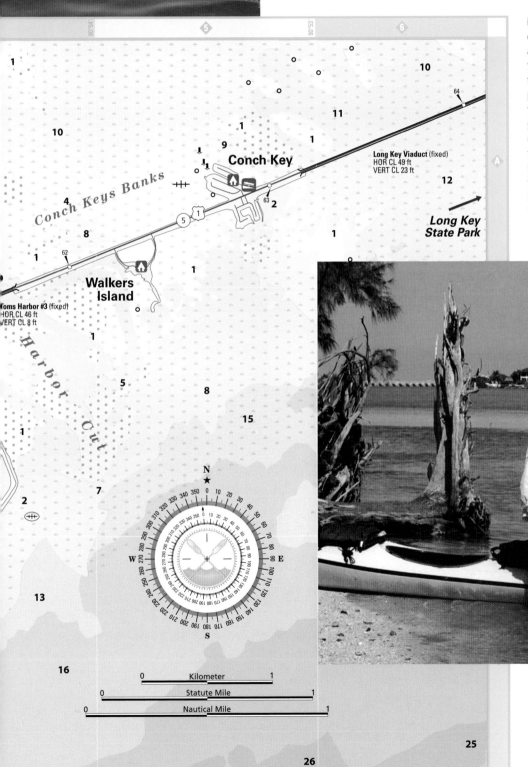

Go-to Points: 1–5; 6 (Crawl Key Sound); 7 (Deer Key); 8 (Coco Plum Trail)

Off-Chart D/Cs: Toms Harbor Keys; Sister Creek; 33rd Street Ramp

Caution: Commercial and charter fishing boats use Coco Plum Channel (C3) to reach the ocean. On weekends the channel sees heavy recreational boat traffic.

Go-tos 2 and 3 mark low bridges on Coco Plum Drive and Sadowski Causeway,

respectively. Clearance is 4 feet, possibly less at high tide.

Navigation: Distance to Go-to 1 (Toms Harbor Keys): 3.5 miles from Curry Hammock State Park.

Public Land: Curry Hammock State Park (B3, B4) has new campsites, a "Keys beach," picnic area, playground, and bathrooms. At the time of publication, the park was considering creating a paddler-only primitive campsite on the bayside of US 1 and restoring tidal flow between Long Point Key and Fat Deer Key.

CURRY HAMMOCK STATE PARK

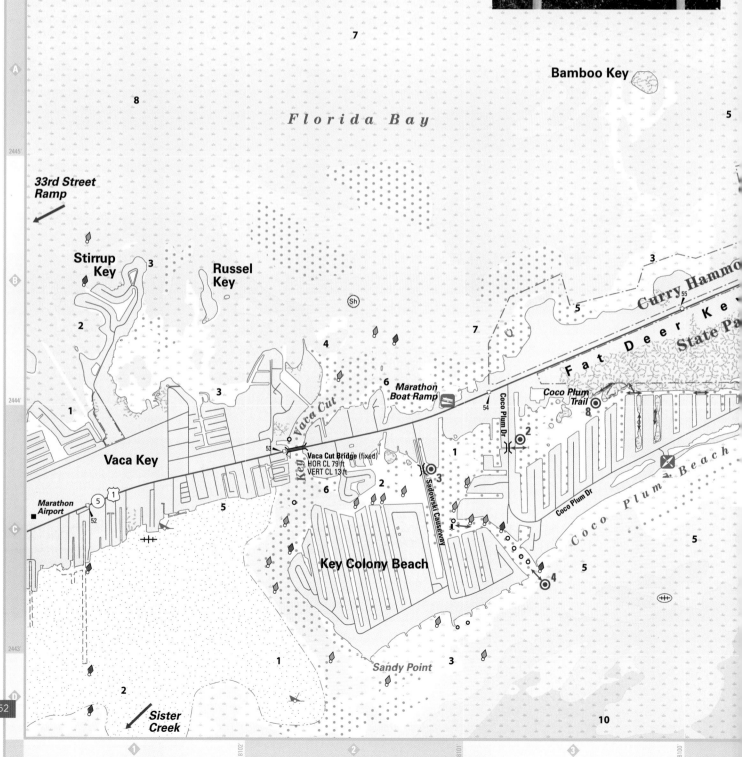

Paddling: Go-to 6 (Crawl Key Sound) (B5) is an ideal day trip for recreational kayakers. There is a small beach, mangrove creeks, old home canals, and guaranteed shelter from ill-blowing winds.

The 1.5-mile paddle around Little Crawl Key (B4) is an easy afternoon trip. Add 1.2 miles to the trip if it includes Deer Key. A mangrove tunnel begins at Go-to 1 passes beneath the park access road and winds through mangrove to emerge in a lagoon between Little Crawl Key and Deer Key.

Deer Key (B4) is the only undeveloped island within Curry Hammock State Park. A no-motor

zone around the island ensures a quiet spot for bird-watching.

Fat Deer Key, better known as Key Colony Beach and Coco Plum Beach, has felt the heavy hand of development. A building moratorium left seven home canals on Coco Plum Channel abandoned. Mangrove are overgrowing two canals (C3), and the deep water and shelter make these particularly good spots for kayak fishing.

Go-to 8 (Coco Plum Trail) (B3) is a paddler's ticket into a fine creek. Tall overarching red mangroves frame the tunnel that runs a half mile to Coco Plum Channel. Use caution when entering the boat channel.

Nature: A visual survey of Fat Deer Key's carved-up shoreline reveals a profusion of Australian pines and sea grapes. Both are invasive exotics that quickly colonize disturbed areas throughout the Keys.

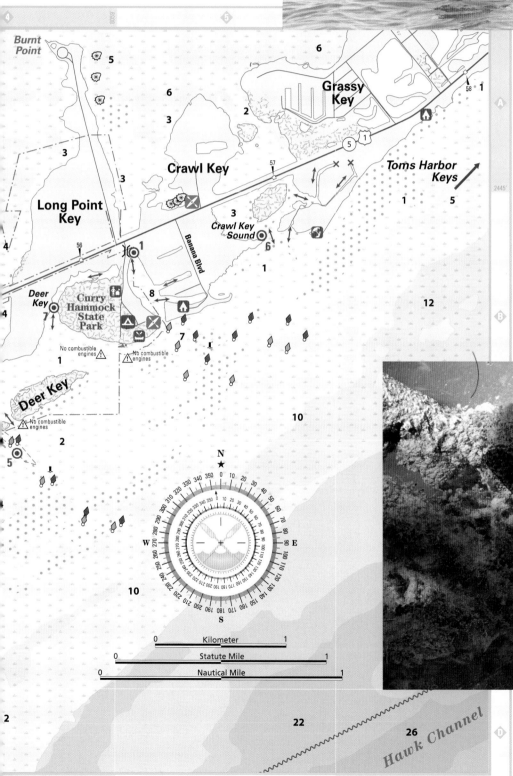

Go-to Points: 1–5; 6 (Whiskey Creek); 7 (Boot Key Mangrove)

Off-Chart D/Cs: Curry Hammock State Park; Molasses Key; Pigeon Key

Caution: Charter fishing boats use the channel offshore of the 33rd Street Ramp (B4). Also, shallow submerged rocks mark the far edge of the channel.

Alerts: The 33rd Street Ramp (B4) is the most reliable put-in for a Seven Mile Bridge crossing. There is a 48-hour parking limit here.

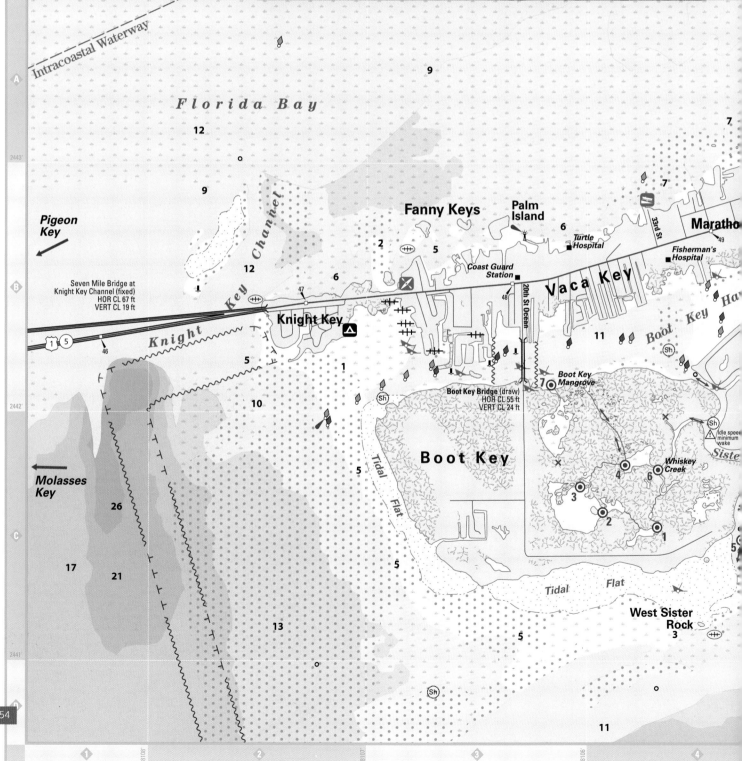

Tidal flats landward of West Sister Rock (C4) are impassable at low water.

Don't be fooled by distance: A trip through Whiskey Creek mangroves (Go-to 6, Whiskey Creek, C4) averages only 2 miles but fills a day with exploring.

Navigation: Route-finding in Whiskey Creek mangroves is a challenge. Here's a trick to finding your way: If you bear left from Go-to 6 (Whiskey Creek) (C4), all subsequent turns are *right* to return to the starting point. If bearing right at Whiskey Creek, all subsequent turns are *left* to the return to the starting point.

Public Land: Along with Bahia Honda State Park and Smathers Beach in Key West, Sombrero Beach in Marathon (C4) is one of the Key's best. There are bathrooms, outdoor showers, and picnic sites. Kayaks may land near the fishing and observation pier on Sister Creek. Entry is free. N 24°41.526′ W81°05.174′.

Paddling: On a 1.3-mile loop through Whiskey Creek mangroves (C4), bathe in a sun-warmed swim hole, watch schools of mullet rainbow out of the water upon approach, and spy white ibis, egrets, and herons amid the shelter and solitude of a small lake.

The narrow creek that runs north from Go-to 4 (C4) follows an adventurous half-mile course entirely under cover of mangroves. Watch out for skinny water at the exit into Boot Key Harbor.

Go-to 7 (Boot Key Mangrove) (B3) is a mere hint of a creek in the far corner of Boot Key Harbor. Once through the mangroves, a shallow lake spreads before you. Mark the inside entrance/exit to relocate the way out.

Landmarks: Crane Point Hammock Museum and Nature Center (A5), MM 50 B/S, US 1, preserves a pioneering Keys homestead. Its colorful mural facing US 1 will likely draw your attention first. A museum, visitor center, the Adderley Town Black Historical Site, and nature trails are open to visitors. Rachel Key, just offshore of Crane Point, is a bird rookery and nesting site. Admission is charged. Hours vary. (305–743–9100, www.cranepoint.org)

The Turtle Hospital (B3), MM 48.4 B/S, US 1, has daily tours of the turtle rehabilitation area. Advance reservation suggested. (305–743–2552, www.theturtlehospital.org)

Outfitters: Marathon Kayak, 6365 Overseas Highway O/S (A5) rents and offers half-day and full-day tours for birders, snorkelers, and mangrove explorers. They also run custom trips to Curry Hammock and Bahia Honda state parks. See appendix for details.

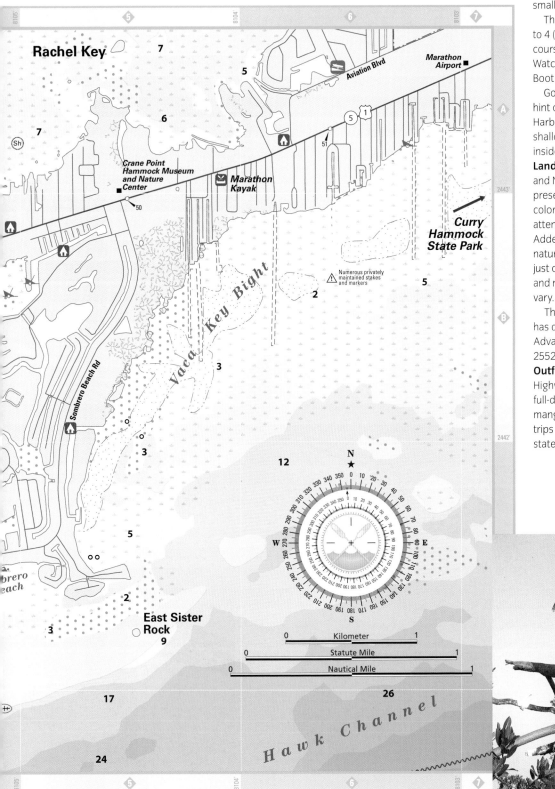

23 Seven Mile Bridge

Go-to Points: 1 (Pigeon Key); 2 (Molasses Key)
Off-Chart D/Cs: 33rd Street Ramp; Sister Creek; Bahia Honda State Park
Caution: Depth and currents produce highly variable conditions around Seven Mile Bridge. In boat channels strong currents can sweep a kayak off-course in a matter of minutes.

An open-water kayak trip, such as a Seven Mile Bridge crossing, requires paddlers be in good physical condition, possess proper skills, and use the right equipment.

Sudden, violent storms rise quickly in the Florida Keys. There is no shelter on open water in heavy winds, lightning, and rough water conditions. Check forecasts before leaving, and consider carrying a weather radio.

Navigation: A crossing of the Seven Mile Bridge by kayak may seem intimidating. Make it manageable by breaking it down into four legs: 1) 33rd Street Ramp to Pigeon Key, 3.8 miles; 2) Pigeon Key to Molasses Key, 2.5 miles; 3) Molasses Key to Money Key, 1.7 miles; and 4) Money Key to Little Duck Key, 1 mile.

Public Land: Pigeon Key (B6) is owned by

Monroe County and leased by the Pigeon Key Foundation, a nonprofit for education and preservation. Landing is permitted on a beach on the north shore of the island (Go-to 1, Pigeon Key).

Paddling: A Seven Mile Bridge crossing between the 33rd Street Ramp in Marathon (Chart 22, B4) and Little Duck Key (Chart 23, C2), via Pigeon Key, Molasses Key, and Money Key averages 9 miles one way.

Landmark: Pigeon Key preserves original buildings dating to the Overseas Railroad era. Its museum displays scale models of the original

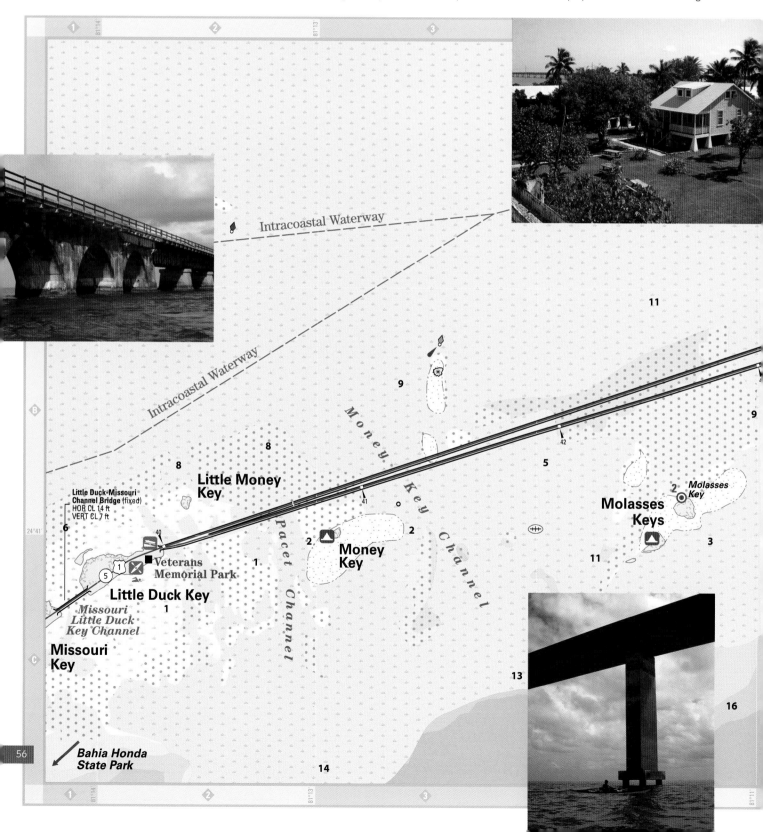

Seven Mile Bridge and preserves documents, photos, and publicity about the period. The island served as a work camp during bridge construction, later as a bridge maintenance camp for the railroad and later the vehicle road. There is a visitor center on Knight Key, MM 47 O/S. Call (305) 743–5999.

Hiking: The historic bridge from Marathon to Pigeon Key is open to hikers, runners, cyclists, and in-line skaters. The state plans to repair the old bridge in the coming year, and access may be restricted.

Photo courtesy of Monroe County Public Library, Mile Markers Project

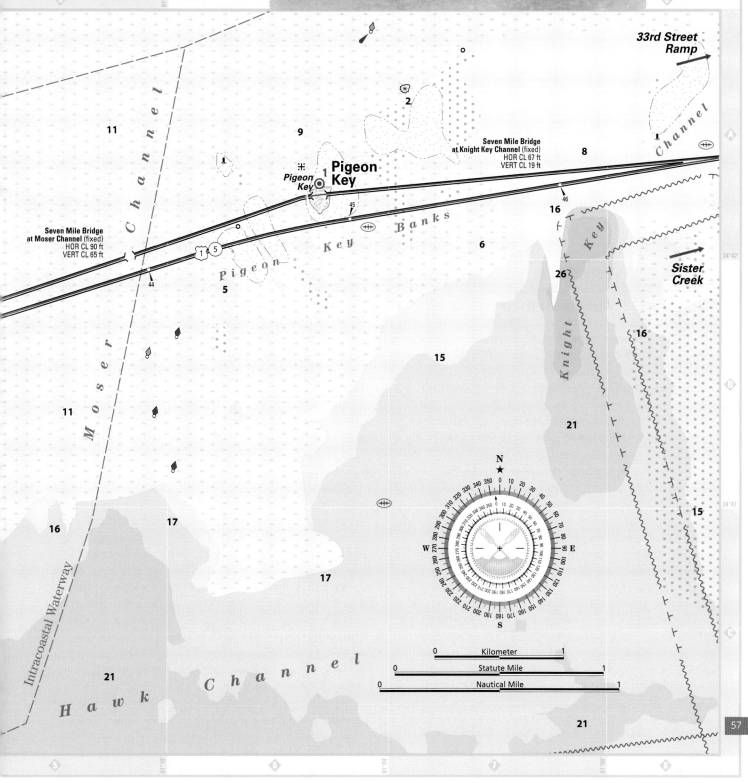

33rd Street Ramp

Seven Mile Bridge
at Knight Key Channel (fixed)
HOR CL 67 ft
VERT CL 19 ft

Seven Mile Bridge
at Moser Channel (fixed)
HOR CL 90 ft
VERT CL 65 ft

Pigeon Key

Pigeon Key

Pigeon Key Banks

Moser Channel

Knight Key

Sister Creek

Intracoastal Waterway

Hawk Channel

N

W   E

S

0	Kilometer	1
0	Statute Mile	1
0	Nautical Mile	1

Lower Keys

What surprises await a paddler in the Lower Keys?

An array of starfish on the mud bottom of Five Mile Creek.

Negotiating "skinny water" in Old Find's Bight.

Breaking through a tiny mangrove tunnel into Howe Key.

Scooting down a neighborhood canal through the heart of Key West.

Snorkeling amid corals, sea whips, and sea fans at the base of Fort Jefferson.

Watching waves break against rocks at Snipe Point.

Riding the surge of a Gulf tide through Content Passage.

Navigating long tunnels through mangrove forest leading to the Key West salt ponds.

Staring down bonefish over the patch reefs at Newfound Harbor.

Watching a Key deer swim toward your boat, only his head and antlers visible.

The Lower Keys begin and end with Key West: Mile Marker 0 on the Overseas Highway (US 1), end of the line for the Overseas Railroad, a military outpost, Florida's largest city in the mid-1800s, an artists' retreat. "About as un-American as possible, and bearing a strong resemblance to a West Indian town," wrote a visitor 1886. Its earliest businessmen were pirates. The first legitimate occupation was salvaging wrecks out on the reef. Spongers, turtlers, and other commercial fishing enterprises thrived here, then faded. Cubans established a cigar-making industry, and after the Great Depression, a public works rebuilding campaign set the city on a path of renewal that spawned its current industry: tourism.

As with Key West, the Lower Keys are nothing like what precedes them up the island chain. Geographically, the Upper and Middle Keys form a bow-shaped line that arcs southwest. The Lower Keys appear—with a healthy dose of imagination—as if someone smeared them across the shallow waters of the Backcountry. Islands are oriented northwest-to-southeast, and are divided by long, wide channels. Soft corals and colorful sponges predominate in many nearshore hard-bottom environments. The channels, by contrast, are carpeted with turtle and manatee grass.

The explanation of why the Lower Keys appear so different goes back tens of thousands of years. In the Upper and Middle Keys, islands formed from coral reef that was exposed then died when sea levels dropped. By contrast, islands from Big Pine to Key West evolved from giant shoals formed from deposits of oolitic sand. This tidbit of geology helps explain, in part, why deer, rabbits, mud turtles, and alligators are found on Big Pine, No Name, Sugar-

loaf, the Torches, and Cudjoe—but not elsewhere in the Keys. In the summer and fall wet seasons, freshwater collects in depressions in the solid oolitic caprock. (In the Upper Keys, the limestone is porous and, in most areas, rainwater seeps through.) These wetlands are seasonal and quite rare, but serve as critical habitat for animals specially adapted to them. During the rainy summer months, around upland pine forests, it's not uncommon to hear frogs on the edge of an ephemeral freshwater marsh. Migrating birds flock here, attracted by freshwater food sources like crayfish. Lower Keys marsh rabbits, an endangered species, munch on the fresh shoots of cattails and sedges, while mud turtles, a reptile endemic to the Lower Keys, wallow about.

Gulfside of the Lower Keys, more than 200,000 acres of water and small islands form what is commonly called the Lower Keys Backcountry. Here visitors can view the great white heron—a color variant of the great blue heron—hunt the shallows alongside Big Pine Key. Royal terns group on sandbars near the Content Keys, intermingled with laughing gulls and a few oystercatchers. Around the Water Keys, shoals are littered with burnt orange–colored sea cucumbers. As you approach the Mud Keys, ospreys soar overhead and issue sharp-pitched whistles as they scan the water for prey. White and brown pelicans, little blue herons, tri-colored herons, great egrets, and snowy egrets work swampy mangrove flats from Cutoe Key to Cayo Agua. West of Key West, loggerhead turtles nest on natural sand beaches.

The Backcountry's watery wilderness, the upland habitat on Big Pine and No Name Keys, and the sandy beaches of Boca Grande

Key and the Marquesas are so unique and important that three national wildlife refuges—National Key Deer, Great White Heron, and Key West—were created to protect them. Combined, they encompass more than 400,000 acres of land and water from East Bahia Honda Key to the Marquesas. National Key Deer Refuge is the best known, with jurisdiction on Big Pine, No Name, and a few of the other larger islands. Great White Heron National Wildlife Refuge covers the Backcountry. Key West National Wildlife Refuge encompasses twelve keys and surrounding waters due west of Key West.

The highlight of the Backcountry has to be the string of remote islands that start at the Content Keys and run southeast to include the Sawyers, Barracudas, Marvin, Snipe Point, Mud, and Lower Harbor Keys. These are as remote as they are beautiful. At low tide miles of sandbars are exposed, and recreational boaters often beach on them for a few hours of lounging in the sand and sun. For a paddler, it is an ambitious open-water journey out to these islands, set as they are between 5 and 7 miles offshore from convenient put-ins. But a trip out to the "edge of the nearshore waters," as we've come to term them, is one not soon forgotten.

Nor is the spirit of the Lower Keys. Here mainland Florida is a distant memory. Off US 1, places like the No Name Pub and Geiger Key Marina don't mimic someone's idea of the Keys—they *are* the

Keys: good food, cold beer, and an ear you can bend with a good story about that 12-foot shark that bumped the boat. An old dog greets you at the Sugarloaf Airport. If you're to believe every story you're told, movie directors use this location for their Third World airport scenes. What's undeniable is the beauty of Fivemile Creek, within sight of the airstrip, and the creeks that wind their way through the deep mangrove forest around Fivemile. In the Lower Keys such creek systems are few and far between, and appreciated all the more because of that.

After two years of paddling the Keys, we recall two encounters that capture the essence of the Lower Keys. After an hour paddling from Big Pine Key, we encountered an older man walking in waist-deep water, trailing a skiff with a rope. He ignored us until we hailed him. "Looking for sponges, different things," he muttered, then returned to ignoring us. A few days later, paddling in shin-deep water offshore of Big Torch Key, a middle-aged couple walked up to our kayaks. This time there wasn't a sailboat in sight. Instead, they hailed from Big Torch. "Just taking a walk in the flats," they said, and pointed to the Torch Key Mangroves, a quarter-mile distant, as their destination.

The Lower Keys: independent, with an eccentric spirit, like the folks who take walks through sponge flats at low tide.

Go-to Points: 1–3
Off-Chart D/Cs: Bahia Honda State Park; Koehn Avenue Boat Ramp
Caution: An open-water kayak trip requires paddlers be in good physical condition, possess the proper skills, and use the right equipment.

Storms rise quickly in the Florida Keys. There is no shelter on open water in heavy winds, lightning, and rough water conditions. Check forecasts before leaving, and consider carrying a weather radio.

Alert: At day's end, paddlers returning to the Koehn Avenue Boat Ramp from points east face a setting sun. The glare can obstruct landforms and makes pinpointing the ramp difficult.
Getting There: Starting points for Horseshoe Keys: Koehn Avenue Boat Ramp, Chart 29, C4; Bahia Honda State Park, Chart 27, C4. See appendix for details.
Navigation: Distances to Horseshoe Keys: 7 miles from Koehn Avenue Boat Ramp via Porpoise Key, Water Key, Johnson Keys; 8.5 miles from Bahia Honda State Park via Teakettle Key, Sandfly Key.

Public Land: East Bahia Honda Key (B7) marks the eastern boundary of the Great White Heron National Wildlife Refuge, a wilderness that ranges 40 miles west to the Bay Keys. This area is referred to as the Backcountry, and its nearly 200,000 acres exist for the protection of wading and migrating birds. Personal watercraft and waterskiing are prohibited; boating, fishing, snorkeling, and wildlife observation are allowed.

A 300-foot no-access buffer surrounds Horseshoe Key (B3) to minimize disturbance to nesting and roosting birds. Heron, willet, and osprey

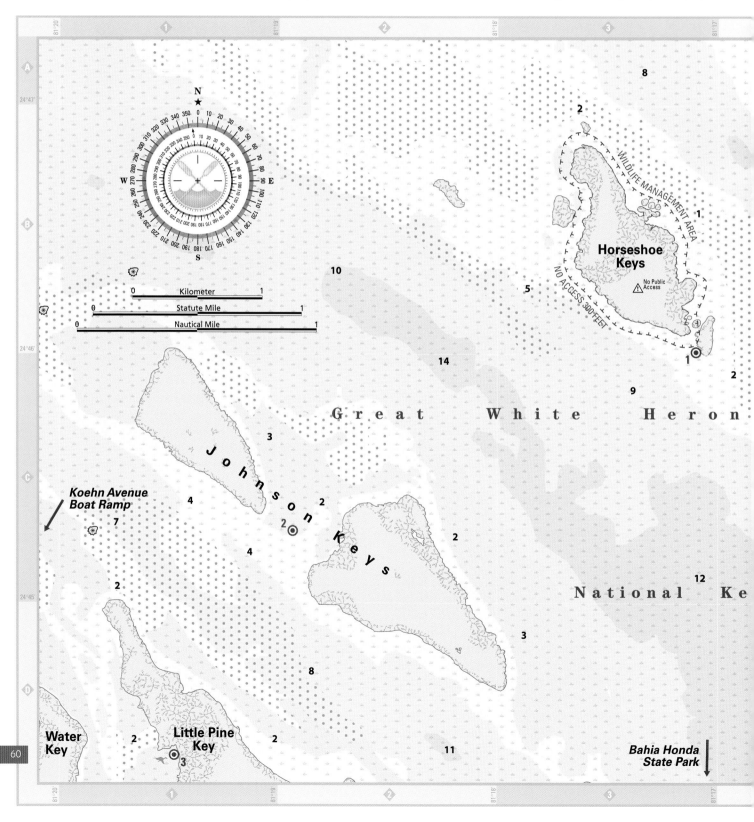

nests have been documented within this wildlife protection area.

Paddling: Johnson Keys, Horseshoe Keys, and West Bahia Honda Key stand well off the chain of inhabited keys. Little Pine Key (D1) had homesteaders in the 1800s, but there are no obvious buildings or sites as you kayak past. Refuge biologists tried introducing Key deer as permanent residents, but the animals swam back to Big Pine Key.

Nature: Most islands in the Lower Keys Backcountry align northwest-to-southeast, a direction that mirrors the channels that separate them. Within the channels, sea grass meadows predominate. Nearshore to many islands, there are extensive hard-bottom communities, with characteristic sponges, algae, and soft corals. Farther offshore the immensity of sky and water dwarfs travelers. On a calm, clear day, the water mirrors sky, and the clouds, tall and billowing, melt into a glassy smooth surface.

Key deer are known to forage on outlying islands during the wet summer season. Encountering a deer swimming toward your boat—essentially a floating head with antlers—is a startling, and not soon forgotten, sight.

Field Notes: Only experienced sea kayakers with a full day and good weather should attempt an ambitious trip to Horseshoe Keys; otherwise, head for the northern tip of Little Pine Key and savor for a moment the wide expanse of blue water and the dark lumps on the horizon. Before you turn back, take a mental snapshot. This is a true modern-day wilderness—a place that will remain untouched and pristine in your imagination.

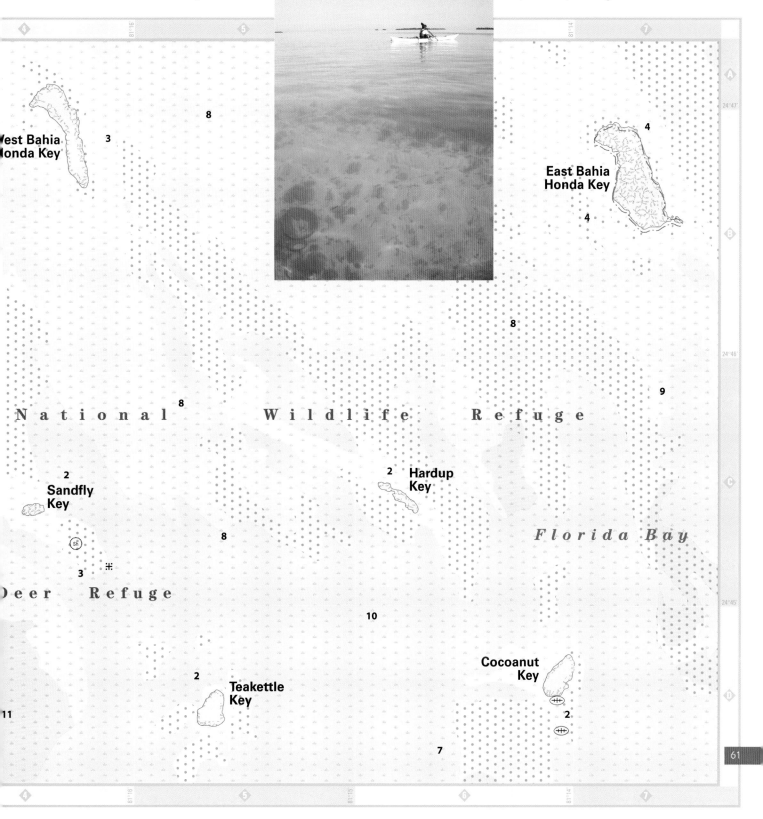

West Bahia Honda Key

3

8

East Bahia Honda Key

4

4

N a t i o n a l   W i l d l i f e   R e f u g e

8

8

9

2
Sandfly Key

2 Hardup Key

Florida Bay

8

3

Deer   Refuge

10

2
Teakettle Key

Cocoanut Key

2

11

7

Go-to Points: 1; 2 (Little Pine Key)
Off-Chart D/Cs: Bahia Honda State Park; Koehn Avenue Boat Ramp
Caution: Any long open-water kayak trip requires paddlers be in good physical condition, possess the proper skills, and use the right equipment.

Sudden, violent storms rise quickly in the Lower Keys Backcountry. There is no shelter on open water in heavy winds, lightning, and rough water conditions. Check forecasts before leaving, and consider carrying a weather radio.
Alert: At day's end, paddlers returning to the Koehn Avenue Boat Ramp from points east face a setting sun. The resulting glare obstructs landforms and makes pinpointing the ramp difficult.
Getting There: Starting points for Horseshoe Keys: Koehn Avenue Boat Ramp, Chart 29, C3; No Name Key Launch #2, Chart 26, C3. See appendix for details.
Navigation: Distances to Go-to 2 (Little Pine Key): 3.1 miles from Koehn Avenue Boat Ramp via Porpoise Key; 2.1 miles from No Name Key Launch #2 via No Name Key.

Public Land: Little Pine Key is part of the Great White Heron National Wildlife Refuge. The refuge protects a variety of migratory wading birds, shorebirds, hawks, and eagles that nest, roost, or feed on more than 30 uninhabited mangrove islands. Personal watercraft and waterskiing are not allowed in the refuge. Fishing, boating, diving, snorkeling, and wildlife observation are permitted.

The National Key Deer Refuge, with landhold-

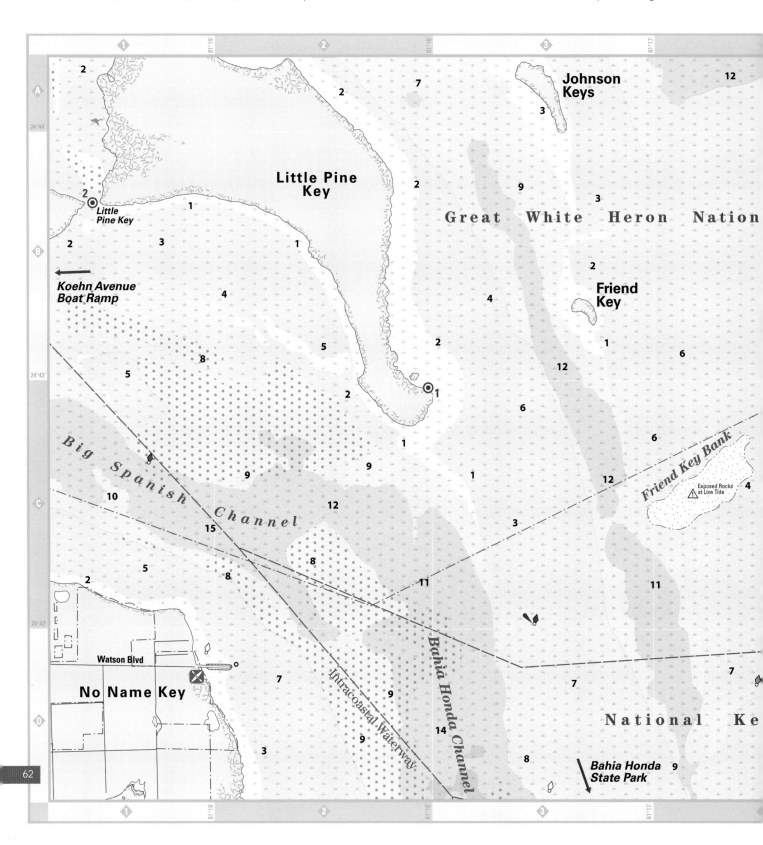

ings on No Name Key (C1, D1), was created in 1957 for protection of then-dwindling Key deer.

Paddling: Circumnavigating Little Pine Key is a rewarding full-day paddle for those who can tolerate sitting for up to six hours in a boat. The bottom habitat along the island's east side is patchy sea grass that looks like dusty gray confetti blowing in the wind. There is usually shark activity north of Go-to 1.

At Go-to 2 (Little Pine Key), paddlers will see colorful orange sponges, soft corals, vase and basket sponges, and lesser starlet coral. The craggy rock bottom hides lobsters and other crustaceans.

See Chart 26 for details on paddling No Name Key.

Field Notes: The wrack and tree debris on Little Pine's eastern side is typical of east-facing shorelines in the Lower Keys. They seem to catch the brunt of storms, as well as whatever flotsam the current carries past.

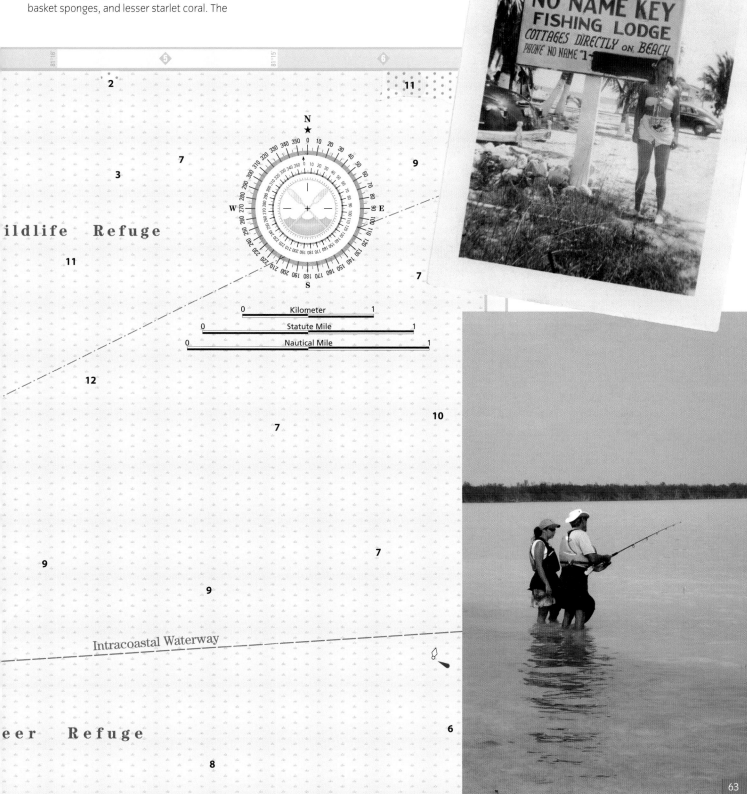

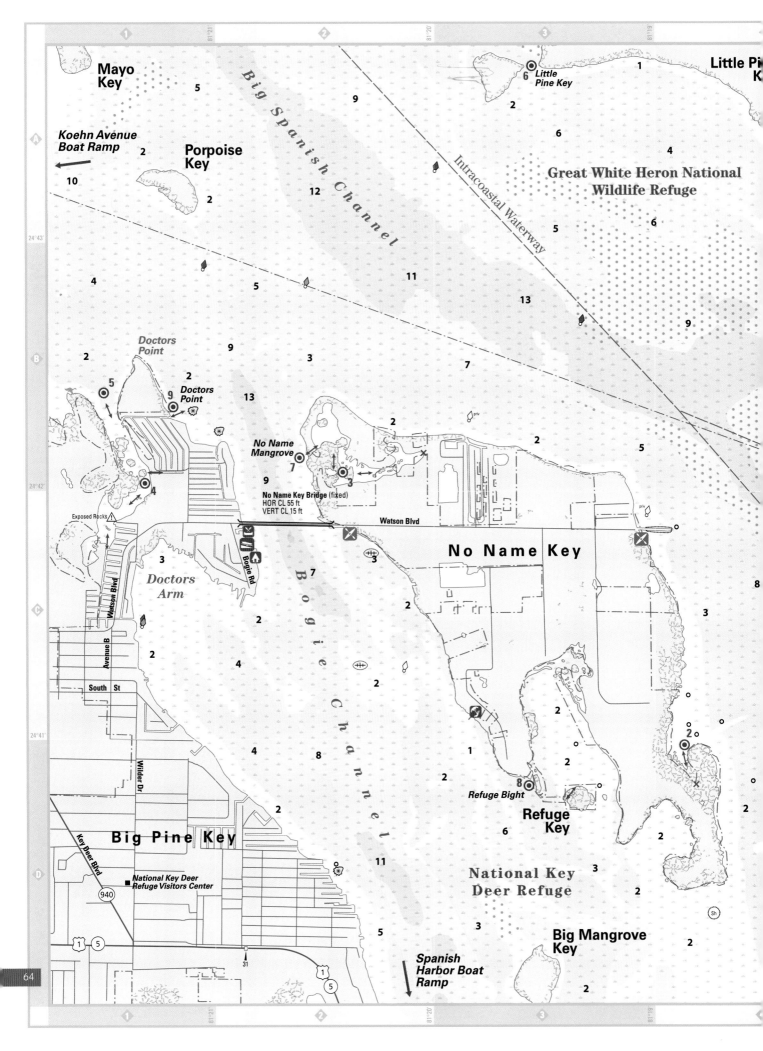

Mayo
Key

*Koehn Avenue
Boat Ramp*

Porpoise
Key

*Doctors
Point*

*Doctors
Point*

No Name
Mangrove

Big Spanish Channel

Intracoastal Waterway

Little
Pine Key

Little Pi
K

**Great White Heron National
Wildlife Refuge**

No Name Key Bridge (fixed)
HOR CL 55 ft
VERT CL 15 ft

Watson Blvd

No Name Key

*Doctors
Arm*

Exposed Rocks

Bogie Rd

Watson Blvd

Avenue B

South St

Wilder Dr

Key Deer Blvd

Big Pine Key

Bogie Channel

National Key Deer
Refuge Visitors Center

940

1   5

31

1

5

*Spanish
Harbor Boat
Ramp*

Refuge Bight

**Refuge
Key**

**National Key
Deer Refuge**

**Big Mangrove
Key**

Sh

24°43'

24°42'

24°41'

81°21'

81°20'

81°19'

81°18'

A

B

C

D

1

2

3

1

2

3

priv

priv

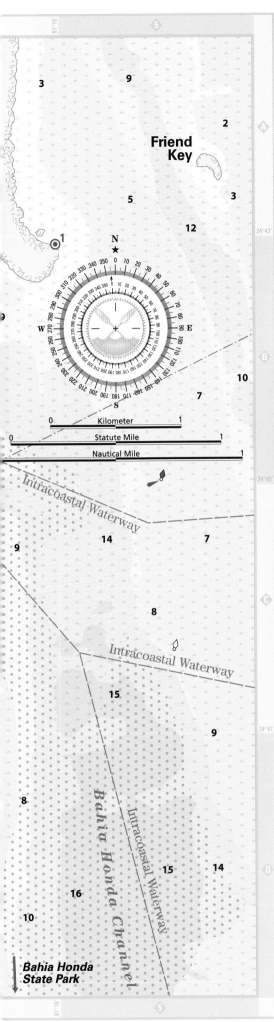

Go-to Points: 1–5; 6 (Little Pine Key); 7 (No Name Mangrove); 8 (Refuge Bight); 9 (Doctors Point)

Off-Chart D/Cs: Koehn Avenue Boat Ramp; Spanish Harbor Boat Ramp; Bahia Honda State Park

Alert: Consider bringing a bright marker—surveyor's tape, a bandana, or an extra hat—to tag the entrance and exit of the interior lake at Go-to 3 (B2). Remove your marker as you leave.

Navigation: Distance around No Name Key: 9 miles from No Name Key Launch #1 (C2) via Refuge Bight, east shoreline, and No Name Mangroves.

Paddling up the east side of No Name, the landmass on the horizon is Little Pine Key. Rounding the northeast corner of No Name, a small pass is visible between Little Pine and an unnamed island (Go-to 6, Little Pine Key, A3).

impractical anytime but high water.

Lay back and float down a creek that bisects Refuge Key (D3). Pelicans and double-crested cormorants roost on this island. As you pass through, listen for their croaking noises from deep within the mangroves.

Landmarks: The National Key Deer Refuge Visitors Center (D1) is in the Big Pine Key Plaza on Big Pine Key, 0.2 mile north of the traffic

Public Land: No Name and Big Pine Keys form the nucleus of the National Key Deer Refuge. Its namesake deer, a diminutive version of the familiar white-tailed deer, will range onto outlying islands, but No Name and Big Pine have reliable year-round supplies of freshwater that the deer need to survive.

Paddling: See Chart 25 for details on paddling Little Pine Key (A4).

See Chart 30 for details on paddling behind Doctors Arm (C1).

A labyrinth-like journey begins at Go-to 7 (No Name Mangrove) (B2). Initially wide and clear, the route becomes narrow, twisty, and intuitive, then empties into an interior lake. The route may be impassable due to overgrown mangrove roots.

Go-to 8 (Refuge Bight) (D3) is a shortcut into wide, shallow Refuge Bight. Near to the shore, sponges are visible on the sandy bottom. At the bight's northern reaches, passage is

light on US 1. (305–872–0774, www.fws.gov/nationalkeydeer)

The Old Wooden Bridge Marina (C2) is on Watson Boulevard on Big Pine Key (at the west end of the ridge to No Name Key). You'll find a marine store with guest cottages, hotel, and marina.

History: Ferries plied the 40-mile stretch between Lower Matecumbe and No Name Keys from 1928 until construction of US 1 on Grassy Key and Key Vaca in the 1930s. The old ferry landing at the end of Watson Road (C3) is now a great kayak launch, albeit from a soupy shoreline that gets socked in with rafts of dead sea grass.

Outfitters: Big Pine Kayak Adventures (C1) operates out of the Old Wooden Bridge Marina on Watson Boulevard. Captain Bill Keogh specializes in Lower Keys Backcountry eco-tours, fishing trips, and catamaran sailing trips.

Go-to Points: 1–2; 3 (Refuge Bight); 4 (South Sound)

Off-Chart D/Cs: Molasses Key; Newfound Harbor SPA; Old Wooden Bridge Marina

Caution: Boaters may encounter strong currents and large swells in Bahia Honda Channel (C3). A strong north wind causes especially rough boating conditions.

Navigation: It is 2 miles, straight-line distance at a compass bearing of 340 degrees, from Spanish Harbor Wayside Park on West Summerland

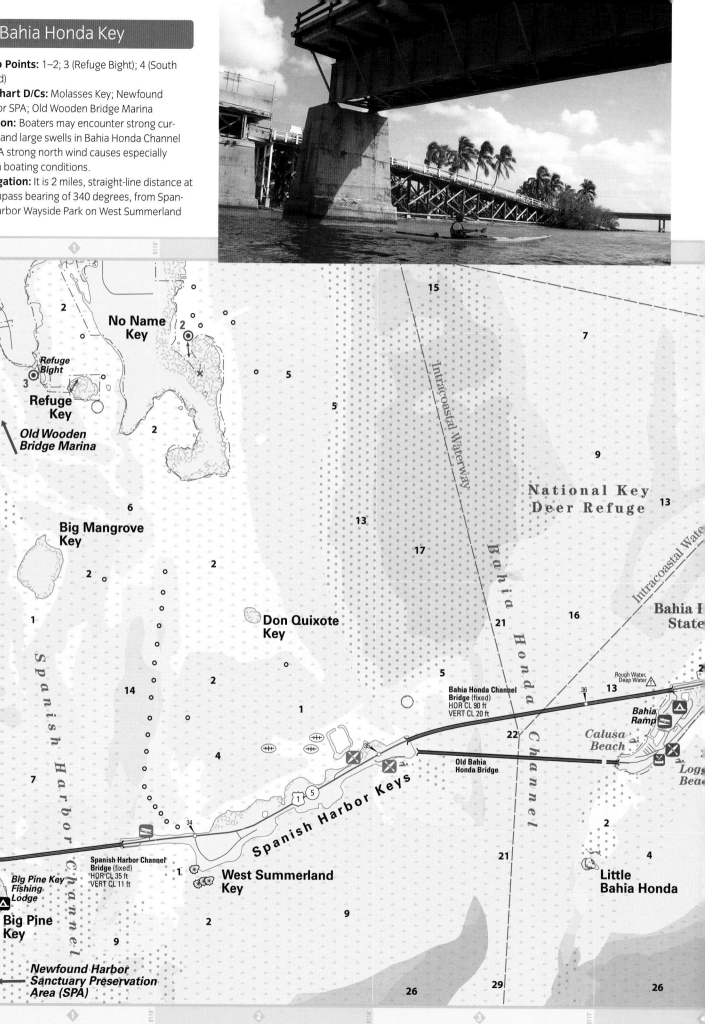

Key (D1) to Go-to 3 (Refuge Bight) on No Name Key (B1).

Public Land: Bahia Honda State Park is famous for its white sand beaches and one-of-a-kind view of the sunset. The entire island lies within the park. There are hiking trails, picnic areas, snorkeling and diving concessions, cabins, developed campsites, and a primitive camping area. See appendix for more information.

A portion of Ohio Key (B6) and the adjacent Rachel Carson Key are part of the National Key Deer Refuge.

Rest Area: The low-tide beach at Go-to 1 (C4) makes a good rest spot or a destination unto itself. The occasional powerboaters bring lawn chairs, but more often than not it is a quiet place. It's also the last reliable rest stop on the Gulf side of Bahia Honda.

Paddling: A circuit around Bahia Honda averages 6 miles, but varying conditions make this an ambitious trip. There are shallow, sheltered waters on the Gulf side of the island, breaking surf on the Atlantic, and rough chop in the deep Bahia Honda Channel.

Little Bahia Honda (D3) is a small island next to the Bahia Honda Channel. It is an easy paddle with sit-on-top kayaks, which are for rent on Loggerhead Beach. The island's rocky surface makes it a less-than-ideal place to sunbathe. Snorkeling around the island is popular.

A short paddle from Go-to 4 (South Sound) (C4) leads into a sheltered lagoon inside Bahia Honda. It is uniformly shallow, save for a borrow pit on the north shore that reportedly dates to the Overseas Railroad. By sticking to the edges, paddlers will see plenty of fish and bird activity.

See Chart 26 for information on paddling No Name Key (A1, B1).

Nature: Why does Bahia Honda have such nice beaches? Like real estate, it's all about location. Large gaps in the Middle Keys' offshore reef allow waves to carry sand farther inshore, until it drops out of the surf onto this lucky island's shoreline.

Bahia Honda's beach and dune ecosystem, in the southeast corner of the island, is unique in the Keys. So, too, are some of the plants that grow here: railroad vine, sawgrass, cattails, and the rare West Indian satinwood, which is found nowhere else in Monroe County.

Camping: If campsites at Bahia Honda State Park are full (in season, they are booked a year in advance), a campsite at Big Pine Key Fishing Lodge (D1) is a good backup.

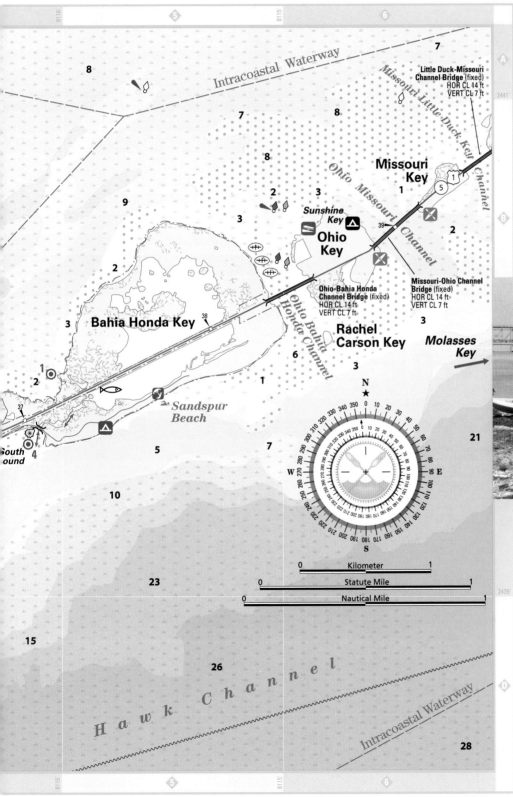

History: Bahia Honda's 35-foot-deep channel was the deepest encountered between Homestead and Key West during construction of the Overseas Railroad. A soft bottom further complicated plans. The uncertainty of how bridge pilings would hold was underscored during a 1910 hurricane when a central piling shifted under the force of the wind and waves. This is the only bridge on the 156-mile route with a superstructure for additional support.

Name: Bahia Honda is Spanish for "deep bay."

Ohio and Missouri Keys (B6) were named by homesick railroad workers constructing the Overseas Railroad.

Go-to Points: 1–4; 5 (Cutoe Key)
Off-Chart D/Cs: Old Wooden Bridge Marina; Koehn Avenue Boat Ramp; Content Keys.
Caution: The penalty for misreading tides on a trip to Cutoe is a long slog around the shallow sea grass meadows that border the channel.
Getting There: Starting points for Cutoe Key: Koehn Avenue Boat Ramp, Chart 29, C4; Key Deer Boulevard Put-in, Chart 29, C3.
See appendix for details.

Navigation: Distance to Cutoe Key Go-to 1: 3.6 miles from Koehn's Avenue Boat Ramp via Big Pine Key, Howe Key; 2.8 miles from Key Deer Boulevard Put-in via Big Pine Key, Howe Key.
Public Land: Cutoe and Annette Keys are part of the Great White Heron National Wildlife Refuge, which covers nearly 200,000 acres in the Lower Keys Backcountry. The refuge protects nesting and roosting habitat for the great white heron, a white morph of the great blue heron whose range is restricted in the United States to South Florida and the Keys.

Paddling: At Go-To 5 (Cutoe Key) (C3), there are three small lagoons connected by short creeks and passes. Juvenile sharks congregate in these pools in late spring.

Mangroves are slowly overgrowing tidal flats at the south end of Cutoe Key (Go-tos 1, 2). The creeks here are some of the most extensive and accessible in the Lower Keys.

On the east side of Cutoe, a small creek penetrates a few hundred feet into the island, then dead-ends in a pile of downed trees (C3). Submerged roots and limbs in this tuck-away make

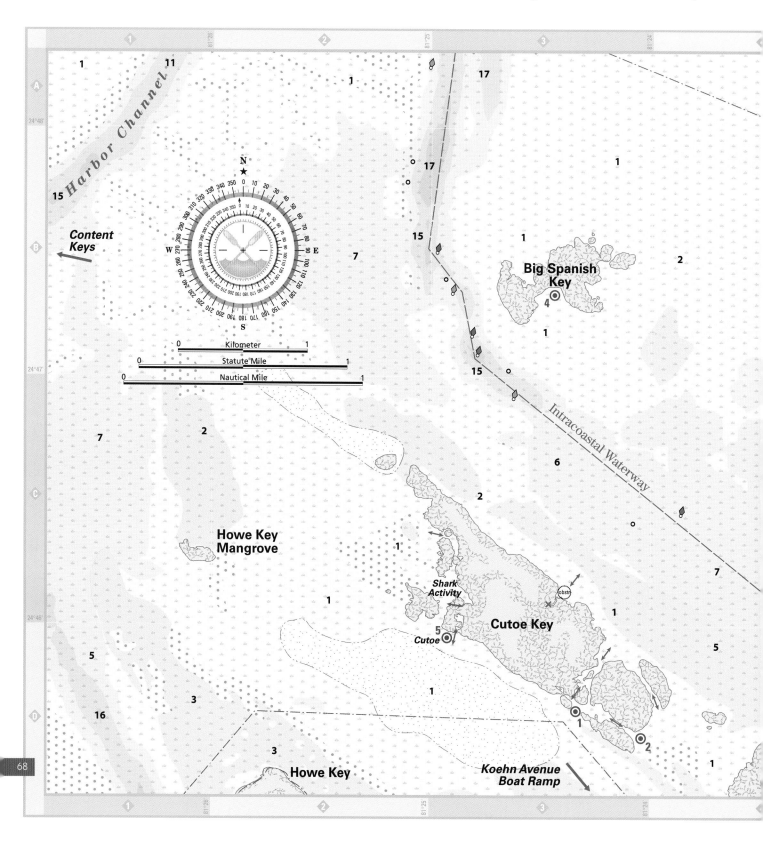

great fish havens. Access to the creek may be restricted to high tide.

Nature: A trip around Cutoe Key presents contrasting views of two bottom types typical of the Lower Keys: hard bottom and sea grass. On Cutoe's east side the bottom appears as flat, misshaped plates of rock strewn about like pieces of a jigsaw puzzle. A thin coat of gray silt covers the bottom and the plant life. This is preferred habitat for whelks, sea stars, black sponges, and soft and hard corals, to name a few. By contrast, in sea grass meadows that pre-

dominate off the western shore of Cutoe and Annette, the bottom is soft. Here, a web of life, from small shrimp and young fish to hungry

sharks, relies on the seagrass beds for shelter and food during formative years.

Great White Heron National Wildlife Refuge

National Key Deer Refuge

Little Spanish
Key Mangrove

Little
Spanish
Key

Big Spanish Channel

Annette
Key

Old Wooden
Bridge Marina

Crawl Key

Little Pine
Key Mangrove

29 Annette Key

Go-to Points: 1–5; 6 (Howe Key Creek)
Off-Chart D/Cs: Old Wooden Bridge Marina; Eden Pines Boat Ramp; Middle Torch Causeway
Alert: When traveling between Annette and Big Pine Keys, keep in mind the adage: "If it's brown, run aground." If you can see tips of sea grass out of the water, it may be too shallow to pass through. Local boat channels are marked by white sticks throughout the Backcountry.
Navigation: A local boat channel wraps around the north tip of Big Pine Key. South of here,

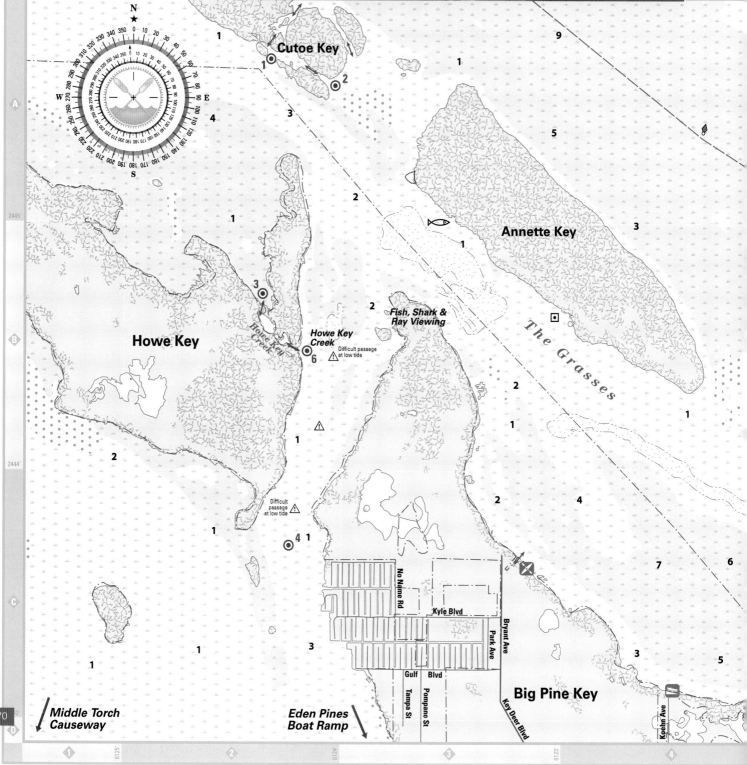

Cutoe Key

Annette Key

The Grasses

Howe Key

Howe Key Creek

Fish, Shark & Ray Viewing

Difficult passage at low tide

Difficult passage at low tide

Big Pine Key

No Name Rd

Kyle Blvd

Park Ave

Bryant Ave

Gulf Blvd

Tampa St

Pompano St

Key Deer Blvd

Koehn Ave

Middle Torch Causeway

Eden Pines Boat Ramp

sharks prowl and stingrays cruise the nearshore waters.

Outside the canal that leads from the Key Deer Boulevard Put-in (C3), line up Porpoise Key at a 110° bearing, Mayo Key at a 75° bearing, and the north side of Annette Key—which appears to merge with the northern tip of Big Pine Key—at a 345° bearing.

Public Land: Howe and Annette Keys are part of the Great White Heron National Wildlife Refuge. Nearly 200,000 acres of water and islands are preserved in the refuge. Great white herons and a variety of other herons, egrets, hawks, eagles,

gulls, terns, and shorebirds forage, roost, and nest here.

The National Key Deer Refuge is headquartered on Big Pine Key, in the Big Pine Key Plaza, 0.2 mile north of the traffic light (see Chart 26, D1).

Paddling: Enter and exit Howe Key Creek (B2) at Go-to 6 (Howe Key Creek) or Go-to 3. This kayak-only creek links two very shallow lagoons. The second lagoon is heavily silted in, but there is passable water tight against the mangroves.

The channel between Howe Key and Big Pine Key (B2, B3) is shallow in all seasons. Go-to 4 is an established local boat channel. Moving north, paddlers will find deeper water closer to Howe Key.

Just off Annette Key's northwest tip (A3) is a hard-bottom flat with soft corals and sponges. From this point south, for a half mile the shoreline is also "soft." A kayaker can poke around beneath overhanging red mangrove branches, where there's sure to be a few white ibis and plenty of fish.

Nature: Prop scars are long, narrow trenches in sea grass meadows dug by motorboat propellers. Several are visible in sea grass beds between Big Pine and Annette Keys. Often, a trough blows out during high winds or rough weather, starting an ever-widening erosion pattern that threatens larger swaths of sea grass than the original impacted area. Inexperience in navigating shallow Backcountry waters is most often the culprit in this destructive practice.

It's estimated only 25 to 80 Key deer were alive in 1955. The deer, which lives nowhere else in the world, was declared an endangered species in 1967. Today, population estimates are 500 to 800 deer, within a range from No Name Key to Sugarloaf Key.

Hiking: Visitors can walk any trail or fire road on National Key Deer Refuge property that is not marked as closed. Pets are welcome, on a leash.

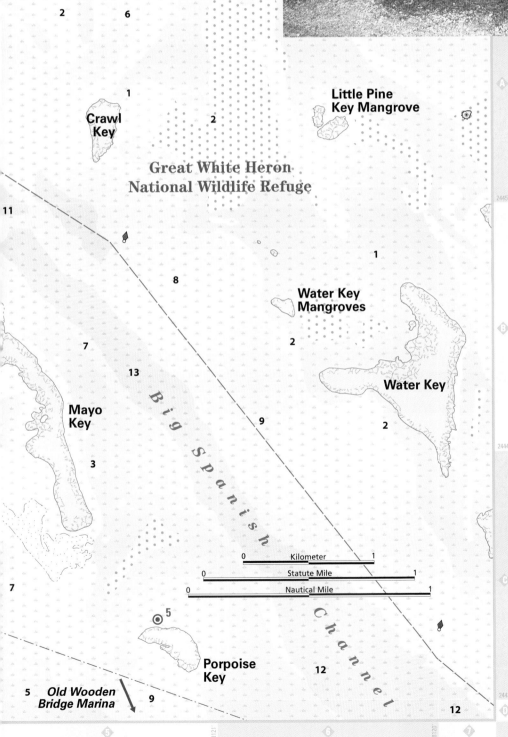

Crawl Key

Little Pine Key Mangrove

Great White Heron National Wildlife Refuge

Water Key Mangroves

Water Key

Big Spanish Channel

Mayo Key

Porpoise Key

Old Wooden Bridge Marina

0	Kilometer	1
0	Statute Mile	1
0	Nautical Mile	1

Go-to Points: 1–5; 6 (Doctors Point); 7 (No Name Mangrove)

Off-Chart D/Cs: Spanish Harbor Boat Ramp; Koehn Avenue Boat Ramp; Howe Key Channel

Caution: The west exit of a home canal on Doctors Point, near Go-to 5 (A5), shallows to less than a foot deep. Coral bedrock may be exposed at low tide. Similar conditions exist in the home canal south of Go-to 4 (A5).

Alert: Obey posted speed limits and watch out for Key deer on the roads of Big Pine and No Name Keys. Cars, and the people who drive them, are the Key deer's number one killer.

Navigation: A trip around Middle Torch requires paddlers to navigate beneath two highway bridges: Torch-Ramrod Channel and Torch Key Viaduct (Chart 31, A2 and A3). The bridges have a vertical clearance of 8 and 9 feet respectively. Tidal flats around the bridges may be impassable at low tide.

It is 1.2 miles from the Eden Pines Boat Ramp (B4), through the home canals, and out into Pine Channel. From the canal entrance, it is another 3.5 miles north to Go-to 4 on Chart 29, C2.

Public Land: Pilot Whale Park, also known as the Old Swimming Hole (C4), became locally famous when marine mammal rescuers rehabilitated stranded pilot whales here in 2003. Sailboaters use the swim hole as a dinghy dock and as a harbor when big storms blow through the Keys.

The National Key Deer Refuge's 8,800 acres are scattered across numerous islands between Big Pine Key and Summerland Key. The bulk is contained on Big Pine and No Name Keys.

Paddling: See Chart 26 for tips on paddling around No Name Key.

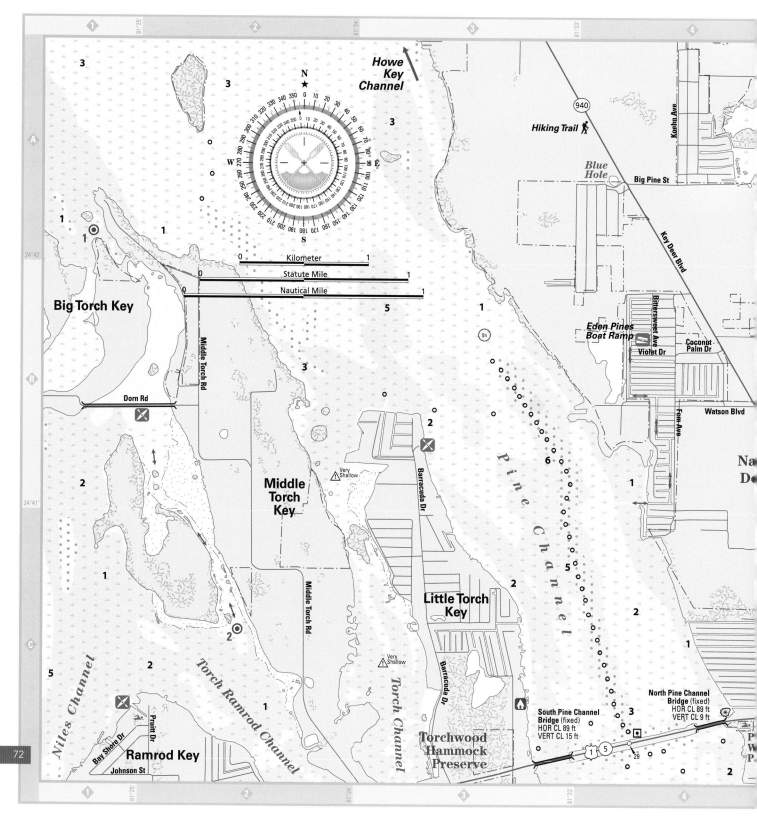

The mangroves behind Doctors Point (A5) is a sheltered spot for kayakers on a windy day. There is good bird-watching in the flats between Go-tos 4 and 5.

For paddlers circumnavigating Middle or Big Torch, Go-to 1 (A1) marks a passage that may be easily missed. There are quiet, sheltered lagoons south of this point.

Head south to Go-to 2 (C2) on days when the wind blows strong out of the north or northeast. Expect skinny water paddling, even at high water, between Middle Torch and the outlying island.

Landmarks: The National Key Deer Refuge Visitors Center (C5) is located in the Big Pine Key Plaza off Key Deer Boulevard, 0.2 mile north of the traffic light. (305–872–0774, www.fws.gov/nationalkeydeer)

Blue Hole (A4) is 3 miles north of the US 1/Key Deer Boulevard intersection on Big Pine Key. At this old limestone quarry turned freshwater pond, alligators—a rarity in the Lower Keys—lurk about, mingling with turtles, birds, and Key deer.

Nature: Weighing between 25 and 90 pounds, the endangered Key deer is the smallest subspecies of the North American white-tailed deer.

About 800 are found on 26 islands in the Lower Keys between Big Pine Key and Summerland Key. Capable swimmers, they will travel between islands in wet seasons, but during dry winter months, movement is restricted to islands with permanent freshwater sources. Big Pine Key and No Name Key contain two-thirds of the total population of the deer.

Hiking: The Jack C. Watson Wildlife Trail (A4) is a two-thirds-mile loop through forest and freshwater wetland. The Fred C. Manillo Wildlife Trail (C3) is 800 feet long and wheelchair accessible. It ends at a platform overlooking a freshwater wetland. Parking is a quarter mile north of the Blue Hole on Key Deer Boulevard.

Outfitters: Captain Bill Keogh of Big Pine Kayak Adventures, based out of the Old Wooden Bridge Marina (B6) on No Name Key, offers rentals, guided eco-tours, and custom backcountry tours. Guide Emily Graves runs Reflections Nature Tours, also headquartered at the marina. She trailers kayaks to select locations throughout the Lower Keys. See appendix for details.

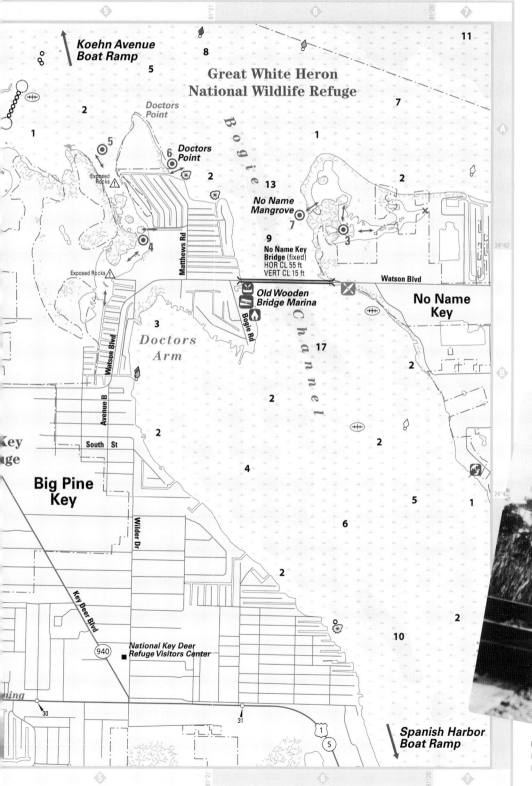

Photo courtesy of Monroe County Public Library, Mile Markers Project

Go-to Points: 1–7; 8 (Coupon Bight); 9 (Coral Heads); 10 (Mangrove Tunnel)

Off-Chart D/Cs: Spanish Harbor Ramp; Tarpon Creek

Alerts: Four large yellow balls mark the Newfound Harbor Sanctuary Preserve Area boundaries. Use smaller white balls with a single blue as mooring balls.

Kayakers should snorkel with one or more partners and be skilled at reentering a boat from in the water. One paddler should remain in his or her boat at all times to assist with rescues. Always use a dive flag, and never use an anchor, which can destroy coral.

The Boy Scouts of America owns Big Munson Island (C3, C4). The public is prohibited from landing.

Navigation: The southeast corner of Coupon Bight (Go-tos 2, 3, and 8; B5 and B6) can be disorienting: One mangrove island looks like another, and every shoreline is unnervingly similar. If you're lost, head southeast toward the sounds of cars on Long Beach Road. As you approach, count four telephone poles left from the first home roof, and follow that mark to the launch.

When heading north from Go-to 8 (Coupon Bight) (B6), locate a replica lighthouse on the far shore and keep it left of your bow. This track leads to a bird rookery northwest of Horseshoe Crab Beach (Go-to 1, A6).

Getting There: It is 2.5 miles one way from the Long Beach Road #1 Put-in (B7) to Go-to 4 (C5). From here, coral heads and patch reefs are widely spread in a line parallel to shore. New-

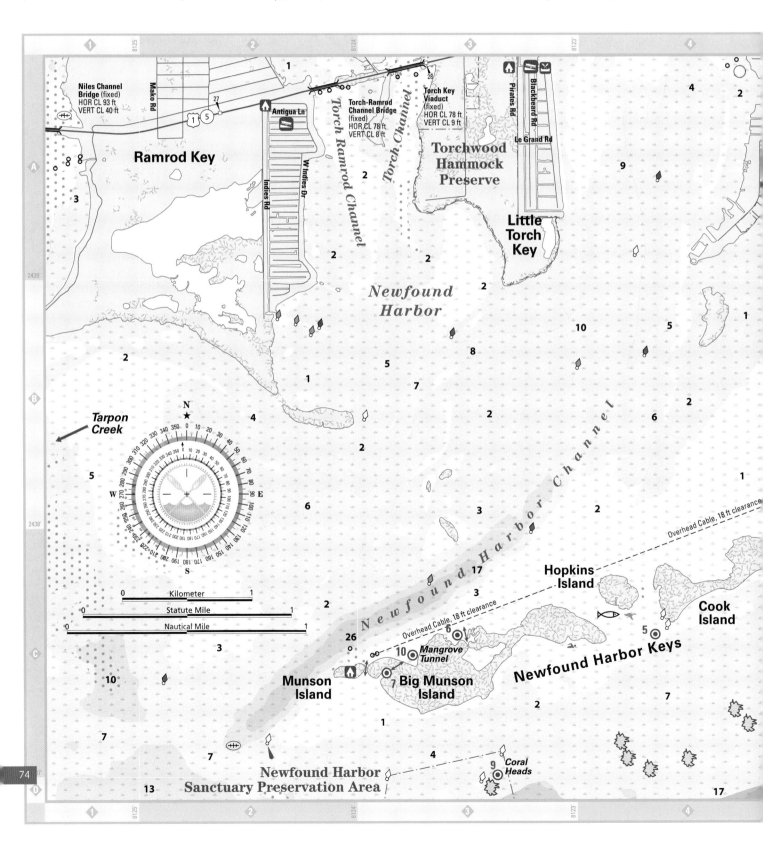

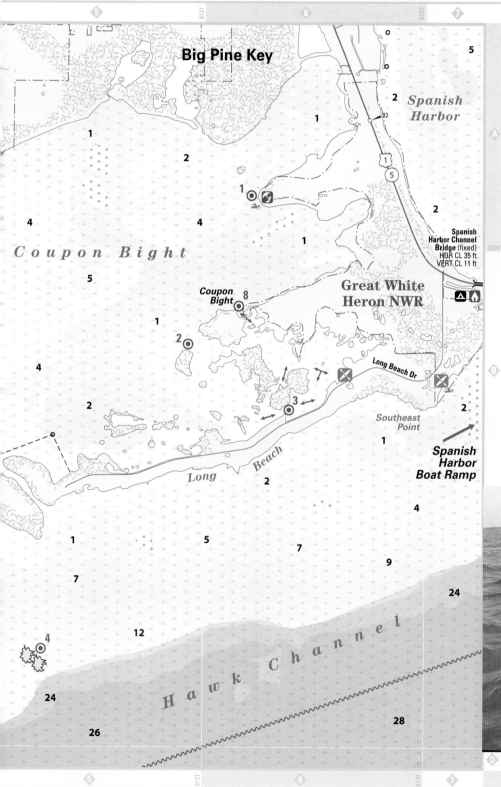

found Harbor Sanctuary Preservation Area is 3.7 miles one way from the put-in.

Public Land: Coupon Bight State Aquatic Preserve is a sanctuary for juvenile sharks, stingrays, and horseshoe crabs. All submerged land, plants, and marine life in the preservation area are protected.

Newfound Harbor Sanctuary Preservation Area (C3), the only protected inshore patch reef in the Lower Keys, is located less than a half-mile offshore of Big Munson Island in water ranging to 18 feet.

Paddling: Coupon Bight is a species-rich habitat of red mangroves, wading birds, sharks, horseshoe crabs, and a host of other marine life. Paddlers will find plenty to see nearshore to Go-to 8 (Coupon Bight) (B6) and Go-to 1 (A6).

A tight mangrove creek (Go-to 7, C3) twists through the west end of Big Munson Island and empties into a channel near Little Palm Island Resort. A quiet lagoon on the backside of Big Munson is accessed by Go-to 6 (C3).

Nature: Red mangroves in the swampy southeast corner of Coupon Bight (A6, B6) seem shorter and less dense than normal. In hard-bottom habitats like this, where only a thin layer of sediment covers bedrock, mangroves won't achieve the familiar solid wall of green. Rather, young tree shoots spread in meadow-like formation and rarely grow more than head high. Older trees send their roots out like tendrils, seeking a soft spot in the rock-hard bottom.

We nicknamed Horseshoe Crab Beach (Go-to 1, A6) for the many carapaces of this ancient creature scattered about the shore. Beach habitat, even one as small as this, serves as important breeding and molting grounds for the crab. Females lay eggs above the low-tide line. Later, maturing crabs crawl ashore and molt. Humans crawl ashore here, too, but mostly for rest, relaxation, and, judging by a fire ring, a little camping. (This is refuge property and camping is illegal.)

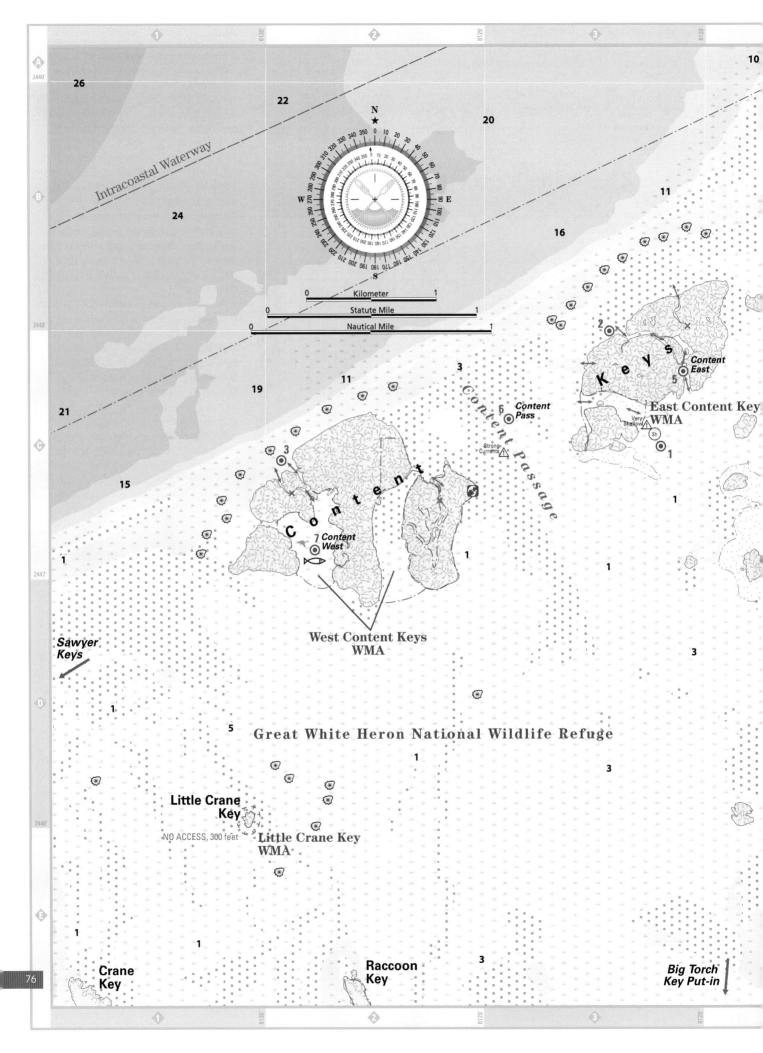

Intracoastal Waterway

N

Kilometer
Statute Mile
Nautical Mile

Content Passage

Content Pass

Content East

East Content Key WMA

Very Shallow

Sh

K e y s

C o n t e n t

Content West

West Content Keys WMA

Sawyer Keys

Great White Heron National Wildlife Refuge

Little Crane Key

NO ACCESS, 300 feet

Little Crane Key WMA

Crane Key

Raccoon Key

Big Torch Key Put-in

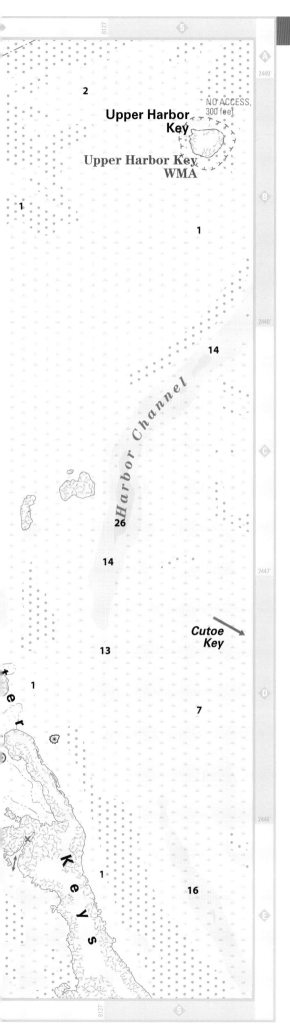

Go-to Points: 1–4; 5 (Content East); 6 (Content Pass); 7 (Content West)

Off-Chart D/Cs: Cutoe Key; Big Torch Key Put-in; Sawyer Keys

Caution: A trip to the Content Keys requires an open-water crossing of nearly 6 miles one way. Any long open-water kayak trip requires paddlers be in good physical condition, possess the proper skills, and use the right equipment.

Sudden, violent storms rise quickly in the Lower Keys Backcountry. There is no shelter on open water in heavy winds, lightning, and rough water conditions. Check forecasts before leaving, and consider carrying a weather radio.

A strong north or northeast wind creates swells in Content Passage and breakers along the beach (C2) on West Content Key. Kayakers should know how to make a surf landing and launch in a kayak.

Alert: Kayakers should avoid approaching within 300 feet of any occupied bird nest. Flushing a bird from its nest saps strength and energy needed for survival or migration.

Getting There: Starting point for Content Keys: Big Torch Put-in, Chart 33, C3. See appendix for details.

If you don't have the equipment or stamina for a trip to the Backcountry, see appendix for companies that offer kayak charters.

Navigation: Distance to Content Keys Go-to 1: 5.5 miles from Big Torch Put-in via Torch Key Mangroves, Water Keys.

Distance to Go-to 7 (Content West): 5.5 miles from Big Torch Put-in via Torch Key Mangroves.

The Water Keys (Go-to 4, D4) make a nice lee in heavy northeast or east winds as you travel to and from the Contents. Be aware that tidal flats north of the largest Water Key may be impassable at low water.

Public Land: The Content Keys are part of the Great White Heron National Wildlife Refuge, a water and island preserve covering nearly 200,000 acres of Lower Keys Backcountry. Day use is permitted on beaches, except where signs prohibit entry or landing. Use of personal watercraft and waterskiing are prohibited inside the refuge.

The Upper Harbor Key Wildlife Management Area encompasses this small island (B5) known for roosting ospreys, frigatebirds, double-crested cormorants, and a host of herons, among them the great white, little blue, and tri-colored. A 300-foot no-access buffer surrounds the island.

Tidal creeks in the East and West Content Keys Wildlife Management Areas (C2, B3) are zoned idle speed/no wake for motorboats.

The Little Crane Key Wildlife Management Area (D1) is a roosting spot for the magnificent frigatebird and nesting American egrets and cormorants. A 300-foot no-access buffer surrounds the island.

Rest Areas: A popular beach on the northeast point of the West Content Keys (C2) gets crowded on weekends and holidays, when recreational boaters pull their craft onto the tidal flats. There are signs of camping activity, although legally none is allowed within the National Key Deer Refuge. N 24°47.384′ W 81°29.064′.

In heavy winds, paddlers can find shelter in a small V-cut in a small island offshore of Water Key's north tip (D4). N 24°46.072′ W 81°27.772′.

Paddling: At low tide the sandbar at Go-to 1 (C3) is welcome landfall after a long trip up from Big Torch Key. On the approach, burnt-red sea cucumbers are visible on the shallow, white sand bottom. Pockets of deeper water are a Caribbean blue-green color. Out on the horizon, it can sometimes be hard to tell where the water ends and sky begins.

The tidal creek bisecting the East Content Keys (Go-to 2, B3) widens and narrows several times, and sharks prowl in its deeper pools. Halfway down, Go-to 5 (Content East) is a pass into a sheltered lake. There is considerable shoaling at the south exit of this creek.

The marshy mangrove fringes of Water Key's western shore (D4, E4) deserve hours of exploring unto themselves. The shoreline forms several points of land, and behind each it is quiet and sheltered. Little blue herons, American egrets, and other wading birds forage here.

Nature: Studies show that bird activity decreases wherever people are present or approach too closely. Approaching on foot or by kayak, no matter how slowly or stealthily, is more apt to flush a bird than a boat traveling at high speed in a boat channel. A good rule of thumb: If a bird stands up, notices you, and appears ready to flee, you've come too close.

Go-to Points: 1–4; 5 (Big Torch Mangroves); 6 (Water Keys); 7 (Raccoon Key)

Off-Chart D/Cs: Howe Key Channel; Ramrod Key Swim Hole; Niles Road Launch; Blimp Road Boat Ramp; Sawyer Keys

Public Land: The Great White Heron National Wildlife Refuge spans 40 miles of Lower Keys Backcountry and nearly 200,000 acres of islands and water. It was created in 1938 to protect migratory wading birds from plume and egg

hunters who pursued them to near extinction. Personal watercraft and waterskiing are prohibited inside the refuge.

The National Key Deer Refuge, which covers a portion of Big Torch Key, protects several endangered species, among them the Lower Keys marsh rabbit. With its habitat cut up by subdivisions and roads, the rabbit's population is fragmented and declining. Feral cats, a problem throughout the Keys, are its biggest predator.

Rest Area: Tarpon Belly's (C1) rough "Keys beach" gets heavy use from recreational powerboaters. The southern of the two large islands is privately owned; tall Australian pines, rather than mangroves, mark this island. Speculation as to why canals are carved through Tarpon Belly range from an abandoned shrimp farm to canal-digging aliens.

Paddling: See Chart 34 for details on paddling Knockemdown Key (D3, D4).

See Chart 35 for details on paddling the Little Swash Keys (D1).

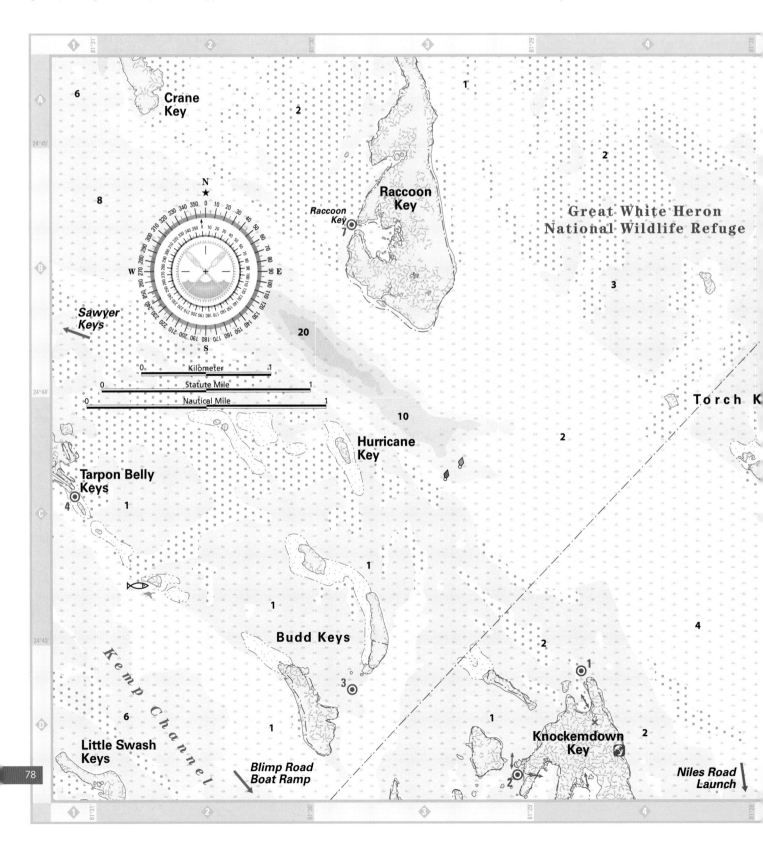

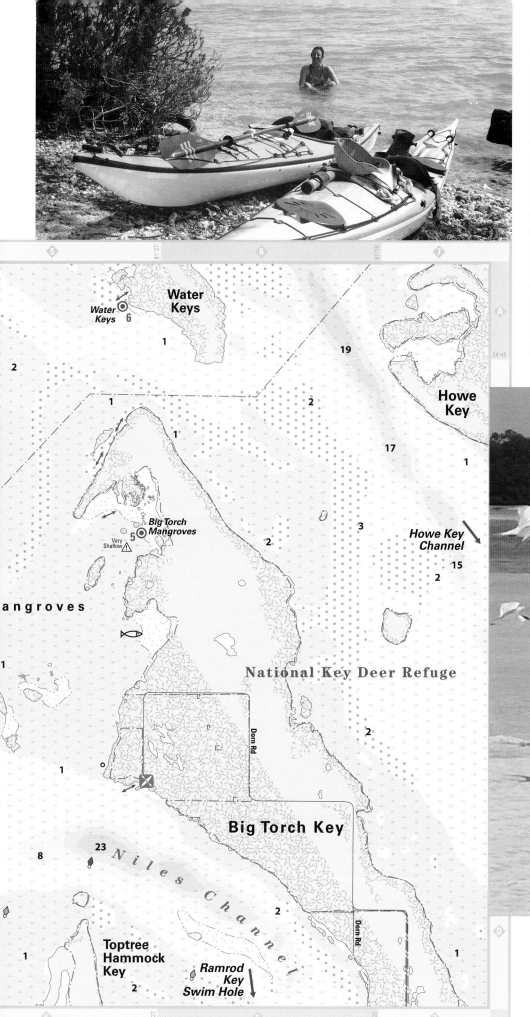

The northern reaches of Howe Key (A7), Big Torch Key (B5), and Knockemdown Key (D3, D4) share much in common. The water is shallow and the bottom is dotted with orange and red sponges. Soft corals, as well as the hard golfball coral and lesser starlet coral, are visible. Blacktip sharks favor areas like this. A "swoosh" of water near your boat and a receding "hump" signals a stingray's hasty flight.

Landmark: Paddlers may have the *Fat Albert* blimp overhead while paddling the Backcountry waters. See Chart 34 for details on these tools in the "war on drugs," and the communist regime in Cuba.

History: A medical supply company used Raccoon Key (B3) for breeding and holding rhesus monkeys from 1976 to the late 1990s. There are visible remains of the facility on the island.

Name: Big Torch Key was named for the torchwood, a tree so resinous, a torch made from it burned twice as long as pine.

Map labels

Water Keys

Water Keys 6

Howe Key

Big Torch Mangroves

Very Shallow

Howe Key Channel

angroves

National Key Deer Refuge

Big Torch Key

Dorn Rd

Dorn Rd

Niles Channel

Toptree Hammock Key

Ramrod Key Swim Hole

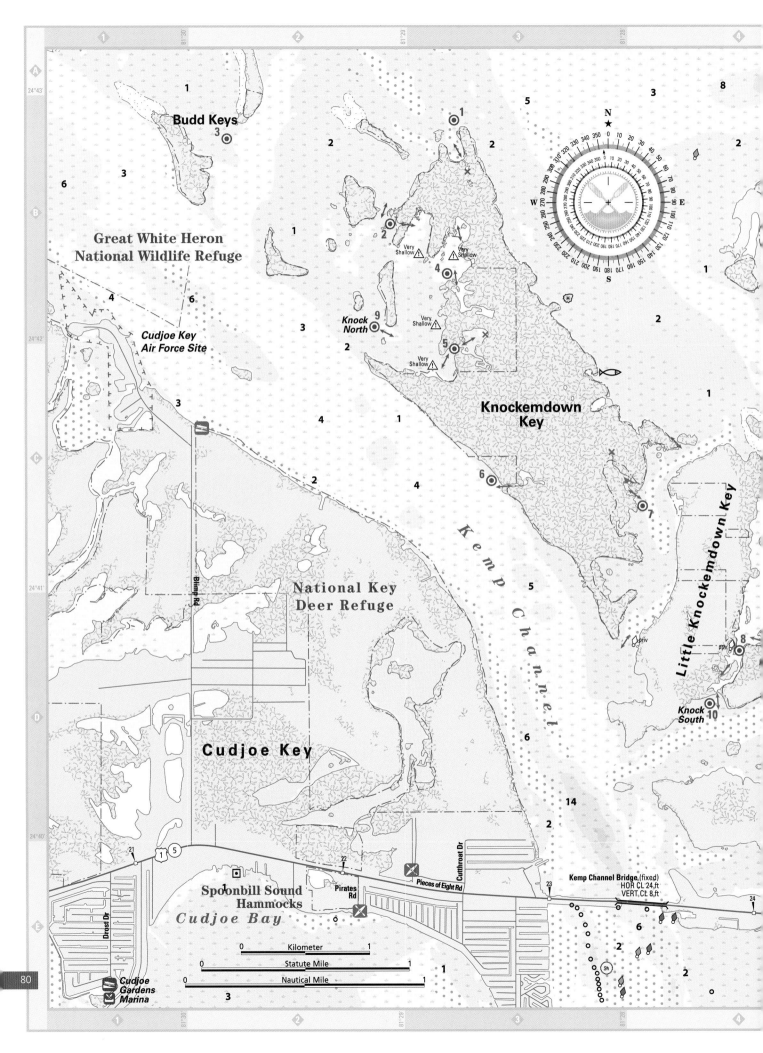

Budd Keys

Great White Heron National Wildlife Refuge

Cudjoe Key Air Force Site

Knockemdown Key

Knock North

Very Shallow

Very Shallow

Very Shallow

Very Shallow

National Key Deer Refuge

Cudjoe Key

K e m p   C h a n n e l

Little Knockemdown Key

Knock South

Blimp Rd

Drost Dr

1 5

22

Cutthroat Dr

Pirates Rd

Pieces of Eight Rd

Spoonbill Sound Hammocks

Cudjoe Bay

23

Kemp Channel Bridge (fixed)
HOR CL 24 ft
VERT CL 8 ft

24

Sh

Cudjoe Gardens Marina

N
★

0	Kilometer	1
0	Statute Mile	1
0	Nautical Mile	1
3

Go-to Points: 1–8; 9 (Knock North); 10 (Knock South)

Caution: See Chart 35 for restrictions on paddling around the Cudjoe Key Air Force Site.

Navigation: It is 2.7 miles one way from the Blimp Road Boat Ramp to Tarpon Belly Key (Chart 33, C1).

It is a 6-mile one-way paddle from the Blimp Road Boat Ramp to the Sawyer Keys (Chart 37, B3 and B4).

To reach the Big Knockemdown mangroves (B3), take a 45° bearing to a small island offshore of the Blimp Road put-in. From there, head east to Go-to 9 (Knock North) (B2). This is a pass between a point of land on the right and a mangrove island on the left.

Rest Area: See Chart 35 for information on Picnic Park (E5).

Small nooks along the east shore of Big Knockemdown Key offer respite from the wind.

Paddling: See Chart 35 for details on paddling Cudjoe Key.

The north end of Big Knockemdown Key (B2, B3) features extensive low-growing mangroves in a diffuse swamplike setting. Go-tos 4 and 5 (B3) are cues for two rewarding, but dead-end, routes. Shark-viewing potential: high.

Landmark: Known as *Fat Albert,* the large white blimp visible high above Cudjoe Key Air Force Site (B1) is a "Tethered Aerostate Radar System" aircraft, or TARS. It makes a great visual cue as you paddle about the vast Lower Keys Backcountry. When not serving as a paddler's beacon, the blimp conducts low-level radar surveillance for drug trafficking and transmits TV Marti, an American television signal, into Cuba. There are two blimps that are used on a rotating basis. Each can rise up to 15,000 feet and is twice the size of the Goodyear blimp.

Field Notes: Go-to 6 (C3) leads inside Big Knockemdown where, halfway up the creek, mangroves squeeze water into a chute. At the height of an outgoing tide, I recorded speeds of 5 mph in my kayak. It is as close to river conditions as you'll find anywhere in shallow water around the Knockemdowns.

Hiking: A yellow gate at the end of Niles Road (C5) marks the start of a 1-mile trail onto Wahoo Key. The island, owned by the state and managed by the Florida Fish and Wildlife Conservation Commission, protects a piece of the fast-disappearing tropical hardwood hammocks of the Florida Keys.

See Chart 35 for details on hiking Spoonbill Sound Hammocks (E2).

Name: One theory holds the name *Cudjoe* is an abbreviation of the term *Cousin Joe.* The name may also derive from a runaway or freed black man who lived on the island at the time of a survey in 1849. Visit Key Names on the Web (http://keys.fiu.edu/gazetteer) for other curious Keys name origins.

Services: Need to drop off recyclables? Turn bayside onto Blimp Road from US 1 at MM 21.4. In 1 mile, turn left. There is a county recycling drop-off site at the end of this road.

Go-to Points: 1–8; 9 (Knock North); 10 (Knock South)

Caution: No trespassing signs are posted in a shallow pass directly north of the Cudjoe Key Air Force Site. Continue north about 200 yards to a creek entrance (Go-to 1, A2) for access to Cudjoe's interior lakes.

Navigation: Exploring Cudjoe from Blimp Road Boat Ramp (B3): 1 mile to Go-to 1 (A2); 1.5 miles to Go-to 3 (B2); 3 miles to Go-to 2 (A1); 5 miles to Blimp Road Boat Ramp (B3).

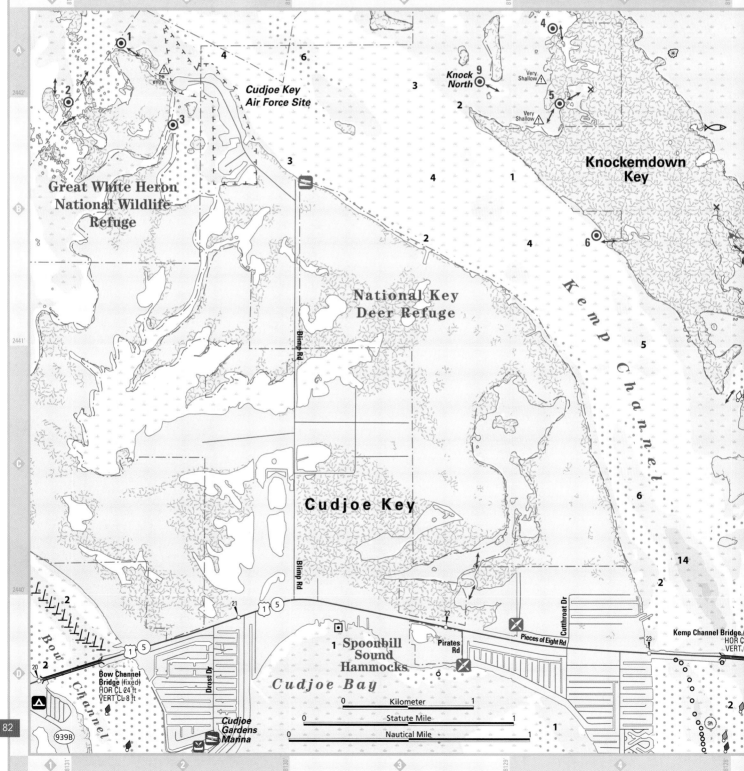

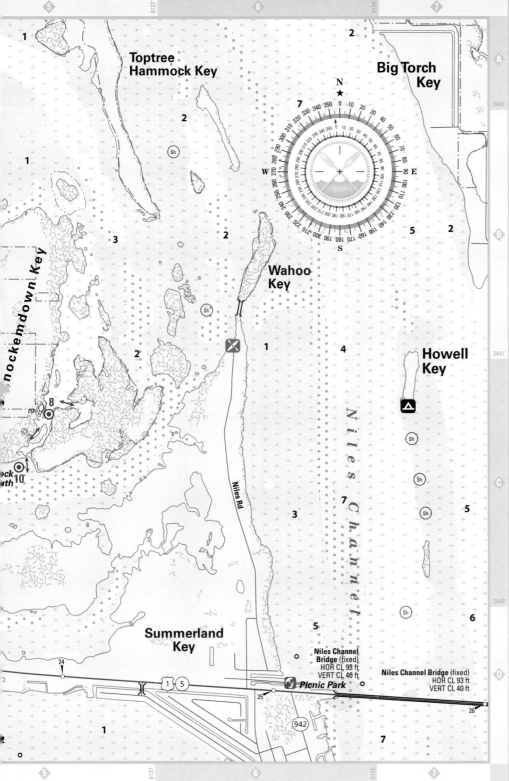

Cudjoe Gardens Marina (D2) or the public launch on Pirates Road (D3) are convenient launch sites for an open-water crossing to Key Lois (see Chart 36 for details).

Public Land: The National Key Deer Refuge protects critical habitat for endangered species such as the Key deer and the Lower Keys marsh rabbit.

Rest Area: There's a small spot to pull up a kayak at Picnic Park on Summerland Key (MM 25.1 G/S). Key West Fishcutters operates a lunch counter/take-out restaurant. The canal is lined with fishing boats, charter boats, and lobster traps. N25°39.688′ W81°26.396′.

Paddling: It is a 6-mile trip around Little Knockemdown Key from the launch on Niles Road (B6). Go-tos 10 (Knock South) and 8 (C5) bookend a short passage through tight mangrove quarters. Fish camps and old homes visible from the water on Little Knockemdown are private property.

Cudjoe's mangrove swamps (A1, B2) and the Little Swash Keys (a portion of which appears on Chart 33, D1) are a nice day paddle of 3 to 5 miles, depending on how "lost" paddlers choose to get. Go-to 2 (A1) is a general reference for paddling here.

Go-to 3 (B2) is an exit from the interior lakes of Cudjoe Key. The tall red mangroves that line this creek stand in contrast to low, shrubby mangroves elsewhere. A daily tidal flush in this creek keeps water clear enough to see the fish and sharks that congregate here.

Nature: Tropical hardwood hammocks harbor a floral diversity that "far surpasses that of any other forest in the continental United States," according to the Audubon Society of Florida. These hammocks are also fast disappearing, which in turn has prompted the state to start buying remaining undeveloped parcels throughout the Keys. Wahoo Key (B6) and Spoonbill Sound Hammocks (D3) are two such areas. A trailhead for Spoonbill Sound Hammocks is on Pirates Road, MM 22.2 O/S, on Cudjoe Key. There is plenty of poisonwood along the trail, so wear long pants.

Hiking: Chart 34 has information on hiking Wahoo Key (B6).

Camping: Howell Key (B7 and C7) is privately owned. See appendix information on primitive camping there.

Name: One possible source for the name *Cudjoe* comes from the fragrant cudjoewood tree once abundant on the island.

36 Tarpon Creek

Go-to Points: 1; 2 (Tarpon Creek); 3 (Key Lois)
Off-Chart D/Cs: Sugarloaf Creek Oceanside; Cudjoe Gardens Marina; Spoonbill Sound Hammocks.
Caution: At its north end, Tarpon Creek (C2) merges with a motorboat channel between Upper Sugarloaf Sound and the Atlantic. There are several blind corners at the west end of this channel (Go-to 1, C1).
Navigation: Distances to Key Lois Go-to 4: 3.5 miles from Cudjoe Gardens Marina (Chart 35,

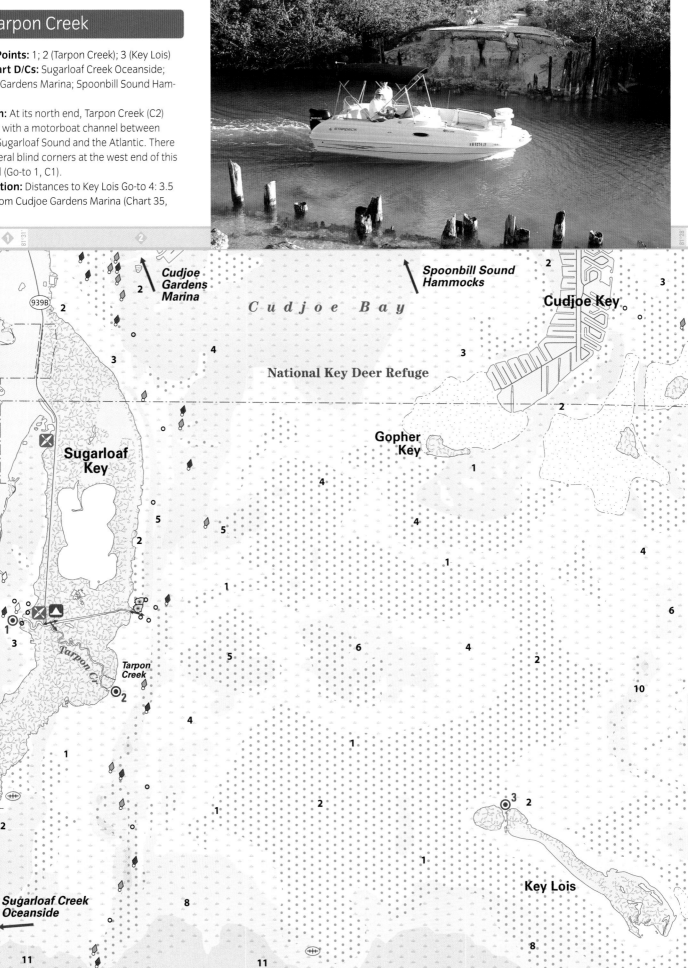

Cudjoe Gardens Marina

Spoonbill Sound Hammocks

Cudjoe Key

C u d j o e   B a y

National Key Deer Refuge

Gopher Key

Sugarloaf Key

939B

Tarpon C.

Tarpon Creek

Sugarloaf Creek Oceanside

Key Lois

D2); 3.5 miles from Spoonbill Sound Hammocks (Chart 35, D3); 2.5 miles from Tarpon Creek (Chart 35, C1).

Rest Area: The old bridge abutment at Tarpon Creek (C2) is a launch as well as a rest area and primitive campsite for paddlers on the Florida Keys Overseas Paddling Trail. Rather than scramble up the steep banks, paddle up a channel on the north bank for a more kayak-friendly takeout.

Paddling: The distance from the old Tarpon Creek bridge (C2) to Go-to 2 (Tarpon Creek) (C2) is only slightly more than a half mile, but the mangrove tunnels make it feel much farther. At the south end, the first left fork runs beneath high-arching mangroves before emptying into open water. Several other tunnels loop back to Tarpon Creek.

Landmarks: Key Lois (C4, D4) was the site of a rhesus monkey breeding site, operated by Charles Rivers Laboratories until 1999. After nearly 30 years of operation, extensive defoliation of mangrove trees by free-roaming monkeys raised protests that ultimately doomed the business. Buildings and boardwalks are visible, and Key deer and raccoons are plentiful on the island.

History: The road that once crossed Tarpon Creek on a wooden bridge was part of SR 4A, the original highway to Key West. The highway name was changed to US 1 in 1939, and during WWII this section of road was bypassed for a more direct route built on the Overseas Railroad right-of-way.

Outfitters: Florida Keys Kayaks and Canoes is located at Cudjoe Gardens Marina (Chart 35, D2). See appendix for more details.

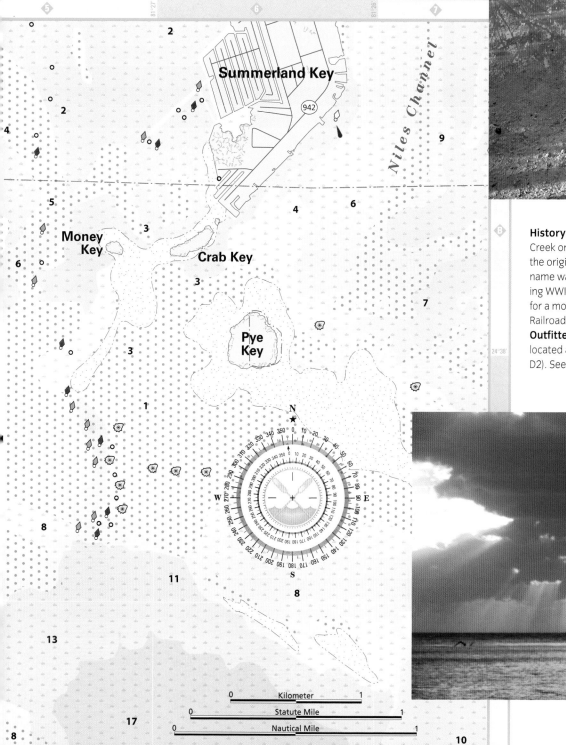

Go-to Points: 1–2; 3 (Sawyer South); 4 (Sawyer North)

Off-Chart D/Cs: West Content Keys; Blimp Road Boat Ramp; Barracuda Keys

Caution: A trip to the Sawyer Keys requires an open-water crossing of 6 miles one way. Any open-water kayak trip requires paddlers be in good physical condition. Be sure to use proper equipment, and bring all necessary gear.

Sudden, violent storms rise quickly in the Lower Keys Backcountry. There is no shelter on open water in heavy winds, lightning, and rough water conditions. Check forecasts before leaving, and consider carrying a weather radio.

Getting There: Starting Point for Sawyer Keys: Blimp Road Boat Ramp, Chart 35, B3.

If you don't have the equipment or stamina for a long day's paddle to the Backcountry, see the appendix for companies that offer kayak charters.

Navigation: Distance to Sawyer Keys: 6 miles from Blimp Road Boat Ramp via Tarpon Belly, Cudjoe Channel, Riding Key.

If tides favor your direction of travel, use Cudjoe Channel to speed a trip to or from the Sawyer Keys. If the tides are counter to your direction, paddle outside the channel.

Go-to 2 (C5) is a boat channel through the sand bank extending south of Riding Key. There is another mile of paddling to reach the Sawyer Keys from here.

It is 4.75 miles, straight-line distance, at a 60-degree bearing between Go-to 4 (Sawyer North) and the Content Keys (Chart 32, Go-to 3, C2).

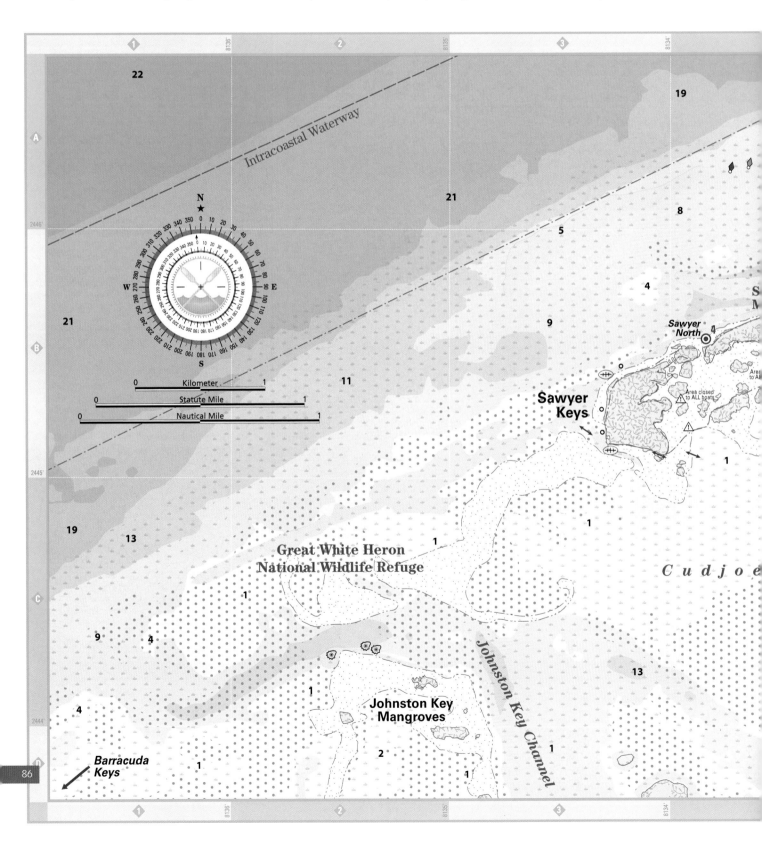

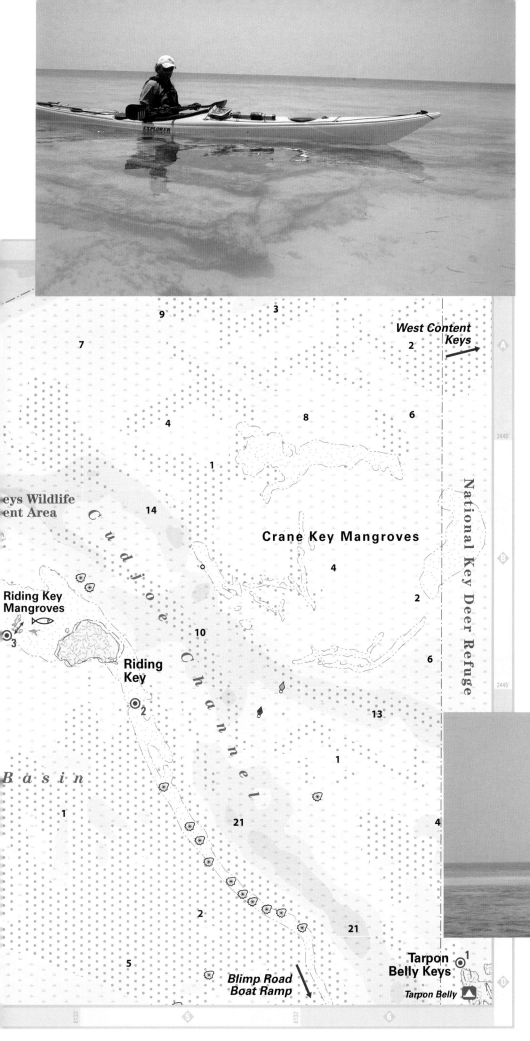

From the northwest corner of the Sawyer Keys, it is approximately 3 miles, straight-line distance, at a 220-degree bearing to Go-to 4 (Barracuda East) on Chart 38 at the easternmost tip of the Barracuda Keys.

Public Land: The Sawyer Keys are within the Great White Heron National Wildlife Refuge. The refuge spans 40 miles and contains nearly 200,000 acres of water and islands for protection of bird roosting, nesting, and foraging habitat. Great white herons and a variety of other herons, egrets, hawks, eagles, gulls, terns, and shorebirds all benefit from this protection.

Tidal creeks on the south side of the Sawyer Keys are protected as a wildlife management area and are closed to the public. Ospreys nest here, and wading birds enjoy quietude in the pristine creeks.

Rest Area: Go-to 1 is a rest area and "Keys beach" on Tarpon Belly (D6). See Chart 33 for details.

Paddling: The Sawyer Keys are part of a line of pristine islands that mark a divide between the Gulf of Mexico and the Backcountry (we call it the "edge of the nearshore waters"). A round-trip around the Sawyer Keys is a 12-plus-mile paddle, all open water. Tarpon Belly (Go-to 1, D6) and a small group of mangroves at Sawyer South (Go-to 3, B4) offer rest and shelter enroute.

Amid the small mangrove islands north of Riding Key (B4), yellow-crowned night herons roost and schooling fish gather in narrow creeks, preying upon food carried in by the fast-moving currents spilling off Cudjoe Channel.

With interior creeks off-limits, circumnavigation is a paddler's only option for the Sawyer Keys (Go-to 4, Sawyer North, B4) Wide, stirring vistas of the Gulf of Mexico from the north side of Sawyer are ample reward for a long day's paddle.

Go-to Points: 1; 2 (Cudjoe); 3 (Johnston Patch); 4 (Barracuda East)
Off-Chart D/Cs: Blimp Road Boat Ramp; Fivemile Creek; Middle Narrows; Sawyer Keys
Caution: A trip to Johnston Key is an open-water paddle of 5 to 7 miles. Any open-water kayak trip requires paddlers be in good physical condition. Be sure to use proper equipment, and bring all necessary gear.

Sudden, violent storms rise quickly in the Lower Keys Backcountry. There is no shelter on the open water in heavy winds, lightning, and rough water conditions. Check forecasts before leaving, and consider carrying a weather radio.
Getting There: Starting points for Johnston Key: Sugarloaf Lodge, Chart 39, B4; Lower Sugarloaf Sound #1, Chart 39, C3; Blimp Road Boat Ramp, Chart 35, B3. See appendix for details.
Navigation: Distances to Go-to 3 (Johnston Patch): 6 miles from Sugarloaf Lodge via Perky Creek, Dreguez, Galdin Key; 7 miles from Lower Sugarloaf Sound #1 via Fivemile Creek, Galdin Key; 5.5 miles from Blimp Road Boat Ramp via Little Swash Keys, Pumpkin Keys.

The large basin between Galdin Key and Fivemile Creek (Chart 39, B2) shallows to 1 or 2 feet at low tide and may be impassable except in established boating channels marked by white PVC posts.
Public Land: Johnston and surrounding islands are part of the Great White Heron National Wildlife Refuge, which covers nearly 200,000 acres of islands and water throughout the Lower Keys Backcountry. The refuge was formed in 1938 to protect migratory wading birds from plume and egg hunters who pursued egrets and herons to near extinction. Personal watercraft

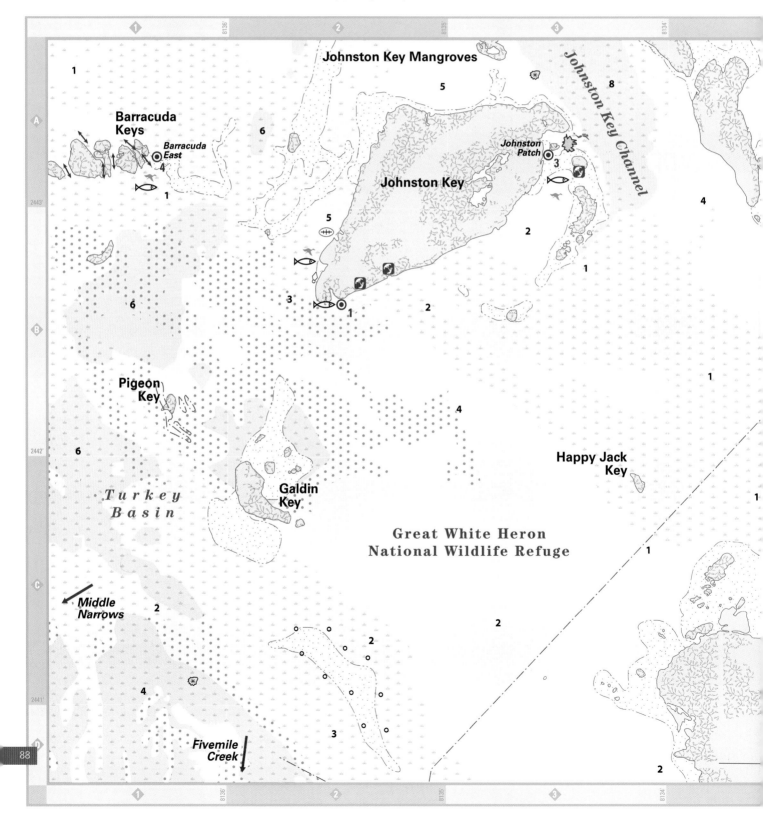

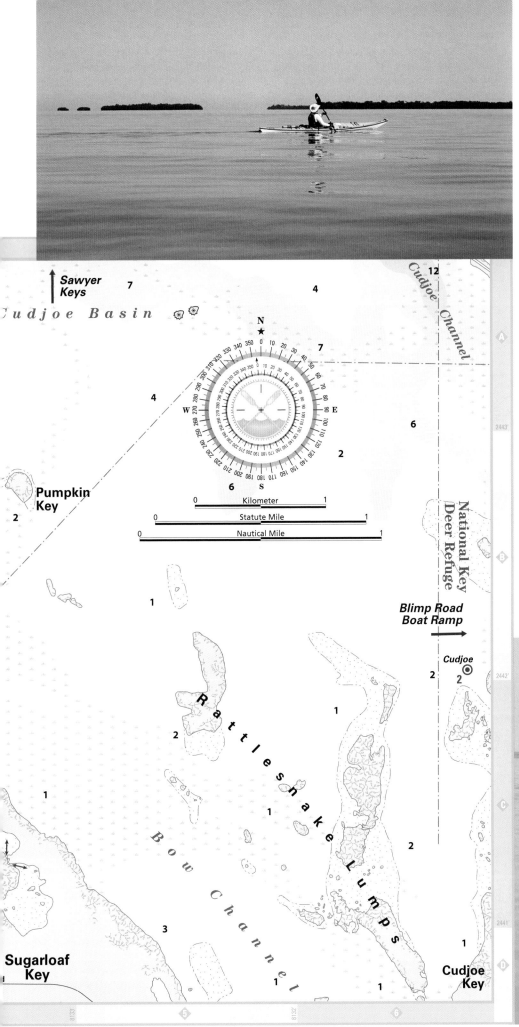

and waterskiing are prohibited inside the refuge.

The north end of Sugarloaf Key is part of the National Key Deer Refuge.

Paddling: Johnston Key and surrounding mangrove islands—collectively known as the Johnston Key Mangroves—are easily overlooked and not often visited by kayakers. Tidal banks surround small mangrove islands that tail off Johnston's southeast corner. At low tide these make nice resting or sunbathing spots.

Older charts and satellite photos show creeks penetrated into Johnston's interior. With time, these have either overgrown or been blocked by storm-felled trees. There is a dead end that begins at the far eastern end of the island, in the vicinity of Go-to 3 (Johnston Patch). There are scores of golfball coral here, so use care if you begin scraping bottom.

Go-to 3 (Johnston Patch) marks coral heads in water about 5 feet deep. Large whelks and starfish may also be visible on the sandy bottom.

See Chart 41 for details on paddling the Barracuda Keys (A1).

The Rattlesnake Lumps (C5, C6) are nearshore to Cudjoe Key and can be explored in conjunction with a trip into Cudjoe's interior lakes. (See Chart 35 for details on paddling the north end of Cudjoe Key.)

Name: A writer traveling down the Keys in 1856 described a man named Happy Jack and his band of merrymaking brothers who were "united a common love: The fragrant goddess of whisky." Happy Jack outlived all his companions, which may explain why Happy Jack Key was named for him.

39 Fivemile Creek

Go-to Points: 1–7; 8 (Fivemile Mangrove); 9 (Fivemile South); 10 (Fivemile North); 11 (Dreguez Cut); 12 (Old Finds #1)

Off-Chart D/Cs: Tarpon Creek; Sugarloaf Creek Soundside; Middle Narrows

Caution: Mangrove creeks at Go-tos 5 and 6 empty into Perky Creek, a motorboat channel. Be alert for speeding boat traffic.

Public Land: The north end of Sugarloaf Key is part of the National Key Deer Refuge.

Paddling: Three passages through the mangroves around Perky offer paddlers a variety of loop options. Go-tos 5 and 6, (B3) are kayak-friendly creeks that thread north and south through the mangroves. Be aware: The lower creek (Go-to 6, B3) shoals up at its west exit.

Fivemile Creek (B2 and C2) actually measures 1.2 miles end-to-end. Long, rambling mangrove creeks branch south off the main channel. Most empty into Lower Sugarloaf Sound.

Landmarks: Allen Morris, in his book *Florida Place Names*, describes Perky's Bat Tower (C3)

as "a Dutch windmill without its blades." Richter Perky built this 35-foot square-sided structure in 1929 to attract bats, hoping they would eat swarming mosquitoes and sand flies. No bats ever came. The tower is now on the National Register of Historic Places.

Sugarloaf Airport, at MM 18.9 G/S, is a small private airstrip that reputedly stood in as a Third World airport in some 30 movies for directors without a budget for the real thing. The airport hangar is an unpainted shack with dogs hanging about. Airplane rides and

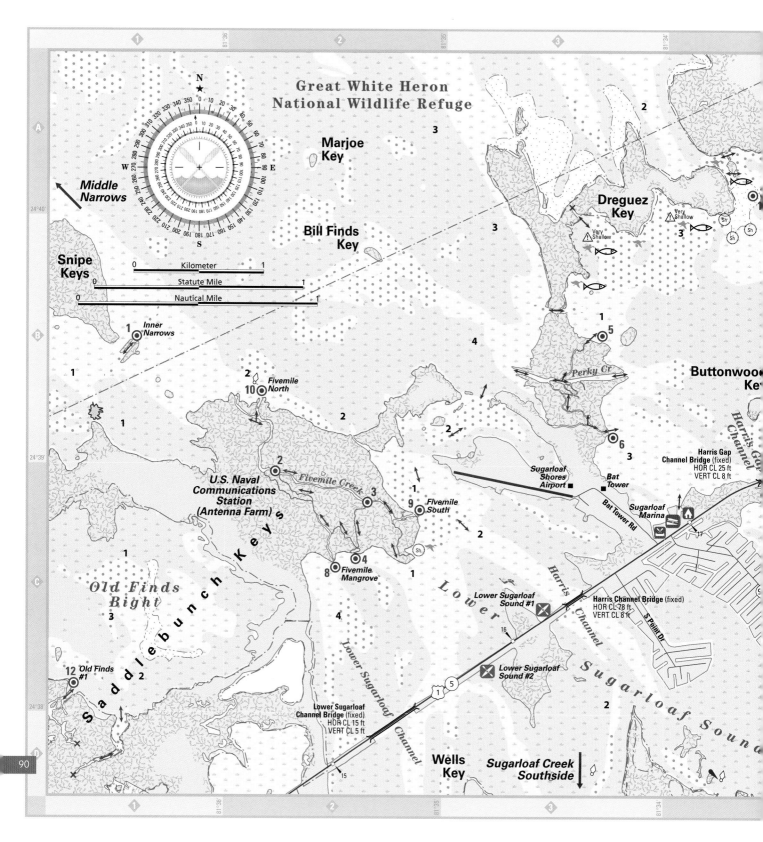

skydiving are offered; call (305) 745–2217.

Field Notes: The inside shoreline of Dreguez Key is flanked by healthy hard-bottom flats, replete with sponges and small corals. Here we experienced two phenomenal events: we saw a skinny fish tailing across the water, prey firmly lodged in its long pointed jaws; a few minutes later, we cupped a seahorse in our hands.

Hiking: Approximately 1 mile of hiking on an abandoned road lies beyond a refuge gate on Crane Boulevard, 1.3 miles north of the US 1 intersection.

History: Sugarloaf Key was the site of a commercial sponging operation prior to World War I. After it went bankrupt, Richter Perky bought up land on Sugarloaf for speculation and rechristened the island in his name. His legacy survives in the names Perky Creek and Perky's Bat Tower.

Outfitters: Several seasonal kayak tour operators and backcountry guides work out of Sugarloaf Marina, MM 17 G/S, US 1. See appendix for details.

Photo courtesy of Monroe
County Public Library, Mile Markers Project

Map

Cudjoe Key

Bow Channel

Acosta Trl

Bow Channel Bridge (fixed)
HOR CL 24 ft
VERT CL 8 ft

Crane Blvd

Sugarloaf Key

Sugarloaf Elementary

1 5

Park Channel Bridge (fixed)
HOR CL 15 ft
VERT CL 5 ft

Very Shallow

Park Key

Park Channel

Upper Sugarloaf Channel

North Harris Channel Bridge (fixed)
HOR CL 78 ft
VERT CL 9 ft

North Harris Channel

Very Shallow

Sugarloaf Sound

Sugarloaf Key

Tarpon Creek

Go-to Points: 1–3; 4 (Missile Pad Creek #1); 5 (Missile Pad Creek #2); 6 (Sugarloaf Creek Sound); 7 (Sugarloaf Creek)

Off-Chart D/Cs: Tarpon Creek; Lower Sugarloaf Sound #2; Geiger Key Marina; Key Lois

Alert: Landscaping along the Overseas Heritage Trail has affected a series of roadside put-ins through the Saddlebunch Keys. Between Mile Markers 10 and 16, the most reliable put-ins are Sugarloaf Sound #1 and #2 (Chart 39, C3), Blue-water Drive (A1), and the Shark Key Boat Ramp (Chart 44, A6).

Getting There: Starting point for Lower Sugarloaf Sound: Lower Sugarloaf Sound #2, Chart 39, C3. See appendix for details.

Navigation: From Bird Island east of Wells Key, Go-to 4 (Missile Pad Creek #1) is 0.6 mile, straight-line distance, at a bearing of 103°.

From Bird Island east of Wells Key, Go-to 5 (Missile Pad Creek #2) is 1.2 miles, straight-line distance, at a bearing of 159°.

From the Lower Sugarloaf Sound #2 launch (Chart 39, C3), it is 2 miles, straight-line distance, at a bearing of 170° to Sugarloaf Creek.

Rest Areas: After navigating a tight squeeze at Go-to 1, (A4), the route opens up and the shoreline on the right is rimmed with sand. Footing is solid.

There is a sandbar off the mouth of Sugarloaf Creek (Go-to 7, Sugarloaf Creek Oceanside, B3).

Paddling: Lower Sugarloaf Sound can disrupt even the keenest sense of direction. Wells Key (A3), a large island in the middle of the sound, lies due south of Lower Sugarloaf Sound #2 put-

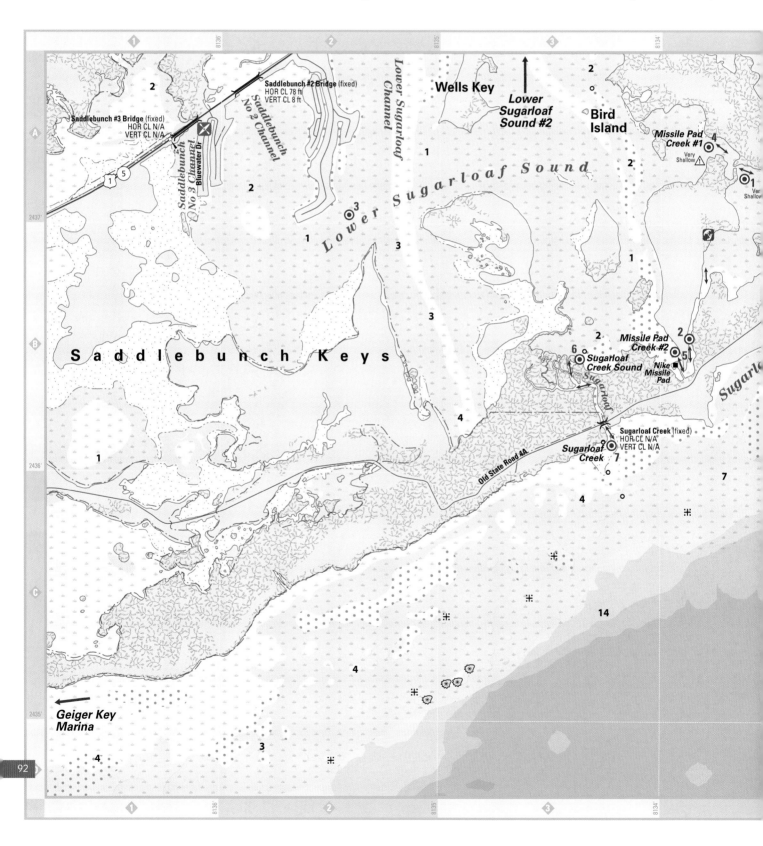

in. A half-mile east of Wells is Bird Island, a small island conspicuous for the dead-standing trees used by roosting birds.

Missile Pad Creek (B4) is our nickname for a route through a corner of Lower Sugarloaf Sound.

At several points between Go-tos 1 and 2, the route appears choked off by mangroves. Keep probing for an opening. The route's name is inspired by a nearby missile launch site activated during the Cuban missile crisis in 1961. It is now abandoned.

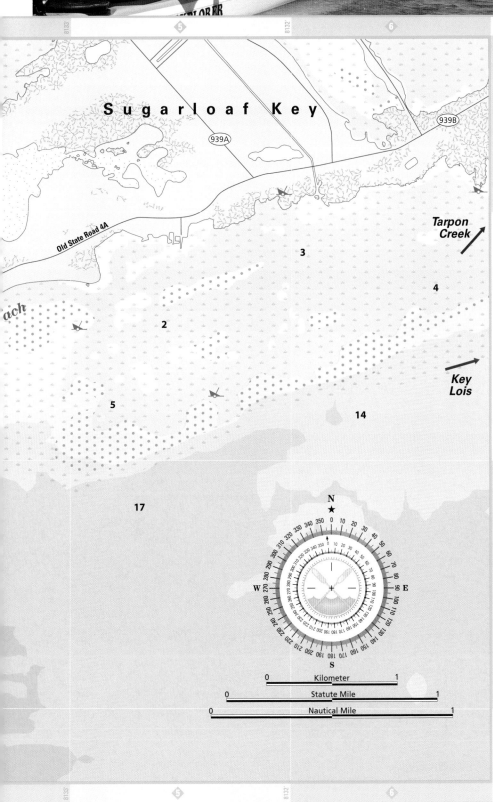

Go-to Points: 1–8; 9 (Barracuda East); 10 (Barracuda West); 11 (Snipe East); 12 (Mud Keys North)

Off-Chart D/Cs: Perky Creek; Fivemile Creek; Shark Key Channel

Caution: A trip to the Snipe, Marvin, or Barracuda Keys requires an open-water crossing of 6 to 8 miles one way. Any open-water kayak trip requires paddlers be in good physical condition. Be sure to use proper equipment, and bring all necessary gear.

Sudden, violent storms rise quickly in the Lower Keys Backcountry. There is no shelter on open water in heavy winds, lightning, and rough water conditions. Check forecasts before leaving, and consider carrying a weather radio.

Getting There: Starting points for Snipe, Marvin, and Barracuda Keys: Boca Chica Bridge, Chart 44, C1 and C2; Cop Land Boat Ramp, Chart 44, A4; Public boat ramp on Shark Key, Chart 44, A6; Lower Sugarloaf Sound #1, Chart 39, C3; Lower Sugarloaf Sound #2, Chart 39, C3. See appendix for details.

If you don't have the equipment or stamina for a long day's paddle to the Backcountry, see the appendix for companies that offer kayak charters.

Navigation: Distances to Snipe Keys Go-to 4: 6.2 miles from Shark Key Boat Ramp via Shark Key Channel, Round Key, Waltz Key; 6 miles from Cop Land Boat Ramp via Waltz Key Basin; 7 miles from Boca Chica Bridge via Channel Key, Fish Hawk Key, Mud Keys; 7.5 miles* from Sugarloaf Sound #1 via Fivemile Creek, Lower and Middle Snipe, Outer Narrows; 8 miles* from Sugarloaf Sound #2 via Lower Sugarloaf Channel, Fivemile Creek, Lower and Middle Snipe, Outer Narrows.

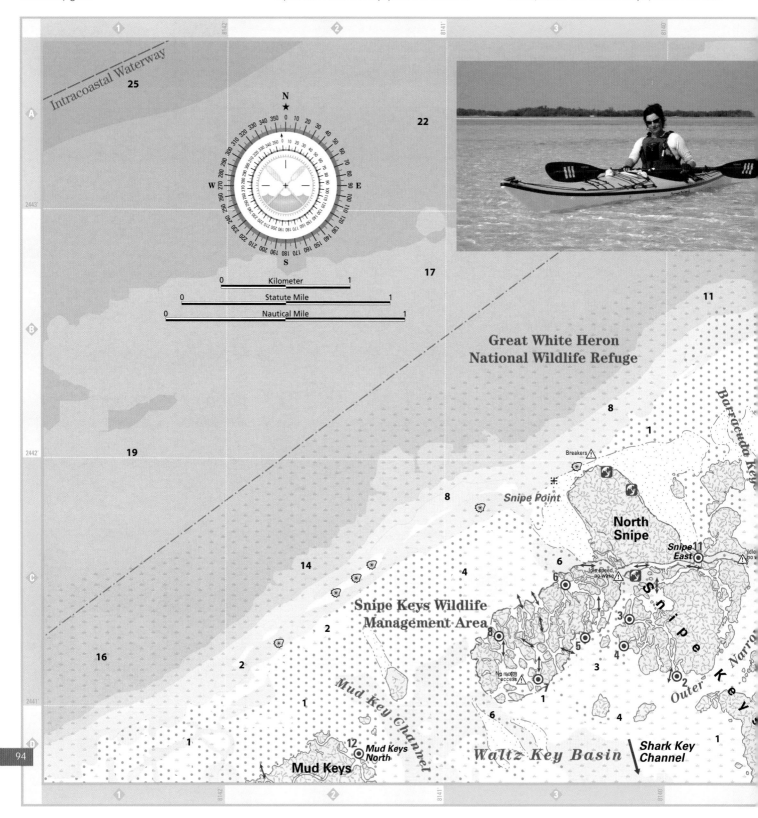

*Paddlers who launch from Sugarloaf Sound #1 or #2 should note that wide tidal flats around Lower Snipe Key may be impassable at low water. See Charts 39 and 42 for a survey of this area.

Public Land: Snipe Point and the Marvin Keys are within the Great White Heron National Wildlife Refuge. However, Snipe Point is state-owned, and the Marvin Keys are private islands. Day use is common on beaches and tidal flats on these islands, except where signs prohibit entry or landing. Use of personal watercraft and waterskiing are prohibited inside the refuge.

The Snipe Keys Wildlife Management Area encompasses the many small tidal creeks between Snipe Point (C3) and the Outer Narrows, which are off-limits to motorboats for protection of herons, egrets, and other birds. The main tidal creek through the Upper Snipes is marked an idle speed/no wake zone for motorboats.

Rest Areas: Snipe Point and creek sandbars around Go-to 4 (C3) are popular day-use areas.

The northernmost of the two Marvin Keys (B5) has a beach and sandy tidal flats on its north, west, and south shores. There is a primitive campsite on the eastern side of the same island.

Paddling: You'll hear the crashing surf long before you reach Snipe Point (C3). This beachhead is popular with recreational boaters on weekends and holidays. Kayakers can approach the point from the sides, rather than head on, for a sheltered landing.

Few places in the Keys rival the mangroves south of Snipe Point for sheer complexity and beauty. The clean, clear water of so many small creeks is a window to a world of red calcareous algae, sponges, soft corals, and fish.

The aqua-blue channels that dissect this chain of small islands are quiet and distinctly beautiful.

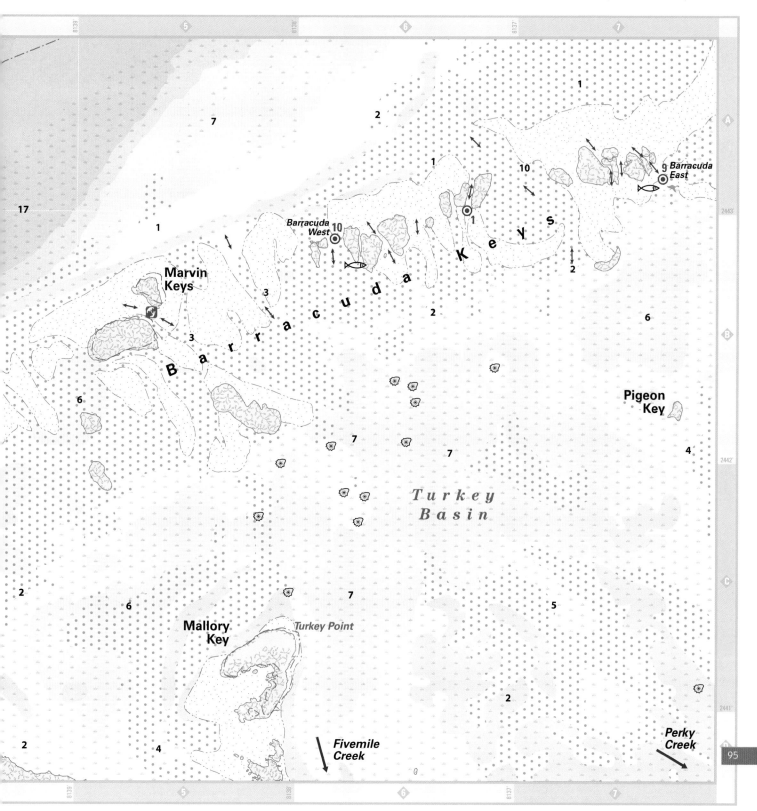

42 Mud Keys

Go-to Points: 1–9; 10 (Mud Keys South);
11 (Mud Keys Middle); 12 (Mud Keys North)
Off-Chart D/Cs: Barracuda Keys; Perky Creek;
Shark Key Channel; Boca Chica Bridge; Lower
Harbor Keys

Caution: A trip to the Mud Keys requires an
open-water crossing of between 5 and 7 miles
one way. Any open-water kayak trip requires
paddlers be in good physical condition. Be sure
to use proper equipment, and bring all necessary gear.

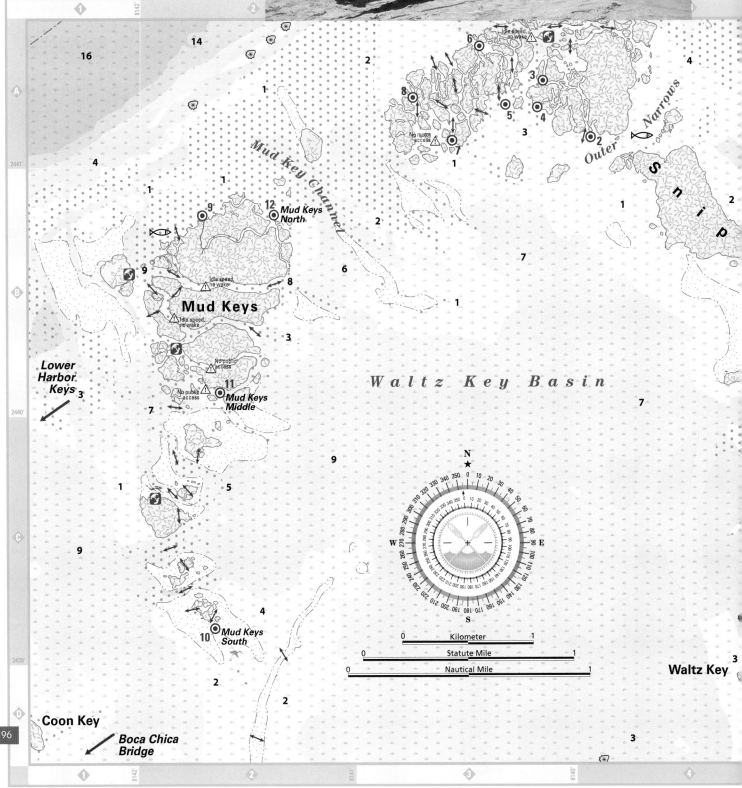

Sudden, violent storms rise quickly in the Lower Keys Backcountry. There is no shelter on open water in heavy winds, lightning, and rough water conditions. Check forecasts before leaving, and consider carrying a weather radio.

Getting There: Starting points for the Snipe and Mud Keys: Boca Chica Bridge, Chart 44, C1 and C2; Cop Land Boat Ramp, Chart 44, A4; Shark Key Boat Ramp, Chart 44, A6. See appendix for details.

If you don't have the equipment or stamina for a long day's paddle to the Backcountry, see the appendix for companies that offer kayak charters.

Navigation: Distances to Go-to 11 (Mud Keys Middle): 6.7 miles from Boca Chica Bridge via Channel Key, Harper Key, Fish Hawk Key, Go-to 10 (Mud Keys South); 5.3 miles from Cop Land Boat Ramp via Duck Key, Fish Hawk Key, Go-to 11 Mud Keys South); 6 miles from Shark Key Boat Ramp, via Shark Key Channel, Waltz Key Basin.

Between Go-to 12 (Mud Keys North) and Snipe Point, it is 1.6 miles, straight-line distance, at a 40° bearing.

Between Go-to 12 (Mud Keys North)

and the Outer Narrows, it is 1.5 miles, straight-line distance, at an 80° bearing. Note that two small islands block the view of the Outer Narrows from this Go-to point.

Public Land: The Snipe and Mud Keys are part of the Great White Heron National Wildlife Refuge. Day use is permitted on beaches and tidal flats, except where signs prohibit entry or landing. Personal watercraft and waterskiing are prohibited inside the refuge.

See Chart 41 for information on the Snipe Keys Wildlife Management Area (A3).

The Mud Keys Wildlife Management Area (B2, C2) protects nesting osprey and a great white heron rookery. The northernmost creeks are idle speed/no wake for powerboaters. Two smaller, southernmost creeks (in vicinity of Go-to 11, Mud Keys Middle) are closed to the public.

Rest Area: A small island (B1) off the northwest corner of the Mud Keys features a white sand beach and an upland clearing with fire rings. This is a popular spot for powerboaters.

Paddling: Go-to 9 is a hard-to-find mangrove creek entrance. Follow it west, then sharply south to its exit into a wide creek. A left turn here leads to Go-to 12 (Mud Creek North) (B2).

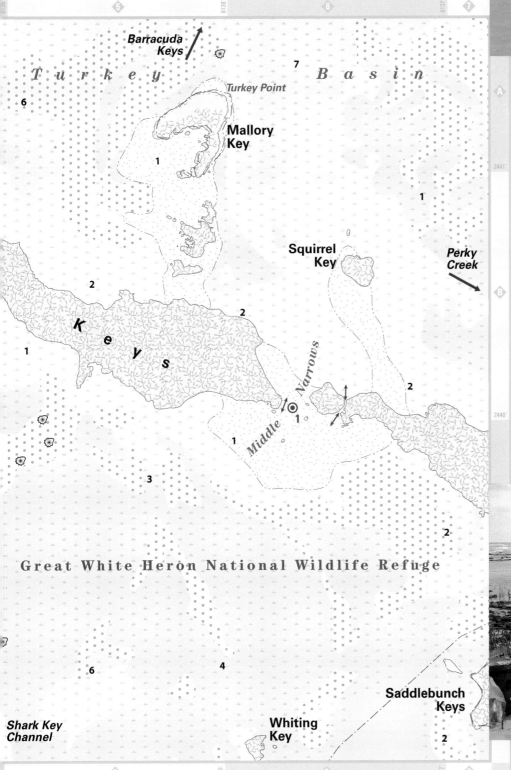

Go-to Points: 1–2; 3 (Jim Pent Point); 4 (Duck Key); 5 (Mud Keys South); 6 (Old Finds #2)

Off-Chart D/Cs: Middle Narrows; Cop Land Put-in; Boca Chica Bridge; Lower Harbor Keys; Snipe Key Mangroves; Old Finds Bight

Caution: Go-to 3 (Jim Pent Point) (C4) marks the entry/exit of a channel into Halfmoon Basin. Kayakers should stay alert for motorboats traveling full speed through here.

Alert: Landscaping along the Overseas Heritage Trail has affected a series of roadside put-ins throughout the Saddlebunch Keys. Between Mile Markers 10 and 16, the most reliable put-ins are Sugarloaf Sound #1 and #2 (Chart 39, C3), Bluewater Drive (Chart 40, A1), and the Shark Key Boat Ramp (Chart 44, A6).

Getting There: Starting points for Old Finds Bight: Lower Sugarloaf Sound #1, Chart 39, C3; Lower Sugarloaf Sound #2, Chart 39, C3; Shark Key Boat Ramp, Chart 44, A6. See appendix for details.

Navigation: Distances to Go-to 6 (Old Finds #2): 4 miles from Sugarloaf Sound #1 via Fivemile Creek, Old Finds Bight; 4.5 miles from Sugarloaf Sound #2 via Fivemile Creek, Old Finds Bight; 4 miles from Shark Key Boat Ramp via Shark Key Channel.

See Charts 41 and 42 for distances and navigating cues for the Mud Keys and Upper Snipe Keys.

Paddling: Duck Key (C3) is surrounded by hard-bottom habitat replete with vase and basket sponges, loggerhead sponges, and small corals. Clear water makes sighting bonefish easy. At 0.1 mile south of Duck Key a cluster of mangrove is-

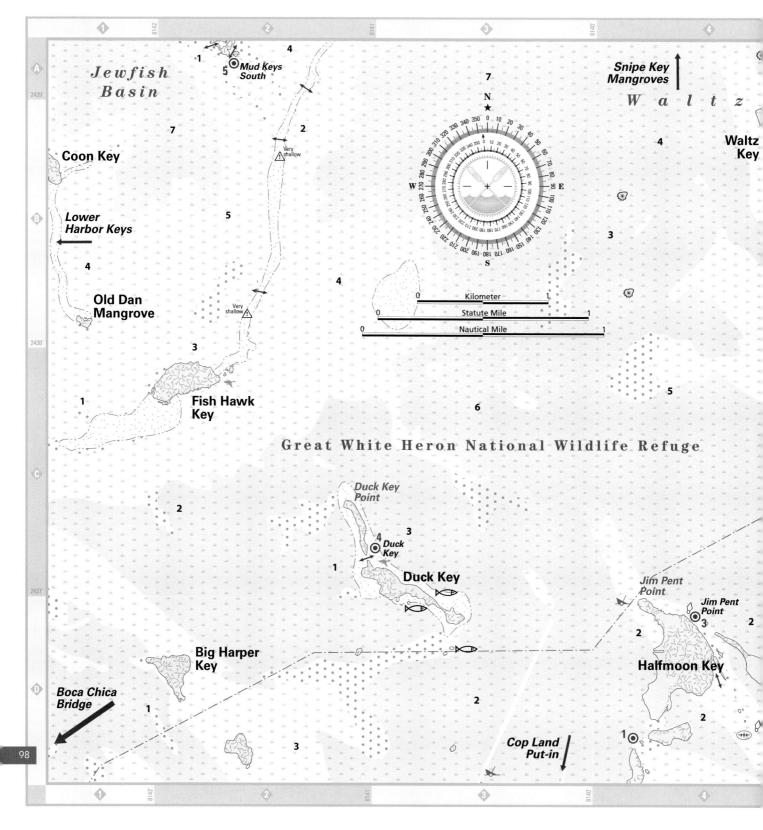

lands surrounded by deep water provides good shelter in the wind, and perhaps a choice spot to toss a fishing line.

There is a small mangrove tunnel through the southeast corner of Halfmoon Key (D4) and extensive mangrove swamps in the vicinity of Go-to 1. Use extra caution if exiting from the mangrove tunnel into the boat channel

Paddling along the bank that tails north off Fish Hawk Key (B2) is bound to yield shark sightings. These predators cruise the flats and trap small fish in shallow water. At low water the bank may be impassable, except in areas marked with white posts.

Tall red mangrove trees stand apart from the low, scrubby mangroves marking the entrance of creeks in Old Finds Bight (Go-to 6, Old Finds #2, B7). Water here is rarely more than 1 or 2 feet deep, and distinctive orange sponges dot the hard bottom. Soft corals, sponges, and other hard-bottom algae are visible in the bight. Small mounds rising from the sandy bottom are signs of marine worms. (See also Chart 39, C1.)

Etiquette: Commercial guides frequent the wide flats around Duck Key. You may be vacationing, but they're working. Give them wide berth, so not to disrupt.

Trip Planning: Paddlers planning a multiday trip into the Lower Keys Backcountry may want to launch from Geiger Key Marina (Chart 44, C6). It adds 4 miles to the trip but offers peace of mind with more secure parking. Conch Republic Kayaks Company is also located at Geiger Key Marina and owner Jason Drevenak can advise you on trip itineraries and local conditions.

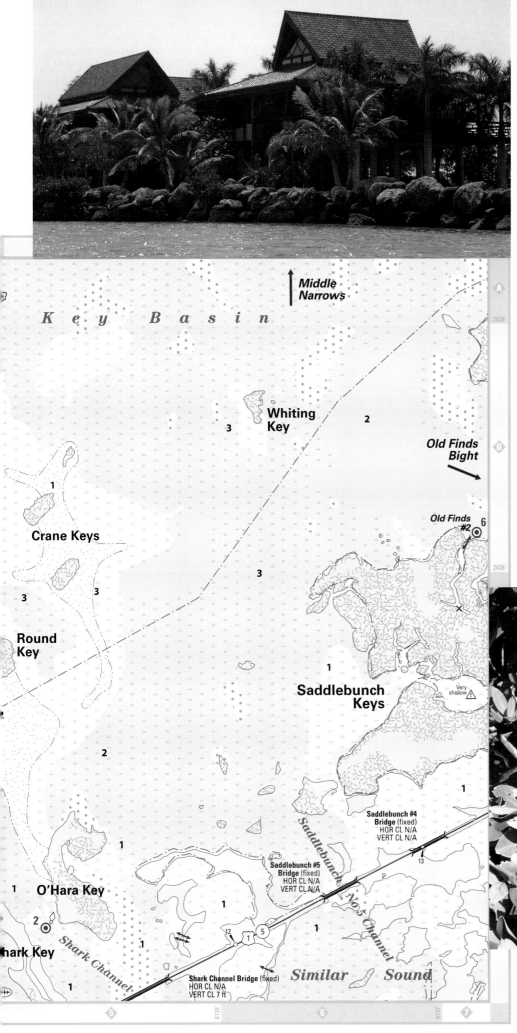

Go-to Points: 1; 2 (Geiger North); 3 (Geiger South)

Off-Chart D/Cs: Sugarloaf Creek; Cow Key Channel; Garrison Bight; Lower Mud Keys

Caution: Keep an eye out for powerboaters in local channels around Pelican and Saddlehill Keys and at a blind corner in a channel that hugs Saddlehill's west side.

Alerts: The lake behind Geiger Key (Go-to 2, Geiger North, C4) is shallow and may be passable only at high tide.

A paddle around Geiger Key is accompanied by the noise of fighter jets taking off and landing at Naval Air Station Boca Chica. NAS pilots train here for, among other things, tactical aviation squadrons (i.e., "Top Guns").

Navigation: From Go-to 2 (Geiger North) (C4), it is 1.5 miles, straight-line distance, at a 55° bearing to the channel that leads beneath Boca Chica Road back into Similar Sound.

The tidal flat between Pelican Key and Saddlebunch Key may be impassable at low tide.

Paddling: See Chart 46 for details on paddling Channel Key (A1).

A circumnavigation of Geiger Key (C5) is about 5 to 6 miles, including a stop at a snorkeling spot on the western end of Saddlehill Key (C6).

The Boca Chica Beach launch offers the quickest access inside Geiger Creek, where red mangroves canopy over a quiet tidal creek. A day trip up this creek and a return to Boca Chica Beach makes a nice 2-mile round-trip.

The 2005 hurricane season brought fresh sand to the oceanside of Saddlehill Key. There's a nice tuck inside the mangroves on the north and west sides of the island. Keep a sharp eye out for small sharks and stingrays in the tidal flat

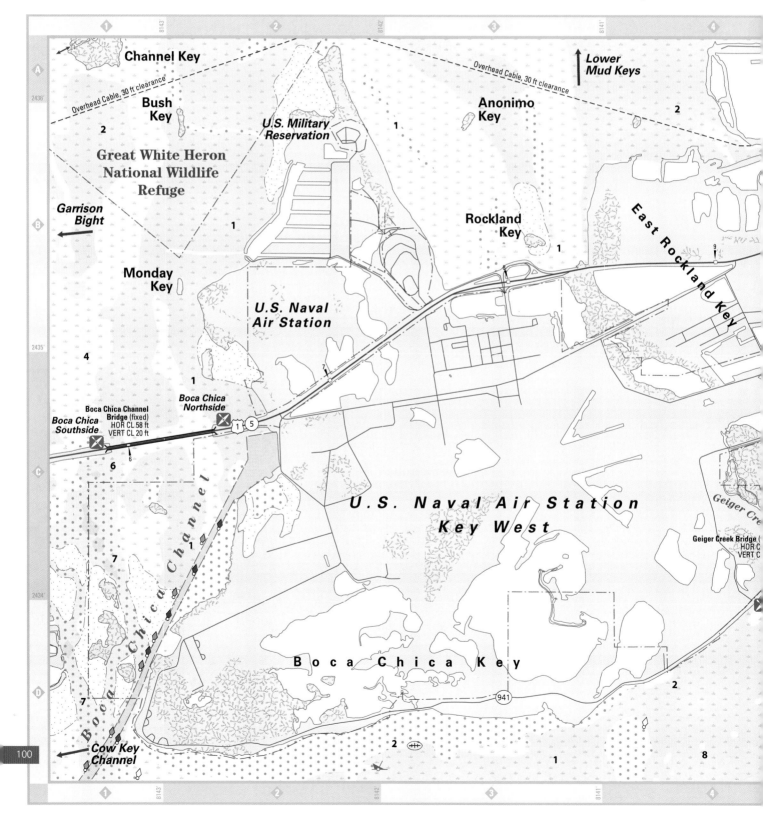

linking Saddlehill and Pelican Keys.

Shallow, clear water in Similar Sound permits top-down views of long-spined urchins clinging to small bits of rubble, and sponges opening and closing in rhythmic dance. Several islands in this sound are privately owned. Contact Conch Republic Kayak Company at Geiger Key Marina for details about camping on one of these islands.

There is a swim hole in a deep channel carved into the northern tip of Bird Key (B6).

Patch reefs lay offshore of Saddlebunch and Sugarloaf Keys along a 3-mile stretch of shoreline between Shark Channel and Sugarloaf Creek. The reefs are not marked, but can be identified as large shadows set in shallow water. There is also a patch reef about a half-mile offshore of Go-to 3 (Geiger South).

Landmark: Geiger Key Marina, nicknamed "The Backside of Paradise," is a locally famous watering hole, restaurant, live music venue, and campground. The food fills you up, the beer is cold, and the company is social.

Nature: The bonnethead shark is instantly distinguished from other sharks by its flat head (think of a miniature hammerhead shark). These small sharks like shallow hard-bottom areas like Similar Sound, where they can feed on crabs, mollusks, and fish.

Outfitter: Conch Republic Kayaks operates out of Geiger Key Marina. See appendix for more information.

History: The old highway to Key West once ran down the oceanside of Sugarloaf and Saddlebunch Keys and crossed Similar Sound to reach Geiger Key. Some charts still show a series of submerged pilings in the area for the old bridge.

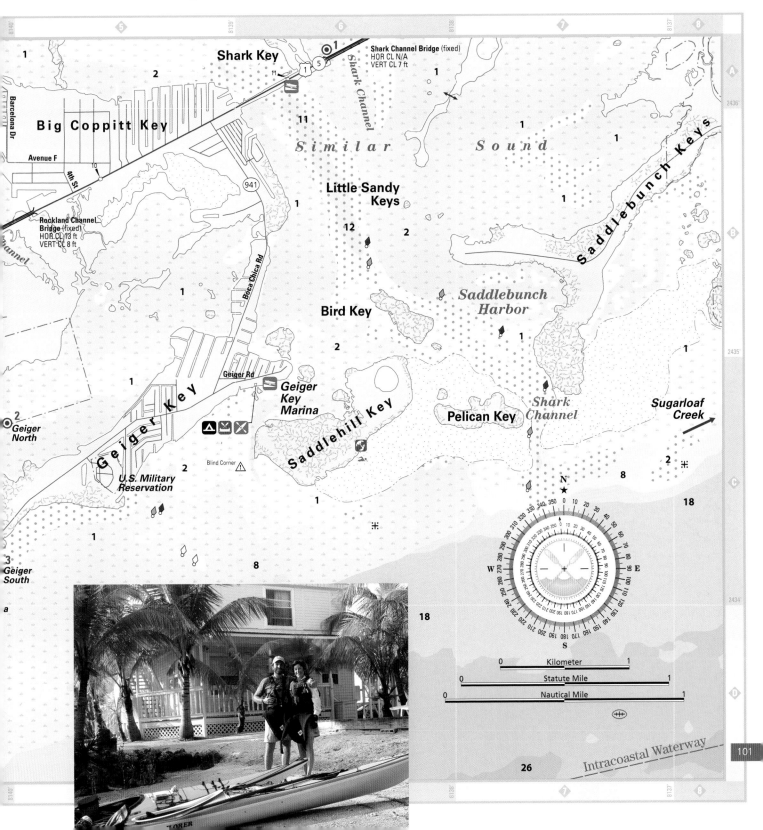

Intracoastal Waterway

Go-to Points: 1–6; 7 (Cayo Agua); 8 (Lower Harbor Lake)

Off-Chart D/Cs: Lower Mud Keys; Boca Chica Bridge; Garrison Bight

Caution: A trip to Cayo Agua and Lower Harbor Keys requires an open-water crossing of 6 to 8 miles one way. Any open-water kayak trip requires paddlers be in good physical condition. Be sure to use proper equipment, and bring all necessary gear.

Sudden, violent storms rise quickly in the

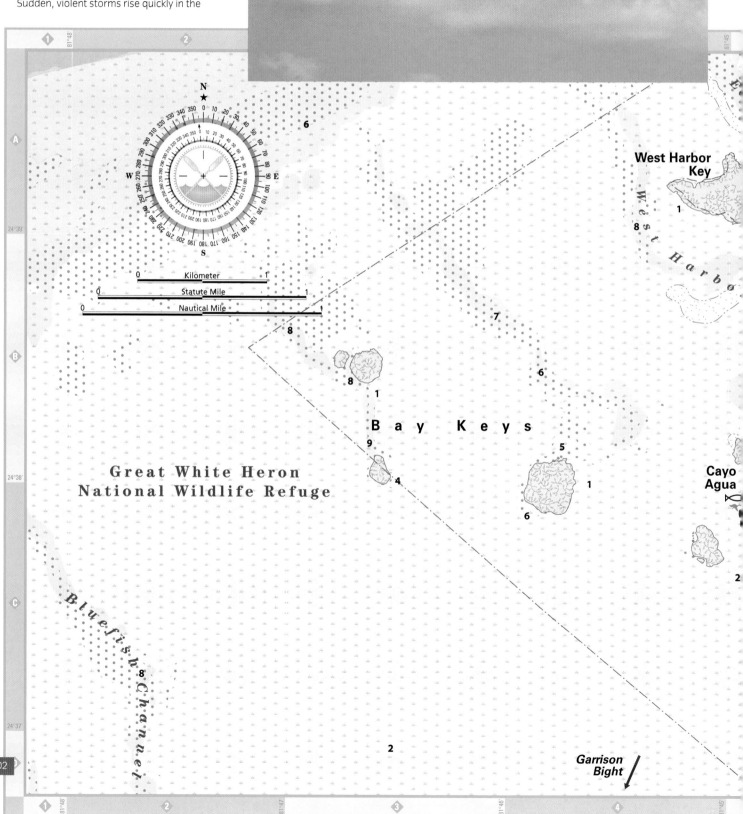

West Harbor Key

Great White Heron
National Wildlife Refuge

Bay Keys

Cayo Agua

Bluefish Channel

Garrison Bight

Lower Keys Backcountry. There is no shelter on open water in heavy winds, lightning, and rough water conditions. Check forecasts before leaving, and consider carrying a weather radio.

Getting There: Starting point for Cayo Agua and Lower Harbor Keys: Boca Chica Bridge, Chart 44, C1 and C2. See appendix for details.

If you don't have the equipment or stamina for a trip to the Backcountry, see the appendix for companies that offer kayak charters.

Navigation: Distance to Lower Harbor Keys Go-to 1: 4 miles from Boca Chica Bridge via Channel Key, Grassy Key, Middle Key.

Getting to Go-to 7 (Cayo Agua) Route: 4.3 miles from Boca Chica Bridge via Channel Key, Grassy Key, Middle Key.

The Mud Keys are northeast of the Lower Harbor Keys. It is 2.75 miles, straight-line distance, at a 48° bearing between Go-to 3 (A6) and the northwest shore of the Mud Keys.

From Go-to 7 (Cayo Agua) (C5), it is 1.1 miles, straight-line distance, at a 42° bearing to Go-to 8 (Lower Harbor Lake) (B6).

Public Land: All navigable creeks through Cayo Agua (B5, C5) are zoned idle

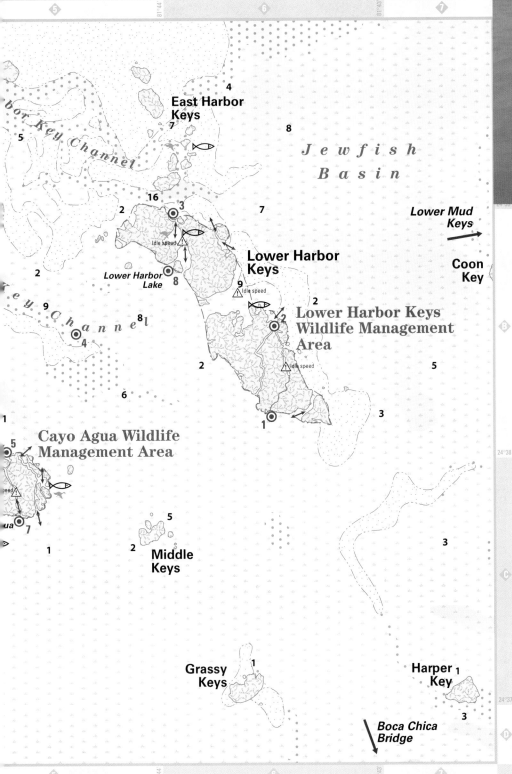

speed/no wake for powerboats. This minimizes disturbances to great white herons and ospreys that roost and nest in this wildlife management area.

In the Harbor Keys Wildlife Management Area, the largest creeks in the Lower Harbor Keys are zoned idle speed/no wake for powerboaters. Great white herons, double-crested cormorants, and ospreys frequent these islands. Also, a 300-foot no-access buffer surrounds the northernmost East Harbor Key (A5).

Rest Areas: A large shell bar, composed of millions of broken shells washed in by the tide, lies just inside the south end of a creek that bisects Cayo Agua (C5). The base is firm and makes a suitable rest area in ankle-deep water.

Paddling: In Cayo Agua's mangrove-fringed tidal creeks, large nurse sharks lie placidly on the deep bottom, seemingly immune to the fast-moving currents. Around the southern and eastern fringes of this island, mangroves colonizing the shallows form a nice windbreak and prime bird-viewing areas.

In the Lower Harbor Keys, a large lake is set between Go-to 8 (Lower Harbor Lake) and Go-to 3 (A6 and B6). In the southern key, a long mangrove creek enters the lower of the two Harbor Keys at Go-to 2 (B6) and winds up, with some tight possibility, exiting at Go-to 1 (B6).

Grassy Key (C6), 3 miles north of the Boca Chica Bridge launch, is an easy paddle that, if linked with Channel Key (Chart 46, A6), can provide a day full of exploring. See Chart 46 for details on paddling here.

Go-to Points: 1–4; 5 (Riviera Canal)
Off-Chart D/C: Cayo Agua
Caution: Fleming Key Cut (C2) is subject to strong tidal currents between 6 and 9 knots at peak flood (eastward current) and ebb (westward current). On windy days this is a dicey passage in a kayak.

Low tide exposes rocks and other hazards offshore of Key West in the area of Sigsbee Park (C4).

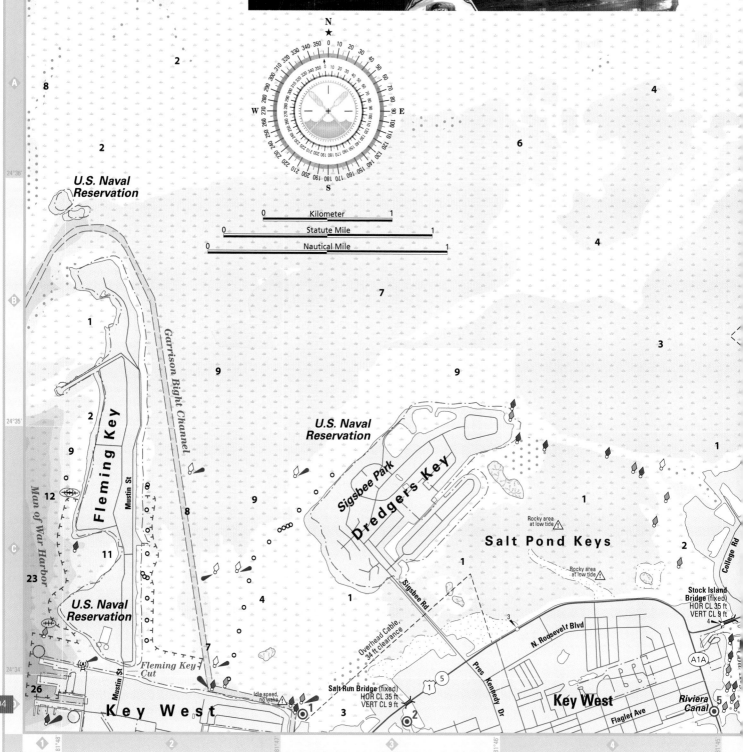

Alert: Watch out for personal watercraft riders zipping through the large creek bisecting Channel Key (A6).

Getting There: If you don't have the equipment or stamina for a long day's paddle to the Backcountry, see the appendix for companies that offer kayak charters.

Navigation: Cayo Agua (Go-to 7, Cayo Agua, Chart 45, C5) is 2.1 miles, straight-line distance, at a bearing of 325° from Channel Key (Go-to 3, A6).

The Lower Harbor Keys (Go-to 1, Chart 45, B6) are 2 miles, straight-line distance, at a 350° bearing from Channel Key (Go-to 4, A6).

The Mud Keys (Go-to 12, Mud Keys South, Chart 42, C2) are 3.6 miles, straight-line distance, at a 28° bearing from Channel Key (Go-to 4, A6).

Paddling: Go-to 2 (D3) is Salt Run Creek, a narrow passage that leads into the heart of Key West and links with Riviera Canal. See Chart 47 for details on using this route in a Key West circumnavigation.

Two creeks divide Channel Key (A6). Go-to 3 marks the west end of the largest creek. A second smaller creek to the north is more kayak-friendly. Go-to 4 is the entrance of a south-running mangrove creek that narrows to a point where kayakers must break down their paddles to half-length or pull through with their hands.

Field Notes: Local boaters use white posts to mark channels—also known as "cuts"—through banks and shallows throughout the Lower Keys Backcountry. The bank that links Channel Key with Bush Key to the south and Grassy Key to the north is marked by several of these local cuts.

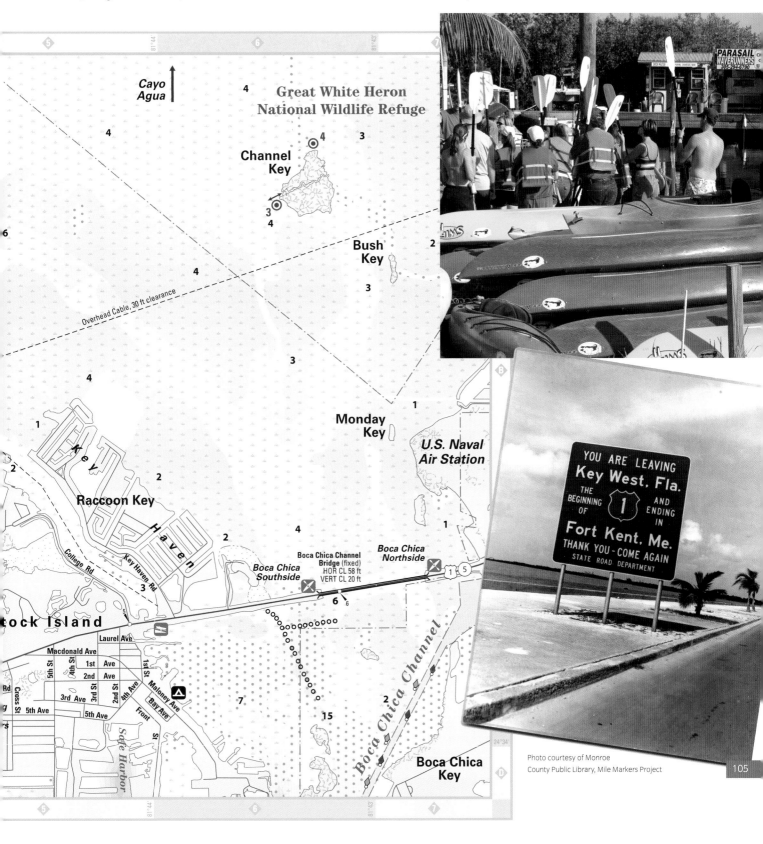

Photo courtesy of Monroe County Public Library, Mile Markers Project

Go-to Points: 1–7; 8 (Riviera Canal)
Off-Chart D/Cs: Cuba, Cayo Agua, Geiger Key Marina, Mud Keys, Boca Grande
Caution: Fleming Key Cut (B3) is subject to strong tidal currents between 6 and 9 knots at peak flood (eastward current) and ebb (westward current). On windy days this is a dicey passage in a kayak.

Powerboaters roar through Turning Basin (C2) at full speed traveling between Key West Channel, Garrison Bight Channel, and Fleming Key Cut.

Kayakers approaching Trumbo Point (C3 and C4) should watch for boats entering and exiting Garrison Bight and the Key West Municipal Marina.
Alerts: Bring a hat, bandana, surveyor's tape, or some other means of marking your entrance/exit from the Salt Ponds (C5).
Getting There: Key West Salt Ponds (C5) are best accessed from Lazy Dog Island Outfitters on Stock Island (B6) or from the 11th Street Boat Ramp (C4).
Public Land: Smathers Beach is Key West's famous white sand Atlantic strip. Do not land or

launch kayaks from designated swim areas. The far east end (C5) is a favored launch site for kite boarders and windsurfers.

Little Hamaca Park (C5) harbors the only native hardwood hammock left in Key West. A boardwalk through the park ends at an overlook on Riviera Canal.
Rest Areas: City of Key West Nature Preserve (C4) is a passive park with a short stretch of Atlantic beach wedged between condominiums and private homes. It is suitable as a landing/rest area, but not available for launching.
N 24°33.006' W 81°46.696'.

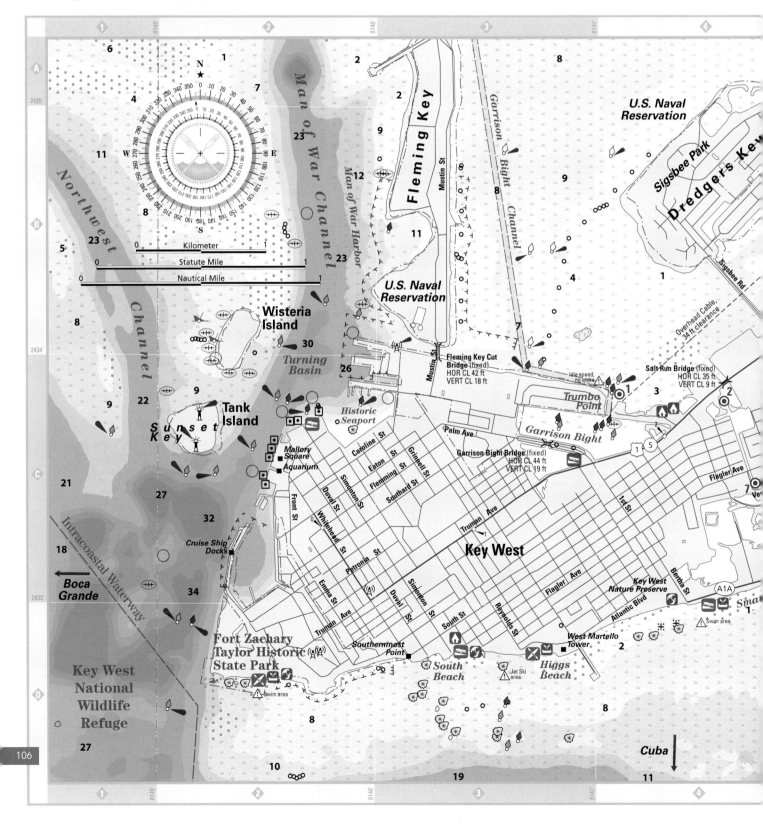

Landing kayaks is allowed at Smathers Beach and the beach at Fort Zachery Taylor State Park (D2). Stay out of marked swimming areas. At Fort Zachery Taylor, use a designated channel set off from the swimming area to reach the landing.

Paddling: A trip around Key West averages 11 miles. Salt Run Channel (Go-to 2, C4) and Go-to 8 (Riviera Canal) (C5), bookend an unexpected treat: a creek and canal through Key West's neighborhoods. The culvert under Flagler Avenue is a tight squeeze for kayaks.

The salt ponds are shallow inland lakes bordering Key West's airport (C5). Access is via two winding mangrove creeks (Go-tos 3, 5) that branch south off Riviera Canal. In the 19th century, salt was distilled from seawater in these shallow basins through a process of solar evaporation. Today the shallow waters are an aquarium of small fish and sharks, sea cucumbers, and cassiopeias (upside-down jellyfish) in water a half-foot deep or less.

Landmarks: Southernmost Point (D3), a large rainbow-colored buoy at the end of Whitehead Street, is visible from the water as you paddle between Fort Zachery Taylor and Higgs Beach.

It is a symbolic marker of the southernmost point in the United States.

West Martello Tower (D3), a Civil War–era fort adjacent to Higgs Beach, is visible from the water. Once the garrison of Union soldiers, the brick fortress houses the Key West Garden Club (305–294–3210), which has built a lush tropical garden on the grounds.

Paddlers can enter the Historic Seaport District (C2), a small bight where tall ship schooners and Mel Fisher's treasure boat are docked along Harbor Walk. Good for sightseeing and boat-watching from the water, but no kayak landing.

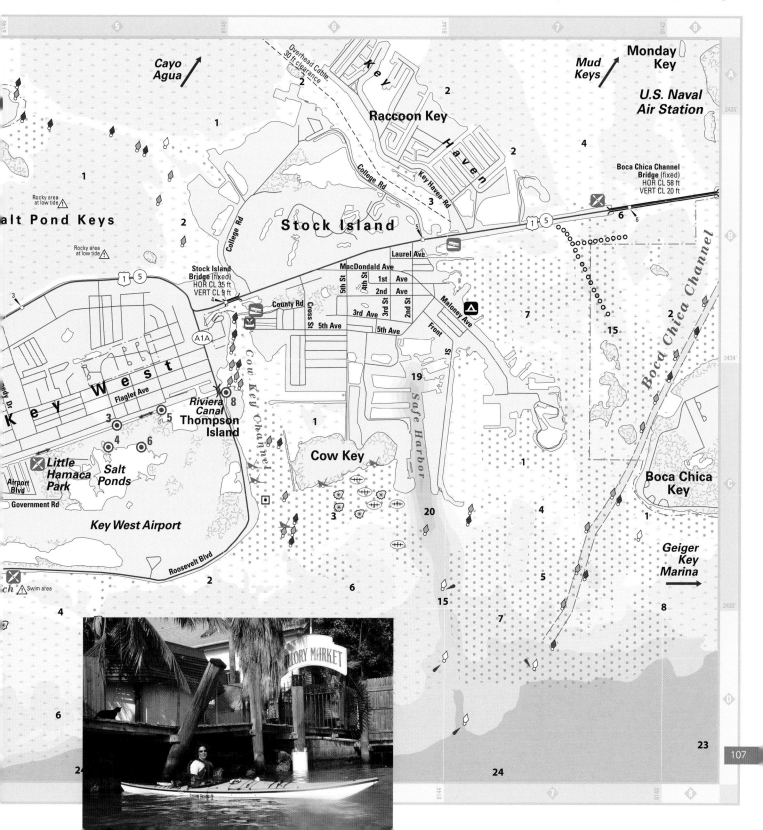

Go-to Points: 1; 2 (Mooney Harbor)

Caution: Boca Grande Channel sees swift currents as water passes through between the Gulf and the Atlantic. Small craft are advised to use caution and to check tide and current predictions and wind speed and direction.

Sudden, violent storms rise quickly in the Key West National Wildlife Refuge. There is no shelter on open water in heavy winds, lightning, and rough water conditions. Check forecasts before leaving, and consider carrying a weather radio.

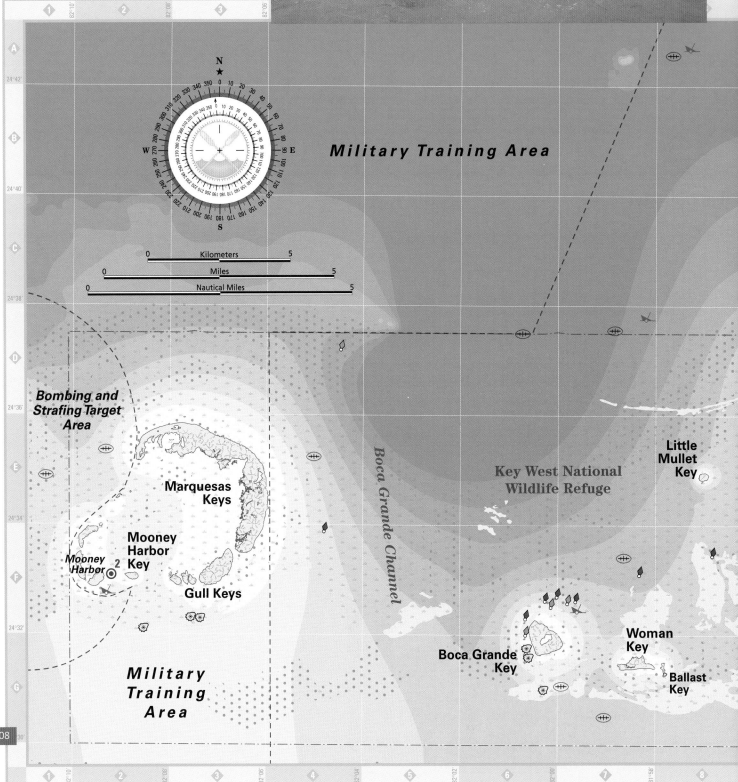

Military Training Area

Key West National
Wildlife Refuge

Little
Mullet
Key

*Bombing and
Strafing Target
Area*

Boca Grande Channel

Marquesas
Keys

Mooney
Harbor
Key

Mooney
Harbor 2

Gull Keys

Woman
Key

Boca Grande
Key

Ballast
Key

*Military
Training
Area*

Getting There: At between 6 and 12 miles one way, a kayak trip into the Key West NWR is impractical. However, loading kayaks onto a motorboat and traveling out to shelter and shallow water is an excellent way to see this pristine environment.

Navigation: The Lake's Passage is a local channel from Key West to Boca Grande Key that cuts across numerous banks and flats. It is advisable that boaters obtain local information about the channel before traveling this route.

Public Land: The Key West National Wildlife Refuge is the largest in Florida and one of the old-

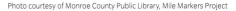
Photo courtesy of Monroe County Public Library, Mile Markers Project

est in America, established in 1908. Within its boundaries are 13 small mangrove islands due west of Key West and a ring of islands called the Marquesas Keys. Several islands—namely Boca Grande and Woman Keys—have gorgeous white sand beaches and dune habitat. These islands are roosting and foraging grounds for migrating gulls and terns, white-crowned pigeons, egrets, herons, falcons, and magnificent frigatebirds. The islands are considered the most important site for wintering piping plovers in the Keys, as well as a nesting site for sea turtles.

The beaches on Boca Grande's south and west sides (G6) are nesting habitat for loggerhead sea turtles, and an interior lake on the island offers important wetland habitat for foraging birds. A portion of the beach is closed. Visitors should restrict activity to beach areas that remain open to the public.

A white sand beach on the southeast side of Woman Key (G7) is nesting habitat for loggerhead sea turtles. Half of the beach and sand spit on the southeast side of the island is closed; restrict activities to portions of the beach that remain open to the public.

Cottrell Key, Little Mullet Key, and Big Mullet Key (D9, E8 and E9) are wildlife management areas for the protection of foraging and roosting egrets, herons, and other birds. Mangrove terrapins, a small turtle, have been documented on Cottrell. A no-motor zone surrounds Cottrell and Big Mullet Keys; a 300-foot no-access buffer surrounds Little Mullet Key.

See Chart 49 for details on the Marquesas Keys wildlife management area.

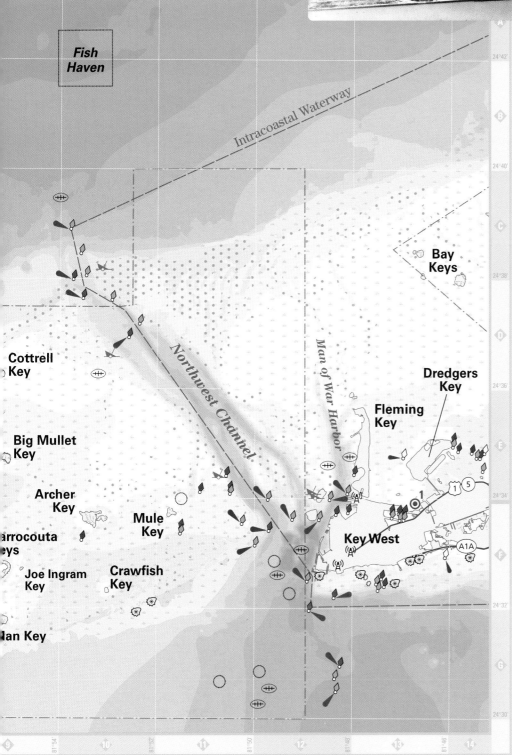

Fish Haven

Intracoastal Waterway

Bay Keys

Cottrell Key

Dredgers Key

Fleming Key

Man of War Harbor

Northwest Channel

Big Mullet Key

Archer Key

Mule Key

Key West

rrocouta eys

Joe Ingram Key

Crawfish Key

Jan Key

Photo courtesy of Monroe County Public Library, Mile Markers Project

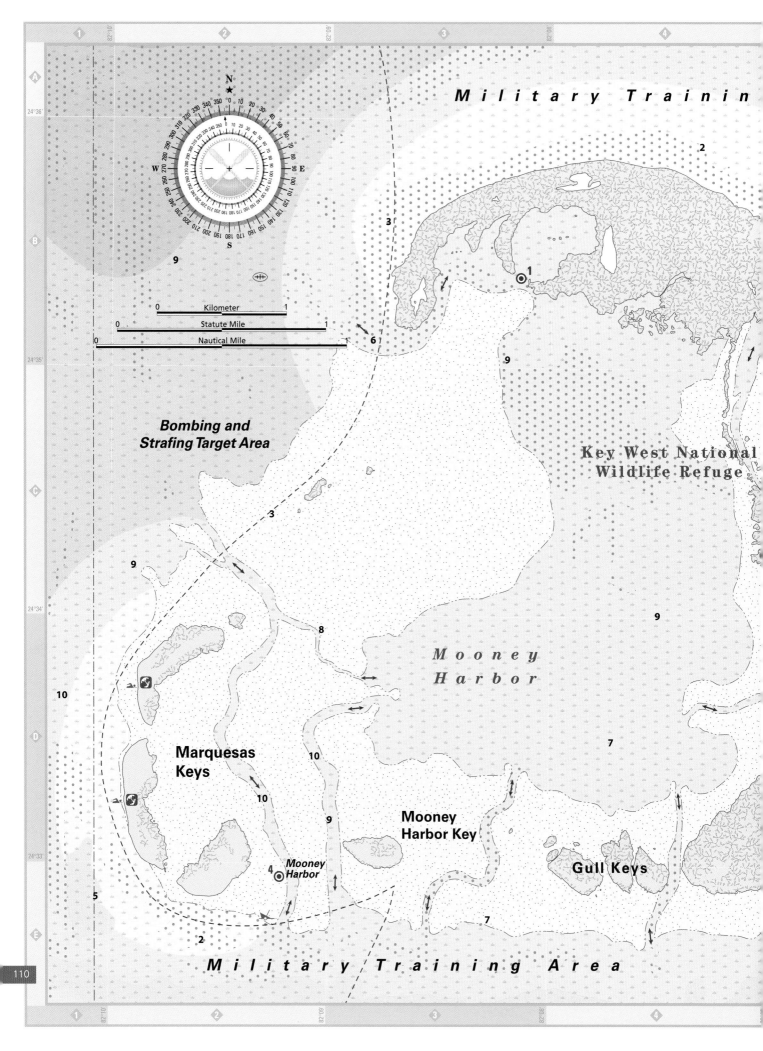

N

W E

S

9

0 — Kilometer — 1

0 — Statute Mile — 1

0 — Nautical Mile — 1

**Bombing and
Strafing Target Area**

3

9

Military Trainin

2

3

1

9

6

9

Key West National
Wildlife Refuge

3

9

8

9

*Mooney
Harbor*

9

7

10

Marquesas
Keys

10

10

10

9

Mooney
Harbor Key

Gull Keys

5

4
Mooney
Harbor

7

2

7

Military Training Area

110

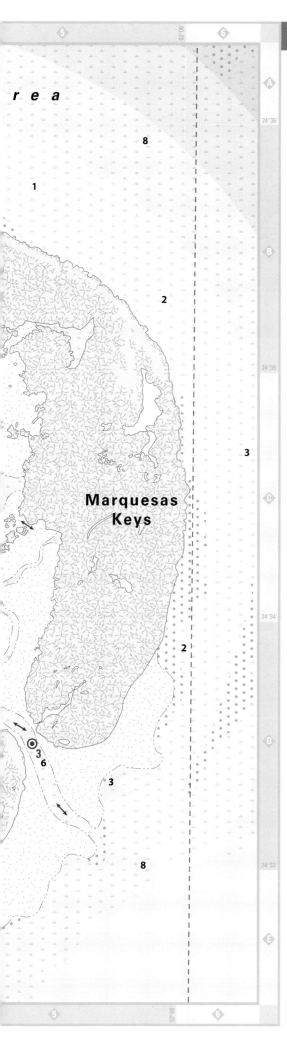

r e a

8

1

2

3

**Marquesas
Keys**

2

3
6

3

8

Go-to Points: 1–3; 4 (Mooney Harbor)
Off-Chart D/Cs: none
Caution: There is a difference in tidal change between the Atlantic and Gulf sides of the Marquesas. Tides at Go-to 4 (Mooney Harbor) are similar to Key West Harbor, but on the Gulf-facing side, tides lag those at Mooney Harbor by an hour or two. This difference varies based on season and time of month.

Sudden, violent storms rise quickly around the Marquesas. There is no shelter on open water in heavy winds, lightning, and rough water conditions. Check forecasts before leaving, and consider carrying a weather radio.

Alert: The Marquesas are a favored sportfishing ground for tarpon, permit, and sailfish. Be respectful of guides who earn a livelihood on the water by maintaining your distance.

Getting There: The Marquesas stand some 20 miles west of Key West, and, as such, it is impractical to reach them by paddling. A number of kayak fishing charters operate from Key West.

Public Land: The Marquesas, 20 miles west of Key West, are part of the Key West National Wildlife Refuge. The natural sand beaches, shallow nearshore flats, and remote location make this a critical site for nesting sea turtles and birds that nest, feed, and roost on the islands. A 300-foot no-motor zone surrounds the three smallest islands in this chain (C2). There is a no-access buffer around one mangrove island (C2), and motorboats must run at idle speed/no wake in the southeast tidal creek (D4).

Nature: The Marquesas Keys form an atoll—barrier islands in a circle with a natural harbor in the middle. As such, they're geologically distinct from the coral islands that form the mainline Keys.

Snorkeling: There are coral heads roughly 300 yards south off Gull and Mooney Harbor Keys.

History: Fishing has long been a staple activity in the Marquesas. In days past, commercial fishermen lived in seasonal shacks built on stilts in the water. The flats are now favored by anglers looking for the Keys slam: tarpon, permit, and bonefish.

The Spanish galleon *Nuestra Senora de Atocha,* part of a treasure fleet sailing from Havana, Cuba, to Spain, was driven from the Florida Straits and in 1622 sank. In 1985, after a 16-year search, treasure hunter Mel Fisher's company found the *Atocha* in the Quicksands, a large sandbar west of the Marquesas. It has yielded Fisher's company and investors more than 40 tons of silver and gold, and $450 million.

Go-to Points: 1–3; 4 (Dry Tortugas); 5 (Loggerhead Key)

Caution: Strong currents run through the boat channel between Garden and Loggerhead Keys. Only kayakers with experience navigating strong currents and rough water conditions should attempt this crossing in a kayak.

Alert park volunteers or staff on Garden Key if you plan to paddle to Loggerhead Key. They are not responsible for your safety, but someone

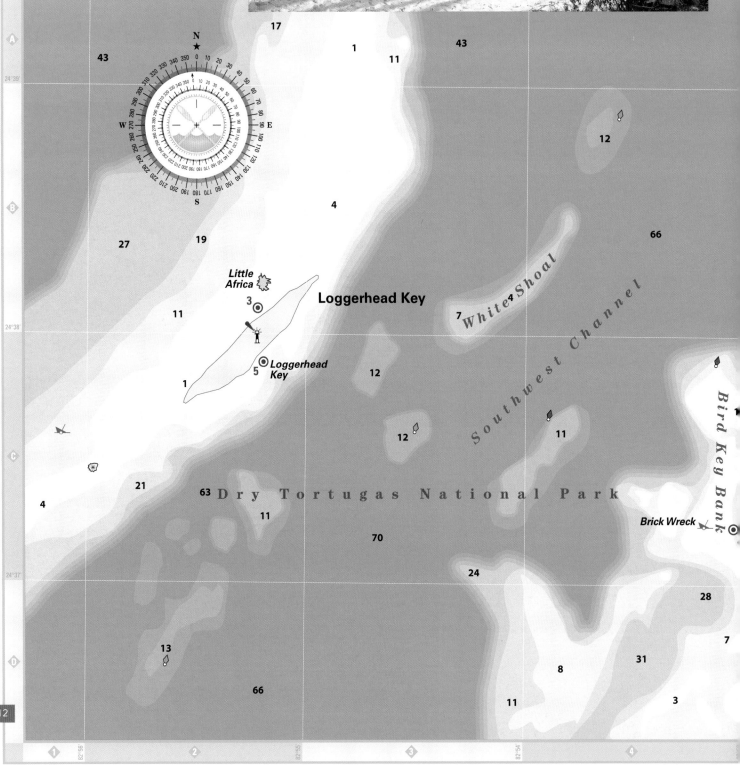

should know whether winds and current have carried you off to the high seas.

Alert: In a no-entry zone over hard-bottom flats off Long Key (C6), scientists conduct research on the behavior and breeding of nurse sharks.

Getting There: It is a two-hour trip (conditions permitting) aboard a high-speed ferry from Key West. Sunny Days (800–236–7937) and Yankee Freedom (800+634–0939) will transport a few kayaks, but call for length restrictions.

Public Land: Dry Tortugas National Park (www.nps.gov/drto) encompasses seven coral, shoal, and sand islands perched on the Straights of Florida. Set 70-miles west of Key West, its remote destination is matched only by the immensity of Fort Jefferson, a Civil War–era fort that never fired a shot in wartime. Park entrance fee.

Paddling: Fort Jefferson's massive brick edifice rising from the water looms larger still from the deck of a kayak. Circling Garden Key is an easy half-day paddle. Launch from Dingy Beach west of the main landing dock.

Bush Key was described in one historical document as being "three-quarters of a mile" from Garden Key. Today visitors can walk across a small channel at low tide and explore this spit of sand and scrub. Circling the island is a 2.3-mile round-trip.

Nature: They are visible from Key Largo to Key West, soaring hundreds of feet overhead, recognizable for their distinctive angled-wing profile. But Long Key in Dry Tortugas National Park is the only site in the United States where magnificent frigatebirds nest. These birds are considered kleptoparasitic, meaning they steal food from victims rather than hunt or gather on their own.

Camping: There is an eight-site primitive camping area in the shadow of Fort Jefferson, on Garden Key.

Snorkeling: There are brain coral, sea fans, and colorful reef fishes in the snorkeling area at the base of the fort moat on Garden Key. Off Loggerhead there are extensive staghorn coral thickets in the Little Africa patch reef.

Swim with a companion. Do not stand on or touch coral and be aware that flippers/fins may inadvertently touch coral. Always use a dive flag.

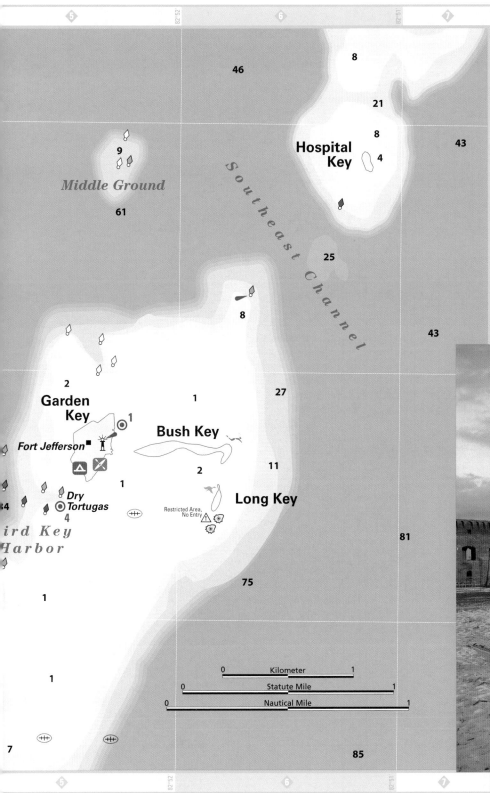

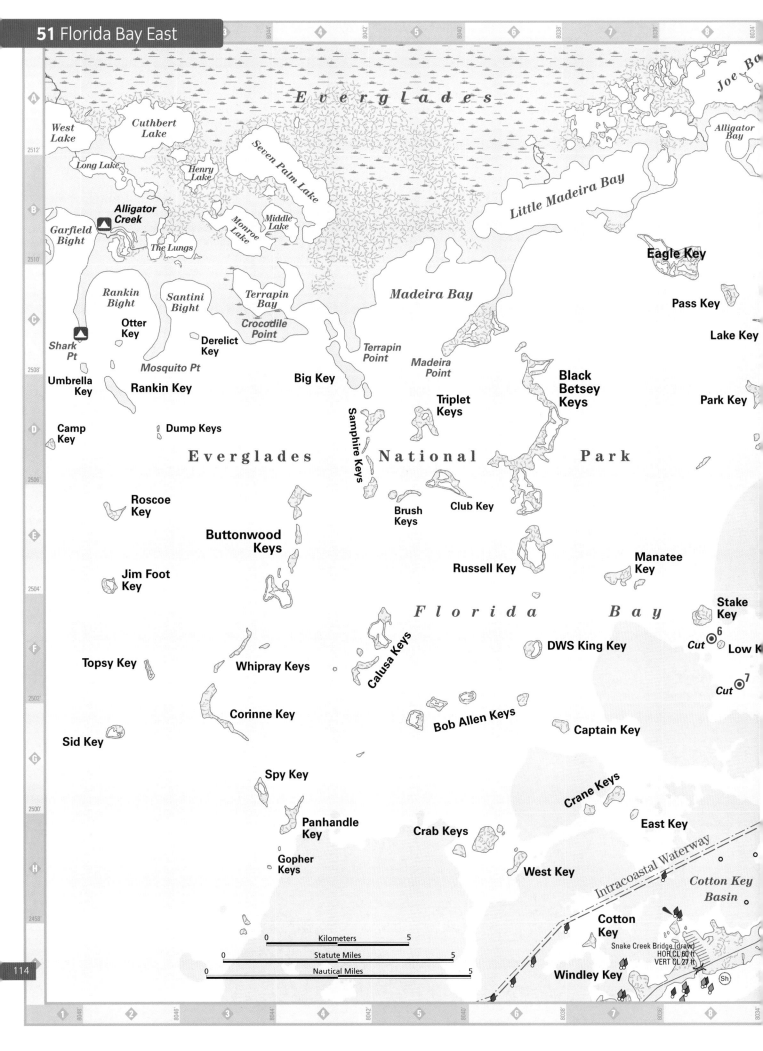

Everglades

Joe Bay

West Lake

Cuthbert Lake

Long Lake

Henry Lake

Seven Palm Lake

Little Madeira Bay

Alligator Bay

Alligator Creek

Garfield Bight

Monroe Lake

Middle Lake

The Lungs

Madeira Bay

Eagle Key

Rankin Bight

Santini Bight

Terrapin Bay

Pass Key

Otter Key

Crocodile Point

Terrapin Point

Lake Key

Shark Pt

Derelict Key

Madeira Point

Mosquito Pt

Big Key

Black Betsey Keys

Umbrella Key

Rankin Key

Park Key

Triplet Keys

Camp Key

Dump Keys

E v e r g l a d e s

Samphire Keys

N a t i o n a l

P a r k

Roscoe Key

Brush Keys

Club Key

Buttonwood Keys

Manatee Key

Jim Foot Key

Russell Key

Stake Key

F l o r i d a

B a y

Topsy Key

Whipray Keys

Calusa Keys

DWS King Key

Cut ⊙6 **Low K**

Cut ⊙7

Corinne Key

Sid Key

Bob Allen Keys

Captain Key

Spy Key

Crane Keys

East Key

Panhandle Key

Crab Keys

Gopher Keys

Intracoastal Waterway

Cotton Key Basin

West Key

0   Kilometers   5

0   Statute Miles   5

0   Nautical Miles   5

Cotton Key

Snake Creek Bridge (draw)
HOR CL 60 ft
VERT CL 27 ft

Windley Key

Ⓢⓗ

Appendixes

Kayak Launches

Directional cues for launches are organized by page and referenced to our charts with a number/letter grid coordinate. The launch name and mile marker is followed by either oceanside (O/S) or bayside (B/S); in the Lower Keys, bayside is gulfside (G/S). In areas where these terms do not apply, we indicate northbound or southbound lane. A brief description of the launch, hazards, and GPS coordinates follows.

Chart 2

D2 **Alabama Jack's,** CS-5, 1500 Card Sound Road, southbound, 0.2 mile north of Card Sound Bridge tollbooth. Funky open-air restaurant on a canal with concrete boat ramp. Fee. Access to Little Card Sound and Ghost Trap Lake. (305–248–8741). N25°17.498′ W80°22.767′

D2 **Card Sound Bridge Boat Ramp,** CS-4.7, Card Sound Road, southbound. A public boat launch between the tollbooth and west side of Card Sound Bridge. Free launch off a concrete ramp; short hand-carry; parking for 7 vehicles. Access to Little Card Sound and Ghost Trap Lake. N25°17.398′ W80°22.526′

Chart 2 and Chart 3

D3 and A2 **Card Sound Bridge,** CS-3.8, Card Sound Road, northbound. A roadside pull-off 0.1 mile east of Card Sound Bridge. Free kayak-only launch from a gravel beach; short hand-carry; parking for 5 vehicles. Access to Crocodile Lake National Wildlife Refuge. N25°17.098′ W80°21.669′

D5 and A4 **Steamboat Creek,** CS 1.7, Card Sound Road, northbound. A popular fishing area with associated debris. Free launch off a dirt boat ramp; short hand-carry; parking for 3 cars. Access to Angelfish Creek and Crocodile Lake National Wildlife Refuge. *Caution:* Parking surface uneven and prone to flooding at high tide. N25°17.035′ W80°19.835′

Chart 4

A1 **South Dade Marina,** MM 115, US 1, northbound. Private marina. Concrete boat ramp; restrooms. Fee. Access to Manatee Bay and Sarge Creek. Gate locks at closing. (305–247–8730, www.southdademarina.com) N25°16.045′ W80°26.376′

Chart 7

A2 **Gilbert's Resort,** MM 107, US 1, southbound. Private resort on Blackwater Sound at south entrance to Jewfish Creek; restaurant and tiki bar on premises. Free kayak-only launch off a sand beach; long hand-carry; plenty of parking. Access to Blackwater Sound. *Caution:* Swimmers and motor craft present. (800–274–6701, www.gilbertsresort.com) N25°10.966′ W80°23.397′ **Note:** Scheduled for conversion into private condominiums. Call ahead for status.

B4 **Garden Cove,** MM 106.5 O/S, Garden Cove Drive, Key Largo, 0.4 mile off CR905A. An abandoned county boat ramp. Free kayak-only launch off a rocky shoreline; short hand-carry; roadside parking for 5 vehicles. Access to North Sound Creek. *Caution:* Busy boat channel offshore of kayak launch. N25°0.257′ W80°2.023′

D2 **Caribbean Club,** MM 104 B/S, US 1, Key Largo. Classic Keys bar. Concrete boat ramp. Fee. Plenty of parking for cars and trailers. N25°8.724′ W80°3.820′

D2 **Florida Bay Outfitters,** MM 104 B/S, US 1, Key Largo. Kayak and canoe outfitter, offering equipment rentals and sales and kayak instruction. Free kayak-only launch off a sand beach; short hand-carry; parking for up to 5 vehicles. Access to Dusenbury Creek and the Boggies. (305–451–3018, www.kayakflorida keys.com) N25°08.700′ W80°23.842′

Chart 9

B3 **John Pennekamp Coral Reef State Park,** MM 102.5 O/S, US 1, Key Largo. Kayak landing, boat ramp, and parking for 50-plus vehicles and boat trailers. Access to Pennekamp canoe trails. Entrance fee. (305–451–1202, www.floridastateparks.org/pennekamp)

B3 **Monroe County Park** (under construction), MM 102 B/S, US 1, Key Largo. Former restaurant property (The Quay) being converted to a public park with kayak launch.

Chart 11

A3 **Harbor Drive,** MM 98.5 O/S, Harbor Drive, Key Largo, 0.1 mile off US 1. A neighborhood boat ramp. Free launch off a concrete ramp; short hand-carry; parking for 5 vehicles. Access to Rock Harbor. *Caution:* Parking area may flood at high tide. N25°05.113′ W80°26.860′

Chart 12,

D6 **Sunset Park,** MM 95.3 B/S, Sunset Road, Key Largo, 0.1 mile off US 1. A county boat ramp; gates lock at closing. Free launch off a concrete boat ramp; short hand-carry; parking for 5 vehicles. Access to Bottle Key. N25°02.996′ W80°29.354′

Chart 13

B3 **Harry Harris Park,** MM 92.5 O/S, Burton Drive, Tavernier, 1.2 miles off US 1. A county park with swimming beach, boat ramp, picnic tables and shelters, playground, restrooms, soda machines, and water. Entry free to Monroe County residents; fee for nonresidents on weekends and holidays. The concrete boat ramp is slippery; instead, use the sandy shoreline left of ramp for kayaks. No overnight parking (vehicles will be towed). Access to Dove Creek and Tavernier Key. N25°01.482′ W80°29.651′

B3 **Dove Creek,** Caribbean Avenue, Tavernier. Access via Burton Drive off U.S. 1, MM 92.5 O/S. Free, rocky launch in a residential neighborhood. No facilities. Very limited street parking. Access to Dove Sound and Dove Creek Hammocks Wildlife Management Area. Nice windy-day paddle. N25° 01.735′ W80° 29.870′

Chart 13, Chart 14, and Chart 15

C1, C5, and A6 **Jo Jean Way Boat Ramp,** MM 92 B/S, Jo Jean Way, Tavernier. Neighborhood ramp at the dead end of Jo Jean Way. Free launch off a concrete boat ramp; short hand-carry; no parking available. Access to Bottle Key. N25°00.751′ W80°31.062′

C2, C6, and A7 **Old Settlers Park,** MM 91.9 O/S, US 1, Tavernier. County park with playground, benches, and picnic shelter. Nice place to land and stretch your legs. Cuban restaurant nearby. The launch is free off a rocky shoreline; long hand-carry; parking for 3 vehicles; no water or facilities. Access to Tavernier Key. N25°00.518′ W80°30.912′

Chart 16

A4 **Snake Creek Bridge, northside,** MM 85.9 B/S, US 1, Islamorada. Dirt road access to fishing area at the north bridge abutment. Free kayak-only launch off a rocky shoreline; 100-foot hand-carry down a steep bank; parking for 6 vehicles. Access to Snake Creek. *Caution:* Strong current, boat traffic, and large shoreline riprap. N24°57.137′ W80°35.237′

A5 **Founders Park,** MM 87 B/S, US 1, Islamorada. Village park with restrooms, picnic tables, and kayak rentals. Launch off a sandy beach between buoys left of the swimming beach; long hand-carry from parking area; parking for 20-plus vehicles. Access to Cowpens and Crab Keys. Entrance free to Islamorada residents and hotel guests; fee for nonresidents. (park: 305–853–1685; kayak rentals: 305–852–5633) N24°57.725′ W80°34.215′

A5 **East Ridge Road Boat Ramp,** MM 86.8 O/S, East Ridge Road, Islamorada, at dead end 0.3 mile off US 1. Neighborhood boat ramp just north of Treasure Village.

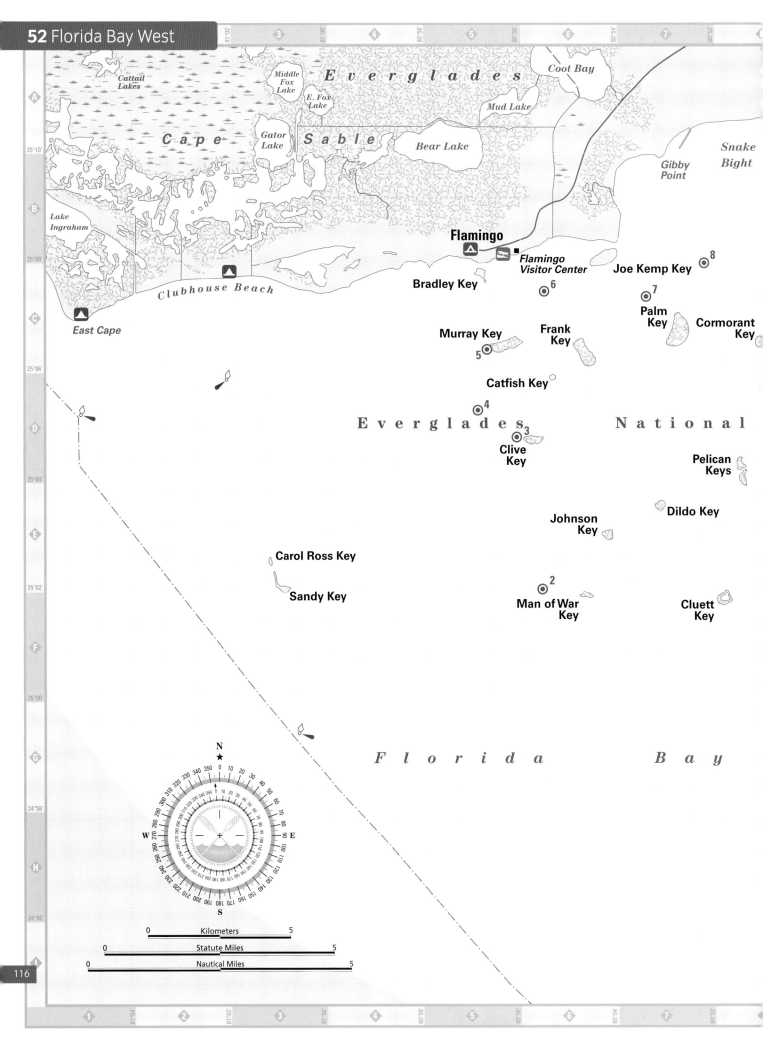

Cattail Lakes

Middle Fox Lake

E. Fox Lake

E v e r g l a d e s

Coot Bay

Mud Lake

Gator Lake

C a p e   S a b l e

Bear Lake

Snake Bight

Gibby Point

Lake Ingraham

Flamingo

Flamingo Visitor Center

Joe Kemp Key ⊙⁸

Bradley Key

⊙⁶

⊙⁷

Clubhouse Beach

Palm Key

Cormorant Key

East Cape

Murray Key

Frank Key

⊙⁵

Catfish Key

⊙⁴

E v e r g l a d e s ⊙³   **N a t i o n a l**

Clive Key

Pelican Keys

Dildo Key

Johnson Key

Carol Ross Key

⊙²

Sandy Key

Man of War Key

Cluett Key

F l o r i d a   B a y

N ★

W   E

S

0   Kilometers   5

0   Statute Miles   5

0   Nautical Miles   5

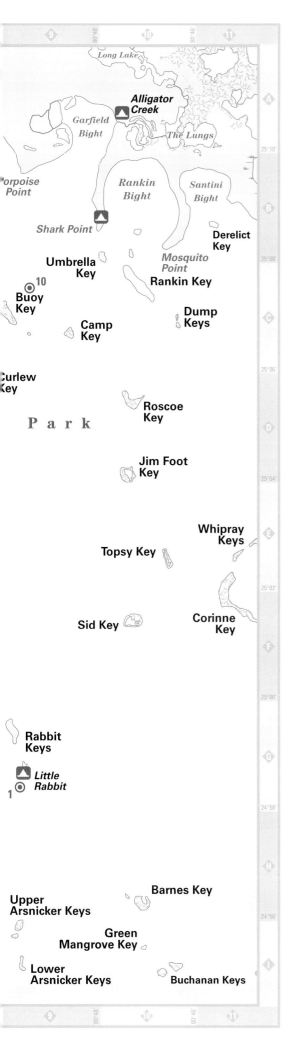

Free launch off a concrete ramp; parking for 3 vehicles. Direct ocean access. N24°57.297′ W80°34.185′

B3 Whale Harbor Channel Bridge, MM 83.9 O/S, US 1, Islamorada. A roadside pull-off on the south end of the bridge. Free kayak-only launch off a rocky shoreline. Access to ocean. *Caution:* Strong currents and boat traffic. N24°56.269′ W80°36.728′

Chart 16 and Chart 17

C1 and A5 Blackwood Road Boat Launch, MM 81.9 B/S, Blackwood Road, Islamorada. A neighborhood boat ramp. Free launch off an old concrete ramp; parking for 5 vehicles; parking lot may flood at high tide. Access to Little Basin. N24°55.215′ W80°38.112′

C1 and A5 Islamorada Library Park, MM 81.6 B/S, US 1, Islamorada, behind the public library. Small village park with picnic tables and restrooms. Free launch off a sandy, sheltered beach into a mangrove-lined canal; long hand-carry; parking for 5-plus vehicles. Access to Little Basin. N24°55.083′ W80°38.240′

C2 and A6 Lorelei's Restaurant, MM 82 B/S, US 1, Islamorada. Restaurant and boat ramp in the heart of Islamorada. Free kayak landing and launching from a gravel beach past the tiki bar; long; hand-carry; plenty of parking. N25°55.326′ W80°38.011′. Concrete boat ramp adjacent to parking lot; fee; N24°55.298′ W80°37.985′. Access to Little Basin. (305–664–4656, www.loreleifloridakeys.com)

Chart 17

B5 La Siesta Marina, MM 80.5 B/S, US 1, Islamorada. Commercial marina with concrete boat ramp; restrooms. Fee. Access to Little Basin and Shell Key. (305–664–2402) Backcountry Cowboy Outfitters operates kayak tours from here. (305–517–4177; www.backcountrycowboy.com) N24°54.467′ W80°38.968′

C2 Indian Key Fill Oceanside, MM 77.8 O/S, US 1, Islamorada. Highway pull-off. Free kayak-only launch off a riprap shoreline; short hand-carry; parking for 5 vehicles. Access to Indian Key. N24°53.066′ W80°41.148′

C3 Indian Key Fill Boat Ramp, MM 78.5 B/S, US 1, Islamorada. Roadside park with historical markers and kiosk for Indian Key and Lignumvitae Key state parks. Free launch off a gravel ramp; short hand-carry; parking for 5-plus vehicles. *Caution:* Busy boat channel parallels the shoreline. N24°53.365′ W80°40.639′

C4 Teatable Fill, MM 79.5 O/S, US 1, Islamorada. Highway pull-off south of the gated entrance to Teatable Key. Free kayak-only launch off a rocky shoreline; short hand-carry; roadside parking. Access to Indian Key. N24°53.793′ W80°39.713′

Chart 17 and Chart 18

D2 and B5 Florida Keys Kayak (at Robbie's Marina), MM 77.4 B/S, US 1, Islamorada. Kayak rentals and tours. Sandy beach left of the kayak shop. Fee. Access to mangrove tunnels and Lignumvitae and Indian Keys. (305–664–4878, www.floridakeyskayakandski.com) N24°52.992′ W80°41.455′

Chart 18

D2 Anne's Beach, MM 74–73 O/S, US 1, Islamorada. 1-mile stretch of county beach along the highway at the southern tip of Lower Matecumbe Key. Two parking areas are connected by a shady boardwalk through mangroves. There are picnic pavilions along the boardwalk, and restrooms and an outdoor shower at the northern parking area. Caloosa Cove Marina is a short walk north with a convenience store, laundry facilities, hardware, bait and tackle, restaurant, and bar. Free launch off sand beach. *Caution:* Depth of nearshore waters is 1 foot or less at low tide. North parking area (MM 73.7): N24°50.924′ W80°44.447′. South parking area (MM 73.3): N24°50.795′ W80°44.651′.

Chart 19

A6 Sea Bird Marina, MM 69.5 B/S, US 1, Long Key. Commercial marina with concrete ramp. Fee. Overnight parking allowed. Access to Long Key Bight. (305–664–2871, www.seabirdmarina.com) N24°50.273′ W80°47.936′

A7 Channel 5 Bridge Causeway, MM 70.7 B/S, US 1. Fishing area pull-off on the west bridge causeway. Free kayak-only launch off a rocky beach; short hand-carry down a steep embankment; ample parking. Access to Long Key Bight. N24°50.409′ W80°46.881′

C3 Long Key Roadside, MM 66.6 B/S, US 1, Long Key. A highway pull-off adjacent to the county landfill. Free kayak-only launch off a beach; short hand-carry; parking for 3 vehicles. *Caution:* There is a 2-foot drop over a seawall to reach this put-in; offshore of launch is shallow and thick with sea grass beds. N24°48.525′ W80°50.111′

C3 Long Key Channel Bridge, northside, MM 65.4 O/S, US 1, Long Key. A fishing area with ocean and bay access via Long Key Channel. Free kayak-only launch off a small, sandy beach at the end of the seawall; long hand-carry over a guardrail and down a grassy embankment; parking for 20 vehicles. N24°48.188′ W80°50.962′

C4 Long Key State Park, MM 67.5 O/S, US 1, Long Key. A state park with canoe rentals and a kayak-only backcountry campsite (permit required). Restrooms and outdoor showers on premises. Entrance fee. Access to canoe trail, Zane Grey Creek, and Long Key Bight. (305–664–4815, www.floridastateparks.org/longkey)

Launch #1: Canoe Trail. Launch off a wooden dock 200 yards past entrance station on the left. *Note:* Parking for this launch is left at the first fork in the camp road. N24°48.888′ W80°49.385′

Launch #2: Picnic Area. Launch off a sandy shoreline; parking for 3 vehicles on grass nearby. *Caution:* Nearshore waters 1 foot or less at low tide. N24°48.707′ W80°49.567′

Chart 20

A5 Bayview Inn & Marina, MM 63 B/S, US 1, Conch Key. Motel, marina, and general store. Beach and concrete ramp. Fee (free for overnight guests). (305–289–1525, www.bayviewinn.com) Sandy beach: N24°47.404′ W80°53.309′. Concrete ramp: N24°47.414′ W80°53.348′.

B3 Toms Harbor Key Access, MM 60.2 O/S, US 1. Fishing area on the northern tip of Grassy Key. Free kayak-only launch off a riprap shoreline; long hand-carry over a guardrail and down rocky embankment; parking for 10 cars. Access to Toms Harbor Keys. N24°46.515′ W80°55.669′

B4 Toms Harbor Cut, MM 61.2 O/S, US 1. Pull-off immediately south of Toms Harbor Cut Bridge. Free kayak-only launch off a beach with riprap; short hand-carry; parking for 5 vehicles. N24°46.893′ W80°54.601′

Chart 21

B2 Marathon Boat Ramp, MM 53.9 B/S, US 1, Marathon. City boat ramp. Free launch off a concrete ramp; short hand-carry; parking for 6 vehicles (no overnight parking). Access to Marathon bayside. N24°43.996′ W80°01.086′

B5 Crawl Key North Sound, MM 56.5 B/S, US 1, Crawl Key. Large borrow pit across from Valhalla Beach Resort. Free kayak-only launch off a gravel beach with a drop-off to deep water; long hand-carry; parking for 5 vehicles. Access to Grassy Key bayside. N24°44.951′ W80°58.669′

B5 Curry Hammock State Park, MM 56.1 O/S, US 1 Little Crawl Key. State park with restrooms, picnic pavilions, a beach, and campground. Kayak-only launch from a small sand beach into a canal, left of the picnic area; long hand-carry; parking for 10 vehicles. Entrance fee. Access to Grassy Key oceanside, Deer Key, and abandoned home canals on Fat Deer Key. (305–289–2690, www.floridastateparks.org/curry hammock) N24°44.498′ W80°58.800′

C3 Coco Plum Beach, MM 54.1 O/S, Coco Plum Drive, Marathon, 1.4 miles off US 1. City beach park with no facilities on premises. Free kayak-only launch off a sandy oceanfront beach; short hand-carry; parking for 10 vehicles. Access to Atlantic Ocean. N24°43.783′ W81°00.081′

Chart 22

A6 **Aviation Boulevard Boat Ramp,** MM 51 B/S, Aviation Boulevard, Marathon, 0.4 mile off US 1. City boat ramp at the west end of the Marathon Airport. Free launch off a concrete ramp into a home canal; short hand-carry; parking for 5 vehicles. Access to Marathon bayside. N24°43.496′ W80°03.550′

B3 **7 Mile Marina,** MM 47.5 B/S, US 1, Marathon. Private marina for charter fishing boats. Free kayak-only launch off small rocky beach; ask in marina office about parking. Access to Seven Mile Bridge. (305–395–0546) N24°42.509′ W81°06.860′

B4 **33rd Street County Boat Ramp,** MM 48.7 B/S, 33rd Street, Marathon, 0.2 mile off US 1. City boat ramp with restrooms and picnic table on premises. Free launch off a concrete ramp; short hand-carry; plenty of parking (48-hour limit). Access to Seven Mile Bridge. N24°42.820′ W81°05.743′

C4 **Sombrero Beach,** MM 50 O/S, Sombrero Beach Boulevard, Marathon, 2.0 miles off US 1. A city beach park fronting the Atlantic Ocean. Free kayak-only launch from a small sand beach adjacent to a fishing pier on Sister Creek; long hand-carry; parking for 10 vehicles. Access to Sister Creek and West Sister Rock. N24 °41.524′ W80°05.227′

Chart 23

C2 **Veterans Memorial Park,** MM 39.8 O/S and B/S, US 1, Little Duck Key. County park and adjacent public boat ramp at the west end of Seven Mile Bridge; restrooms and covered picnic tables at the park. Access to Seven Mile Bridge.

Oceanside: Free kayak-only launch off a sandy beach; short hand-carry; parking for 10 vehicles. N24°40.854′ W81°13.845′

Bayside: Free launch off a concrete boat ramp with parking for boats and trailers. N24°40.947′ W81°13.773′

Chart 25 and Chart 26

D1 and C3 **No Name Key Launch #2,** MM 30.5 G/S, Watson Boulevard, No Name Key (just over the bridge). Free launch off a mud shoreline; short hand-carry; limited on-street parking. Access to No Name Key and Little Pine Key. *Caution:* Obey speed limits on Watson Boulevard; it is a popular Key deer viewing area, so drive with care. N24°41.861′ W81°19.082′

Chart 26

C2 **No Name Key Launch #1,** MM 30.5 G/S, Watson Boulevard, No Name Key (just over the bridge). Roadside launch on the immediate east end of No Name Key Bridge. Free kayak-only launch from small holes in the mangroves on the right side of the road. Parking on either side of Watson Boulevard. *Caution:* Knee-deep soft mud bottom at put-in. N24°41.860′ W81°20.429′

C2 **Old Wooden Bridge Marina,** MM 30.5 G/S, Watson Boulevard, Big Pine Key (just before the bridge to No Name Key). Concrete ramp; store, restrooms, and kayak rentals. Fee. (305–872–2241, www.oldwoodenbridge.com) N24°41.843′ W81°20.909′

Chart 27

B6 **Ohio-Missouri Bridge,** MM 39.1 O/S, US 1, Missouri Key. Roadside put-in at the bridge's north end. Free kayak-only launch off a gravel beach; short hand-carry; parking for 5 vehicles. Access to Ohio-Missouri Channel. N24°40.566′ W81°14.336′

B6 **Ohio Key,** MM 38.9 O/S, US 1. Roadside put-in at the south end of Ohio-Missouri Bridge, part of the Key Deer National Wildlife Refuge. Free kayak-only launch off a sandy shoreline; short hand-carry; limited parking. Access to salt ponds. (305–872–0774) N24°40.403′ W081°14.599′

B6 **Sunshine Key Campground,** MM 38.8 G/S, US 1, Ohio Key. Commercial campground and marina with store and gas station on premises. Concrete boat ramp. Fee. (305–872–2217, www.rvonthego.com) N24°40.348′ W81°14.880′

C1 **Spanish Harbor Wayside Park,** MM 33.8 G/S, US 1, West Summerland Key. Roadside parking and fishing area on the bridge's north end. Free launch off a concrete ramp; short hand-carry; parking for 10 vehicles. Access to No Name Key and Spanish Harbor Channel. N24°38.970′ W81°19.053′

C2 and C3 **Bahia Honda Bridge, southside,** MM 34.9

G/S and O/S, Spanish Harbor Keys. Roadside put-ins at the bridge's south end. Access to Bahia Honda Channel and No Name Key.

Bayside: Free kayak-only launch off a rocky shoreline; extra-long hand-carry to hard-bottom put-in; parking for 5 vehicles. N24 °39.332′ W81°18.124′

Oceanside: Free kayak-only launch off a rocky shoreline; long hand-carry down a roadside embankment to the water's edge. N24°39.279′ W81°17.990′

C4 and C5 **Bahia Honda State Park,** MM 36.8 O/S, US 1, Bahia Honda Key. State park with store, restrooms, and oceanfront beach. Kayak and snorkel rentals are available. Entrance fee. (305–872–2353, www.floridastateparks .org/bahiahonda)

Oceanside: Kayak-only launch off a long sand beach below the public beach parking lot; short hand-carry down a flight of stairs. Access to South Lagoon. N24°39.365′ W81°16.642′

Bayside: Launch off a concrete ramp in the park's boat basin. Access to the north shore of Bahia Honda Key. N24°39.396′ W81°16.690′

Chart 29

C3 **Key Deer Boulevard Put-in,** MM 30.5 G/S, Key Deer Boulevard, Big Pine Key, 4.5 miles off US 1. A canal put-in located near the dead end of Key Deer Boulevard. Free kayak-only launch off a rock embankment; extra-long hand-carry; roadside parking for 5 vehicles. Park on the right 0.1 mile before Key Deer Boulevard dead-ends (this spot is marked by two large coral stones). A trail leads 150 steps, jogging right and then left, to an overgrown canal on the left. *Caution:* Canal bottom is soft; test with your paddle before stepping down. Access to Howe, Annette, and Cutoe Keys. Trailhead: N24°43.616′ W81°23.261′. Put-in: N24°43.630′ W81°23.219′

C4 **Koehn Avenue Boat Ramp,** MM 30.5 G/S, Big Pine Key. County boat ramp. Free launch off a gravel ramp; short hand-carry; roadside parking. Access to Little Pine and Water Keys. National Wildlife Refuge. N24°43.148′ W81°22.498′

Chart 30

B1 **Middle Torch Key Causeway,** MM 27.8 G/S, Dorn Road, 2.6 miles off US 1. Roadside launch on the causeway linking Middle and Big Torch Keys. Free kayak-only launch off road shoulder; short hand-carry; parking for 5 vehicles. N24°41.432′ W81°25.010′

B3 **Little Torch Key,** MM 28.1 G/S, off SR 4A, Little Torch Key, 1.6 miles off US 1. County boat ramp. Free launch off a mud and gravel ramp; short hand-carry; parking for 3 vehicles. Access to Pine Channel. N24°41.274′ W81°23.697′

B4 **Eden Pines Boat Ramp,** MM 30.5 G/S, Bittersweet Avenue, Big Pine Key. Neighborhood boat ramp. Free launch off a concrete ramp; short hand-carry; parking for 4 vehicles across the street. Access to Pine Channel through a maze of home canals. *Caution:* Ramp is very slippery. N24°41.711′ W81°22.670′

B6 **No Name Key Launch #1,** MM 30.5 G/S, Watson Boulevard, No Name Key, on the immediate east side of No Name Key Bridge. Free kayak-only launch from small holes in the mangroves on the right side of the road. Parking on either side of Watson Boulevard. *Caution:* Soft mud bottom offshore of kayak launch. N24°41.860′ W81°20.429′

B6 **Old Wooden Bridge Marina,** MM 30.5 G/S, Watson Boulevard, Big Pine Key (just before the bridge to No Name Key). Concrete ramp; store, restrooms, guest cottages, and kayak rentals. Fee. (305–872–2241, www.oldwooden bridge.com) N24°41.843′ W81°20.909′

C1 **Ramrod Key Swim Hole,** MM 26.7 G/S, off Mako Avenue, Ramrod Key, 1.1 miles off US 1. Old canal and borrow pit. Free kayak-only launch from sandy shoreline; short hand-carry; parking for 5 vehicles. Access to Niles Channel. N24°40.212′ W81°24.992′

Chart 31

A2 **Looe Key Reef Resort,** MM 27.4 O/S, US 1, Ramrod Key. Private concrete boat ramp into a canal; short hand-carry; parking for 5 vehicles. A 15-minute paddle through home canals out into Ramrod Channel. Fee: (free for resort guests). (800–942–5397, www.diveflakeys.com) N24°39.695′ W81°24.356′

A3 **Dolphin Marina,** MM 28.5 O/S, Pirates Road, Little

Torch Key. Private boat ramp. Concrete launch into a home canal. Fee (free to cottage guests). Access via home canal to Newfound Harbor, Munson Island, and offshore coral heads. (800–553–0308, www.dolphinmarina.net) N24°39.911′ W81°23.242′

B6 **Long Beach Road #2,** MM 32.8 O/S, Big Pine Key, 0.9 mile off US 1. A roadside launch on Long Beach Road. Free launch from a small hole in the mangroves on the right road shoulder; short hand-carry; parking for 2 vehicles. Access to Coupon Bight. To reach the put-in, drive 0.9 mile on Long Beach Road from US 1. Park on the right or left just before two stone columns that mark the entrance to Long Beach Estates. N24°38.475′ W081°20.388′

B7 **Long Beach Road #1,** MM 32.8 O/S, Big Pine Key, 0.4 mile off US 1. An oceanfront launch in National Key Deer Refuge. Free kayak-only launch off a wild beach; extra-long hand-carry; parking for 2 vehicles. Access to coral heads off Newfound Harbor Keys. To reach the put-in, park at a yellow gate on Long Beach Road, 0.4 mile from US 1, and walk down a service road. In 0.1 mile, bear left and cross an open area, which is prone to flooding at high tide. Pass through a small stretch of wooded coastal fringe and emerge onto the beach. N24°38.487′ W81°19.901′

Chart 33

C5 **Big Torch Key,** MM 27.8 G/S, at the dead end of Dorn Road, Big Torch Key. Small tidal pond with access to open water at the north end of Big Torch. Free launch off a muddy shoreline; long hand-carry; parking for 3 vehicles. Access to Torch Keys Mangroves and Content Keys. *Caution:* Limestone path to put-in is uneven and slippery. From land: N24°43.297′ W81°27.083′. From open water: N24°43.273′ W81°27.129′.

Chart 34 and Chart 35

C2 and B3 **Blimp Road Boat Ramp,** MM 21.4 G/S, Blimp Road, Cudjoe Key, 2 miles off US 1. County boat ramp at the dead end of Blimp Road. Free launch off a concrete ramp; short hand-carry; parking for 5 vehicles. Access to Bud, Tarpon Belly, and Sawyer Keys. N24°41.701′ W81°29.980′

C5 and B6 **Niles Road Launch,** MM 24.9 G/S, via Horace Street, Northside Drive, and Niles Road, Summerland Key, 1.7 miles off US 1. Free kayak-only roadside launch off a gravel beach; short hand-carry; parking for 6 vehicles. Access to Knockemdown Key. A trail departs right from the parking onto Wahoo Island. N24°41.062′ W81°26.664′

E1 and D2 **Cudjoe Gardens Marina,** MM 21 O/S, Drost Drive, Cudjoe Key, 0.4 mile off US 1. Commercial marina with a store and restrooms. Eco-tours available. Concrete launch on a canal. Fee. Access to Bow Channel (305–294–8007), Tarpon Creek, and ocean. (305–745–2352) N24°39.494′ W81°30.340′

E2 and D3 **Spoonbill Sound Hammocks,** MM 22.2 O/S, Pirates Road, Cudjoe Key, 0.2 mile off US 1. A county nature preserve and boat launch at the end of Pirates Road. Free launch off a rocky shoreline; short hand-carry; parking for 5 vehicles. Access to Cudjoe Bay and ocean. N24°39.737′ W81°29.190′

E3 and D4 **Pieces of Eight Road,** MM 22.7 G/S, Cudjoe Key, 0.4 mile off US 1. A roadside launch on an abandoned road. Free kayak-only launch off a mud and rock shore; short hand-carry; parking for 3 vehicles. Access to adjacent salt ponds. N24°49.979′ W81°28.970′

Chart 36

B2 and C2 **Tarpon Creek,** MM 20 O/S, Route 939B. Two free kayak-only launches along an abandoned, dead-end road. To reach put-ins, turn oceanside onto Route 939B at MM 20. In 0.5 mile, the road becomes dirt and rough; overhanging branches may limit clearance. In 2.2 miles, the road dead-ends at Tarpon Creek and the remains of a blown-up bridge that once spanned Tarpon Creek. Launches provide access to Tarpon Creek and Upper Sugarloaf Sound.

Tarpon Creek #1: In 1.2 miles from US 1, launch from a muddy shoreline on the right side of the road; short hand-carry; parking for 4 vehicles. *Caution:* Waters may be impassable at low tide. N24°38.637′ W81°30.920′

Tarpon Creek #2: In 2.2 miles, launch from a mangrove shoreline on the right side of the road; short hand-carry down a roadside embankment; parking for 5 vehicles. N24°37.880′ W81°30.933′

Chart 39

B5 **Park Key,** MM 18.9 O/S, US 1. A roadside pull-off at a power pole and break in the mangroves. Free kayak-only launch off gravel shoreline; short hand-carry; parking for 5 vehicles on highway shoulder. Access to Park Channel and Upper Sugarloaf Sound. *Caution:* Traffic and roadside parking along a busy highway. N24°39.317' W81°32.270'

C3 **Lower Sugarloaf Sound #1,** MM 16.3 G/S, US 1. A roadside pull-off on the south shore of Harris Channel. Free kayak-only launch off a muddy shoreline; short hand-carry; parking for 2 vehicles. Access to Fivemile Creek. *Caution:* Access to launch is by driving down a steep roadside embankment; the parking area may flood at high tide. N24°38.397' W81°34.556'

C3 **Lower Sugarloaf Sound #2,** MM 16 O/S, US 1. A roadside pull-off. Free kayak-only launch off a rocky shoreline; short hand-carry; parking for 3 vehicles on highway shoulder. Access to Lower Sugarloaf Sound and Fivemile Creek. *Caution:* Traffic, roadside parking; requires a big step-down over riprap to reach water. N24°38.224' W81°34.775'

C4 **Sugarloaf Marina,** MM 17 G/S, US 1, Sugarloaf Key. Private marina and resort with a store, restrooms, kayak tours and rentals, and restaurant. Launch off a wooden kayak-only ramp; short hand-carry; parking for 10 vehicles. Fee. Access to Perky Creek. (305–745–3135, www.sugarloaf keymarina.com) N24°38.831' W81°33.919'

Chart 40

A1 **Bluewater Drive,** MM 14.5 O/S, US 1, Saddlebunch Keys. County-owned property near Belle's Trading Post. Free kayak-only launch off a gravel shoreline; short hand-carry; parking for 5 vehicles. Turn oceanside at MM 14.5 onto Bluewater Drive; the parking area is on the right, just prior to where the road crosses a culvert. *Caution:* Knee-deep drop-off into water, and a strong tidal current. N24°37.405' W81°36.079'

Chart 44

A4 **Cop Land Boat Ramp,** MM 10 G/S, Barcelona Drive via 4th Street, Big Coppitt Key. Neighborhood boat ramp. Free launch off a concrete ramp; short hand-carry; parking for 3 vehicles. Access to Great White Heron National Wildlife Refuge. N24°36.105' W81°40.032'

A6 **Shark Key Boat Ramp,** MM 11 O/S, US 1, Shark Key. County boat ramp. Free launch off a concrete ramp; short hand-carry; parking for 3 vehicles. Access to Similar Sound and Great White Heron National Wildlife Refuge. N24 36.077' W81 38.831'

B6 **Geiger Road Public Boat Launch,** MM 10.8 O/S, via Boca Chica Road, at the end of Geiger Road, Geiger Key. County boat ramp that closes at sunset. Free launch off a hard-packed ramp; short hand-carry; parking for 10 vehicles. Access to Saddlehill Key, Similar Sound, and Geiger Creek. N24°34.921' W081°38.804'

C6 **Geiger Key Marina,** MM 10.8 O/S, Geiger Road, via Boca Chica Road, Geiger Key. Private marina, campground, and restaurant. Kayak rentals and tours provided through Conch Republic Kayaks. Free launch off a concrete kayak-only ramp; short hand-carry; check with marina personnel about parking. Marina property is for sale; call for status. Access to Saddlehill Key, Similar Sound, and Geiger Creek. (305–296–3553, www.geigerkeymarina.com) N24°34.905' W081°38.910'

C4 **Boca Chica Beach,** MM 10.8 O/S, at the dead end of Boca Chica Road. Half-mile stretch of free public beach, picnic tables, and trash cans. Free kayak-only launch off a sand beach; long hand-carry; parking for 5 vehicles. Access to Atlantic Ocean and Geiger Key. N24°34.036' W81°40.298'

Chart 44 and Chart 46

C2 and C7 **Boca Chica Bridge, northside,** MM 6.5 G/S, US 1. A roadside pull-off. Free kayak-only launch in a small opening in the mangroves; short hand-carry; parking for 3 vehicles. Access to Boca Chica Channel and Channel Key. N24°34.716' W81°42.747'

Chart 44, Chart 46, and Chart 47

C1, C6, and B7 **Boca Chica Bridge, southside,** MM 6 G/S, US 1. A roadside pull-off popular with picnickers, fishermen, and sunbathers. Free launch off a gravel beach; short

hand-carry; parking for 10 vehicles. Access to Boca Chica Channel and Channel Key. N24°34.633' W81°43.298'

Chart 46 and Chart 47

C6 and B6 **Stock Island Boat Ramp,** MM 5.3 O/S, US 1. County boat ramp. Free launch off a concrete ramp; short hand-carry; parking for 3 vehicles. Access to bay and ocean. N24°34.499' W81°43.935'

Chart 46 and Chart 47

C5 and B6 **Lazy Dog Island Outfitters,** MM 4.2 O/S, US 1, Stock Island. Kayak outfitter, with restaurant and water-sports complex on premises. Free launch off a floating dock (check in at outfitter before launching); long hand-carry; parking for 5 vehicles. Access to Riviera Canal and Key West salt ponds. (866–293–9550, www.lazydog adventure.com) N24°34.262' W81°44.853'

Chart 47

C2 **Simonton Street Beach and Boat Ramp,** dead end of Simonton Street in Old Town Key West. A small city beach and public boat ramp, with restrooms on premises. Free launch off a sand beach; short hand-carry; metered parking. Access to Gulf of Mexico and sunset paddling. N24°33.721' W81°48.338'

C3 **Key West City Marina,** MM 1.7 G/S, 1801 N. Roosevelt Boulevard (US 1), Key West. Public marina in Garrison Bight with parking and restrooms. Paved ramp. Fee. Access to Key West and the Gulf. *Caution:* Busy boat basin. (305–292–8167) N24°33.592' W81°47.075'

C4 **11th Street Boat Ramp,** 11th Street, Key West. Neighborhood boat ramp. Free launch off a concrete ramp; short hand-carry; on-street parking for 3 vehicles. Access to Riviera Canal, Key West salt ponds, and mangrove tunnels. N24°33.554' W81°46.103'

C4 and C5 **Smathers Beach,** Route A1A, Key West. A public beach fronting the Atlantic Ocean.

  East Beach Launch: Free launch off a sand beach at the east end of Smathers Beach; metered parking up to 12 hours. N24 33.027' W81 46.518'

  West Beach Launch: Free launch off a sand beach at the south end of Smathers Beach; long hand-carry; metered parking up to 12 hours. Kayak and parasailing rentals, and restrooms are near this launch. N24°33.138' W81°45.967'

C5 **Little Hamaca City Park,** Government Road, Key West. A city park. Free launch on a muddy creek shoreline; long hand-carry down a wooded path; parking for 5 vehicles. Access to Key West salt ponds. N24°33.621' W81°45.827'

D2 **Fort Zachary Taylor Historic State Park,** dead end of Southard Street, on Truman Annex, Key West. Free launch off a sandy beach; long hand-carry; parking for 10 vehicles. Access to Atlantic Ocean. Entrance fee. (305–292–6713, www.floridastateparks.org/forttaylor) N24°32.720' W81°48.540'

D3 **Higgs Beach,** Atlantic Boulevard and Reynolds Street, Key West. A city park and beach. Free launch off a sand beach; long hand-carry; parking for 5 vehicles. Access to Atlantic Ocean. *Caution:* Beach is encircled with old pier pilings. N24°32.823' W81°47.261'

D3 **Dog Beach,** dead end of Vernon Street, Key West. Public water access. Free launch off a sandy beach; long hand-carry; limited on-street parking. Access to Atlantic Ocean. *Caution:* Dog poop! N24°32.829' W81°47.571'

Chart 50

C5 **Dry Tortugas National Park,** Garden Key. Free launch off Dinghy Beach on the southeast side of island. *Caution:* Boats are not allowed in the nearby swimming/snorkeling area. (305–242–7700, www.nps.gov/drto) N24°37.618' W82°52.364'

Chart 52

B5 **Flamingo Boat Ramp,** Everglades National Park. Marina, store, canoe/kayak rentals, and hot showers. Kayak launch off a concrete ramp. Entrance fee and launch fee. (park information: 305–242–7700, www.nps.gov/ever; marina: 239–695–3101) N25°08.541' W80°55.394'

Outfitters, Guides, and Kayak Rentals

Chart 7

D2 **Florida Bay Outfitters,** MM 104 B/S, US 1, Key Largo. Tours, rentals, instruction, and extensive selection of gear and boats. Sandy beach launch on Blackwater Sound. (305–451–3018, www.kayakfloridakeys.com) N25°08.700' W80°23.842'

Chart 9

B2 **Doubletree Resort Key Largo,** MM 102 B/S, US 1, Key Largo. Tours, rentals, and instruction; adaptive paddling for those with disabilities. Ask for "Kayak Bob." (305–451–1400, www.doubletreekeylargo.com) N25°07.340' W80°25.090'

B3 **John Pennekamp Coral Reef State Park Concession,** MM 102.5 O/S, US 1, Key Largo. Kayak and snorkel rentals. (305–451–3149, www.pennekamppark.com) N25°07.459' W80°24.433'

Chart 11

B1 **Caribbean Watersports,** MM 97 B/S, US 1, at the Key Largo Grande Resort, Key Largo. Rentals and ecotours. (305–852–4707, ext. 537; www.caribbeanwater sports.com) N25°04.071' W80°28.295'

Chart 16

A5 **Founders Park,** MM 86.5 B/S, US 1, Islamorada. Rentals only, at swimming beach. (305–852–5633) N24°57.725' W80°34.215'

C2 **Backcountry Cowboy Outfitters,** 82.2 B/S, US 1, Islamorada. Tours, rentals, and full outfitting store. (305–517–4177, www.backcountrycowboy.com) N24°55.494' W80°37.662'

Chart 17 and Chart 18

D2 and B5 **Florida Keys Kayak,** MM 77.5 B/S, US 1, at Robbie's Marina, Islamorada. Rentals, ecotours to Indian and Lignumvitae Keys, and small shop. (305–664–4878, www.floridakeyskayakandski.com) N24°52.992' W80°41.455'

Chart 19

C4 **Long Key State Park,** MM 67.5 O/S, US 1, Layton. Canoe and Kayak rentals, at dock just past entrance station. Marked paddling trail in sheltered lagoons. (305–664–4815) N24°48.888' W80°49.385'

Chart 21

B4 and B5 **Curry Hammock State Park,** MM 56.1 O/S US 1, Little Crawl Key. Kayak rentals and launch. (305–289–2690) N24°44.496' W80°58.802'

Chart 22

A5 **Marathon Kayak,** 6363 Overseas Highway O/S, Marathon. Rentals and ecotours. Custom tours of Curry Hammock and Bahia Honda State Parks. Outfitted boats for fishing. Rentals to Sister Creek, Whiskey Creek, Sombrero Beach, and the mangroves inside Boot Key. (305–743–0561, www.marathonkayak.com) N24°43.073' W81°04.125'

Chart 26 and Chart 30

C2 and B6 **Big Pine Kayak Adventures,** MM 30.5 G/S, at Old Wooden Bridge Marina, Watson Boulevard, Big Pine Key. Ecotours, rentals, and backcountry trips with Capt. Bill Keogh. 305–872–7474, www.keyskayaktours.com) N24°41.843' W81°20.909'

Chart 27

C4 **Bahia Honda State Park,** MM 36.8 O/S, US 1, at Loggerhead Beach on Bahia Honda Key. Rentals only. (305–872–3210, www.bahiahondapark.com) N24°39.365' W81°16.642'

Chart 30

Reflections Nature Tours, Big Pine Key. Rentals, ecotours and backcountry transportation. No retail location. (305–872–4668, www.floridakeyskayaktours.com

Chart 39

C4 **Sugarloaf Marina,** MM 17 G/S, US 1, Sugarloaf Key. 2 kayak tour and rental companies operate from here. N24°38.831' W81°33.919'

Mosquito Coast, 305–294–7178, www.mosquitocoast.net

Reelax Charters, 305–744–0263 or 304–1392. www.keyskayaking.com

Chart 44

C6 **Conch Republic Kayak Company,** 10.8 O/S, at Geiger Key Marina, Geiger Road. Rentals, lessons, ecotours, and overnight trips to private island. Owner Jason Drevenak will hook you up and, if you're nice, throw in a white-water play boat demonstration at no extra charge. (305–294–7550, www.kayakkeywest.com) N24°34.905′ W81°38.910′

Chart 46 and Chart 47

C5 and B6 **Lazy Dog Island Outfitters & Outdoor Adventure Co.,** MM 4.2 O/S, US 1, Stock Island. Tours, sales, rentals, and large outfitting store. (866–293–9550, www.lazydogadventure.com) N24°34.262′ W81°44.853′

Chart 47

Blue Planet Kayak Eco-Tours and Rentals, Key West. Environmental scientist-led, 2–3 hour day, sunset, and full-moon tours. Complimentary transportation. No retail location. (305–294–8087, www.blue-planet-kayak.com)

Key West Kayak Fishing. Fishing kayak, gear, and bait provided, as well as transportation by skiff into the Backcountry with Capt. Dave. No retail location. (305–304–0337, www.keyskayakfishing.com)

C4 **Sunset Watersports,** MM 0 O/S, Route A1A, Smathers Beach, Key West. Rentals only. (305–296–2554. www.sunsetwatersports.net) N24°33.027′ W81°46.518′

D2 **Fort Zachary Taylor Historic State Park,** at the end of Southard Street on Truman Annex, Key West. Kayak and snorkel rentals. (305–295–0037, www.fortzacharytaylor.com) N24°32.720′ W81°48.540′

Camping

We classify campgrounds in three categories:

Primitive. Campsites typically have no freshwater or restrooms and are free (exceptions noted in descriptions). We describe how to access these campsites, the physical parameters of the tent area, how many tents will fit, and GPS coordinates.

Commercial. Privately owned campgrounds that typically offer bathhouses and electric hookups (exceptions noted). We describe services offered, identify tent campsites with water access, and give GPS coordinates for campsites with water access and/or the campsite boat ramps.

State parks/national parks. These campgrounds are public and typically will offer bathrooms and electric hookups. Campsites include drive-in, walk-in, and primitive paddle-in. Entrance and camping fees apply. Reservations are made through www.reserveamerica.com, (800) 326–3521. During the high season, January through March, state park campsites in the Keys are often booked eleven months in advance.

Primitive Camping Ethics

The Florida Keys' fragile ecosystem is challenged each year by millions of visitors, so protecting natural areas is a vital concern. Be sure to follow Zero Impact principles:

1. Plan ahead and prepare.
2. Travel and camp on durable surfaces.
3. Dispose of waste properly (pack it in, pack it out).
4. Leave what you find.
5. Minimize campfire impacts (bring a stove; build fires only in fire rings or on beaches, below high tide line).
6. Respect wildlife.
7. Be considerate of other visitors.

Human Waste

In the absence of a toilet, the best course is to pack out human waste. Otherwise, bring a small trowel to dig a hole 6 inches deep, at least 200 feet from water, trails, and camp. Urinate directly in the water. Wash dishes using little, if any, soap, and scatter strained dishwater. Pack out leftover food particles.

The Campsites

Chart 4

B2 **Joe's Beach.** Access from South Dade Marina on US 1 (the "Stretch") or Card Sound Road. A primitive campsite located 1.7 miles from the marina, at the east point of Jim Smith Creek. Room for 2 tents in the mangroves. N25 15.733′ W80 25.185′

B4 **Short Key.** Access from South Dade Marina on US 1 (the "Stretch") or Card Sound Road. A primitive campsite located 3 miles from the marina and 0.2 mile south of Short Key Cut. Room for 10 or more tents under shady pines. **Caution:** Do not leave camp unattended. Theft has been reported at this campsite. N25 15.451′ W80 23.979′

Chart 7

B4 **Dagny Johnson Key Largo Hammock Botanical State Park,** Card Sound Road, Key Largo. Paddler-only campsites are planned as part of the Florida Keys Overseas Paddling Trail. Call John Pennekamp Coral Reef State Park for status and a permit (305–451–1202).

Chart 8

C2 **North Nest Key.** Accessed via the launch at Florida Bay Outfitters, MM 104 B/S, US 1, Key Largo (305–451–3018). A primitive campsite in Everglades National Park located approximately 8 miles from Key Largo. Land on a beach on the northwest side of the island, and pitch tents on dry land in the mangroves. Outhouse and dock. A backcountry permit must be purchased 24 hours in advance through Everglades National Park (239–695–2945). N25 09.053′ W80 30.732′

Chart 9

A3 **King's Kamp,** MM 103.6 B/S, US 1, Key Largo. A commercial campground in a residential RV park, with a few tent sites overlooking Blackwater Sound. Access to Largo Sound and the Atlantic Ocean via nearby Adams Cut. (305–451–0010) N25°08.382′ W°80 24.209′

B3 **John Pennekamp State Park,** MM 102.5 O/S, US 1, Key Largo. A state park campground with canoe/kayak trails, snorkeling and glass-bottom boat trips out to the reef, dive shop, aquarium, nature trails, beaches, deli, and souvenir shop. The picnic area launch is 0.1 mile from campground. (Information: 305–451–1202, www.floridastateparks.org/pennekamp; reservations: 800–326–3521, www.reserveamerica.com. N25°07.365′ W80°24.365′

C2 **Calusa Campground,** MM 101.4 B/S, 325 Calusa Street, Key Largo. A commercial mobile home/RV condo association on Buttonwood Sound. 20 shady tent campsites are a 0.2-mile walk from the boat ramp, which is for guest use only. Tent sites are first-come basis; no reservations. There is no beach, and no campsites have direct water access. Pool, tennis, recreation hall, laundry, and marina on premises. (305–451–0232 or 866–647–0232, www.calusacampground.com) Boat ramp: N25°06.577′ W°80 25 879′. Tent area: N25°06.648′ W°80 25.821′.

C3 **Key Largo Kampground,** MM 101.5 O/S, US 1, Key Largo. A commercial RV park with water access to Pennekamp State Park and South Sound Creek. Tent camping on gravel campsites. The South Beach landing is a 0.2-mile walk from the tent campsites; the campground boat ramp (for guest use only) is adjacent to tent site T31. (305–451–1431 or 800–526–7688, www.keylargokampground.com) South Beach: N25°06.713′ W80°24.885′. Boat ramp: N25°06.800′ W80°24.972′.

Chart 16

B4 **Coconut Cove Resort,** MM 85 O/S, US 1, Islamorada. A small commercial resort on the Atlantic Ocean with tent campsites. Beach, pool and marina; free kayak use for guests. (305–664–0123, www.coconutcove.net) N24°56.810′ W 80 35.949′

Chart 19

C4 and C6 **Long Key State Park,** MM 67.5 O/S, US 1, Layton. A state park campground with drive-in and walk-in full-service campgrounds, canoe and kayak rentals, and a marked water trail. Primitive camping with 6 covered platforms, difficult to access at low tide. (information: 305–664–4815; reservations: 800–326–3521, www.reserveamerica.com) Main campground: N24°48.543′ W80°49.891′. Primitive campsite: N24°48.697′ W80°47.889′.

Chart 20

B2 **Jolly Roger Travel Park,** MM 59.2 B/S, US 1, Grassy Key. A commercial campground with access to Toms Harbor Channel. Laundry and swimming area on premises. The tent campsites feature tiki huts for shade and are located on a small peninsula that sticks out into Florida Bay. This shoreline is surrounded by high riprap, so use the campground boat ramp, which is for guests only. (305–289–0404) N24 °46.290′ W80°56.547′.

C3 **Toms Harbor Keys.** Access via Curry Hammock State Park (MM 56.1 O/S, US 1) or Toms Harbor Keys Access launch (MM 60.2 O/S, US 1). A primitive campsite on a private, uninhabited island offshore of Grassy Key. Tent camping on a beach of the southernmost key. The owners permit use by paddlers, as long as the privilege is not abused. **Caution:** Offshore mud flats may limit access at low tide. N24°46.016′ W80°55.561′.

Chart 21

B4 and B5 **Curry Hammock State Park,** MM 56.1 O/S, US 1, Little Crawl Key. A State Park campground open November1 through May 31, with water access to Deer Key and the Atlantic Ocean. Picnic pavilions, playground, a beach, kayak rentals, and hiking trails on premises. Several campsites are only a short hand-carry from a rocky beach. Otherwise, use the kayak-only launch near the picnic pavilion. A primitive site for paddlers only is being developed. (Information: 305–289–2690; reservations: 800–326–3521, www.reserveamerica.com) Campground landing: N24°44.400′ W80°58.962′ Kayak landing: N24°44.496′ W80°58.802′.

Chart 22

B2 **Knights Key Park Campground & Marina,** MM 47 O/S, US 1, Marathon. A commercial campground with water access to the Seven Mile Bridge. Laundry and marina store on premises. Campsites 9–15, 20–21, 31–33, and 36–54 have water access suitable for landing or launching a kayak. (305–743–4343, www.keysdirectory.com/knightskeyscampground) Waterfront campsites: N24 42.317′ W81 07.100′. Boat ramp: N24°42.319′ W81°07.263′. **Note:** This property slated for development. Call ahead for status.

Chart 23

B3 **Money Key.** Access via 33rd Street Boat Ramp (MM 48.7 B/S, 33rd Street, Marathon) or Veterans Park (MM 39.8 O/S, US 1, Little Duck Key). A primitive campsite on an island offshore of the Seven Mile Bridge. Tent camping in the mangroves on the north or west side of the island. This privately owned island has an established history of public use. Because it is closer to the bridge than Molasses Key, the campsite is subject to louder traffic noise. N24°41.011′ W81°12.905′

C4 **Molasses Keys.** Access via 33rd Street Boat Ramp (MM 48.7 B/S, 33rd Street, Marathon) or Veterans Park launch (MM 39.8 O/S, US 1, Duck Key). A primitive campsite on a private island offshore of the Seven Mile Bridge. Tent camping on the north side of the southernmost Molasses Key. By agreement with the Florida Keys Overseas Paddling Trail, the owners permit use by paddlers, as long as the privilege is not abused. N24°41.013′ W81°11.452′

Chart 27

B6 **Sunshine Key Campground,** MM 38.8 B/S, US 1, Ohio Key. A commercial campground with access to the Ohio-Missouri Channel and Seven Mile Bridge. Campsites 400A–414 are near a sand beach launch suitable for landing or launching a kayak. Marina, store, gas station, laundry, pool, clubhouse, swimming beach, and pier on premises. Free Internet connection is available in the office (305–872–2217, www.rvonthego.com) Boat ramp: N24°40.348′ W81°14.880′. Water-access campsites: N24°40.422′ W81°14.640′.

C4 and C5 **Bahia Honda State Park,** MM 36.8 O/S, US 1, Bahia Honda Key. A state park campground with drive-in and paddle-in campsites. Access to the Atlantic Ocean and Florida Bay. Cabins, a gift shop, marina, snorkel and kayak rentals, dive and snorkel trips, a snack shop, interpretive center, nature trails, and a long, sandy beach. The old trestle bridge is a relic of the Overseas Railroad and makes a great spot for watching the sunset. A primitive paddle-in campsite is planned. (information: 305–872–2353; reservations: 800–326–3521, www.reserveamerica.com) Boat ramp/Buttonwood Campground: N24°39.396′ W81°16.690′. Sandspur Campground: N24°39.645′ W81°15.858′. Bay Side Campground: N24°39.773′ W81°16.475′.

Chart 27 and Chart 31

D1 and B7 **Big Pine Key Fishing Lodge,** MM 32.8 O/S, US 1. A commercial campground, boat ramp, motel, and grocery store. Laundry, recycling, and a small swimming beach on premises. Tent campsites 10–12 and 40–46 have water access suitable for landing or launching a kayak. A nature trail leaves from the campground into the National Key Deer Refuge. Ramp and beach launching are for guests only. (305–872–2351) Water access campsites N24°38.790′ W81°19.712′. Concrete boat ramp: N24°38.890′ W81°19.898′.

Chart 35

C7 **Howell Key.** Access via Niles Road launch (MM 24.9 G/S, at the end of Niles Road, Summerland Key) or Ramrod Key Swim Hole launch (MM 26.7 G/S, Bayshore Drive, Ramrod Key). A primitive campground with 10 campsites on a private 9-acre island in Niles Channel. There is an outhouse on the premises, but there is no freshwater. Fee; reservations required. Island for sale; call for status. (305–797–4789; www.keyscamping.com) N24°40.833′ W81°25.877′

D1 **Sugarloaf Key West KOA,** MM 20 O/S, SR 939B. A commercial campground with water access to Bow Channel, Cudjoe Bay, and Tarpon Creek. Large, shady tent areas, pool, hot tub, pub, laundry, nature trails, kayak rentals, and marina. Tent campsites A–E and J–L have water access suitable for landing and launching a kayak. Kayaks are not allowed on the beach. Mangrove Mama's restaurant is across US 1 from the campground entrance. (305–745–3549, www.sugarloafkeykoa.com) N24°39.654′ W81°31.110′

Chart 36

C2 **Tarpon Creek Bridge.** Water access via Tarpon Creek; land access via Tarpon Creek launch (MM 20, SR 939B, Sugarloaf Key). A primitive campsite at the remains of a bridge that once spanned Tarpon Creek. Tent camping on the abandoned bridge abutment. Bridge embankment: N24°37.846′ W81°30.936′ Level landing area near the bridge: N24°37.880′ W81°30.933′

Chart 37

D6 **Tarpon Belly.** Access via Blimp Road Boat Ramp (MM 21.4 G/S, Blimp Road). A primitive campsite on an island 2.7 miles northwest of the Blimp Road Boat Ramp. Tent camping on exposed coral rock next to an old canal. Room for 5 tents. This island has an established history of public use. N24 43.671′ W81 31.223′

Chart 39

B6 **Lazy Lakes Campground,** MM 19.8 O/S, Johnson Road, Sugarloaf Key. A commercial campground on Sugarloaf Key. This quiet, shady campground does not have an outlet to open water, but there is a 6-acre lake that is nice for paddling around. May be developed; call for status. (305–745–1079). N24°39.312′ W81°31.342′

Chart 44

C6 **Geiger Key Marina,** MM 10.8 O/S, Geiger Road. A commercial campground, primarily for RVs, but they will allow tents. Conch Republic Kayak Company operates from this marina. There are showers, a laundry, and an outdoor restaurant on the premises. Property is for sale; call for status. (305–296–3553, www.geigerkeymarina.com) N°24 34.905′ W81°38.910′

Chart 46 and Chart 47

C6 and B7 **Boyd's Key West Campground,** MM 5 O/S, Maloney Avenue, Stock Island. A commercial campground with water access to Boca Chica Channel. Pool, laundry, and Internet access on premises. Campsites 145–147 have water access suitable for landing and launching a kayak. (305–294–1465, www.boydscampground.com) Boat ramp: N24°34.285′ W81°43.988′. Gravel shoreline kayak launch: N24°34.323′ W81°43.991′. Waterfront campsites: N24°34.246′ W81°43.937′.

Chart 50

C5 **Garden Key Campground,** Dry Tortugas National Park, 70 miles west of Key West. A national park campground on Garden Key. Access via high-speed ferry. The 10 primitive campsites are located on a sandy spit in the shadow of massive Fort Jefferson. Groups of 10 or more must make advance reservations. Composting toilets on premises, but their use is restricted (all island visitors use toilets aboard the high speed ferries while they are docked at Dry Tortugas). There is no freshwater on the island, and campers must carry out their trash. Historical tours of the fort, snorkeling, and bird-watching are available. (305–242–7700, www.nps.gov/drto) N24°37.618′ W82°52.364′

Chart 51 and Chart 52

All primitive camping in **Everglades National Park** requires a backcountry permit (fee). This must be obtained in person, within 24 hours of your reservation, at Flamingo Visitor Center. (Visitors starting their trip in the Keys can obtain a permit by phone.) The visitor center is staffed daily, December through April. From May through November, when camping is minimal due to insects, obtain a permit from the self-service kiosk at Flamingo. All backcountry campsites are primitive and have no freshwater. There are limits on numbers of groups and campers, as well as consecutive nights camping, for each campsite. (239–695–2945, www.nps.gov/ever/visit/campsite.htm)

B2 and A10 **Alligator Creek.** A primitive campsite located 10.5 miles east of Flamingo via Tin Can Pass. Tent camping on the marl north bank of Alligator Creek upstream from where it empties into Garfield Bight. ***Caution:*** Alligators! This site can be wet and buggy, and is difficult to reach at low tide. No fires allowed. Number of people allowed: 8. Number of groups allowed: 3. N25°10.553′ W80°47.492′

Chart 51

C10 **North Nest Key.** Access via the launch at Florida Bay Outfitters (MM 104 B/S, US 1, Key Largo). A primitive campsite located approximately 8 miles from Key Largo. Tent camping on a marl shoreline. Land on a beach on the northwest side of the island, and pitch tents on dry land in the mangroves. Outhouse at dock. No fires allowed. Number of people allowed: 25. Number of groups allowed: 7. N25°09.053′ W80°30.732′

Chart 52

B5 **Flamingo Campground.** A national park campground for tenters and RVs on Florida Bay's northwest shoreline. Restrooms and cold showers on premises; marina store and visitor center nearby. (information: 305–242–7700; reservations: 800–365–CAMP) N25°08.209′ W80°56.280′

C1 **East Cape Sable.** A primitive campsite, approximately 10 miles west of Flamingo, along beach on Cape Sable. Find a nice piece of high land and set up a tent. There was a log fort here during the Seminole wars. Breezes off Florida Bay help keep insects away. Fires allowed only with dead and downed wood, below the high-tide line. Number of people allowed: 60. Number of groups allowed: 15. N25°07.105′ W81°04.797′

C2 **Clubhouse Beach.** A primitive campsite 7 miles west of Flamingo. So named for a clubhouse on stilts built by a land developer in the 1920s to entertain potential buyers. Tent camping on a narrow stretch of marl shoreline interspersed with mangroves. *Beach* is a misnomer. No fires allowed. Number of people allowed: 24. Number of groups allowed: 4. N25°07.721′ W81°02.383′

G9 **Little Rabbit Key.** Access from Florida Keys via Indian Key Fill launch (MM 78.5 B/S, US 1). A primitive campsite on Little Rabbit Key, approximately 12 miles north of Indian Key Fill. Ringed by mangroves, with no beach, camping is in the interior. Land at the dock on the northwest side. Fires allowed only in fire ring. Number of people allowed: 12. Number of groups allowed: 4. N24°58.914′ W80°49.552′

Paddle-Friendly Lodging

Pull up for the night at one of these paddle-friendly lodgings, ranging from colorful mom-and-pop motels to luxurious resorts. We've checked them all for appropriate places to launch and willingness to accommodate guests who bring their own boats. Many provide free kayak use as well.

Unless otherwise noted, launch access is for overnight guests only. If several lodgings are close together, only one symbol is on the chart.

Chart 7

D2 **Azul del Mar,** MM 104.3 B/S, US 1, Key Largo. A small, stylish boutique hotel on Blackwater Sound with modern Jacuzzi suites and a sand beach. Free kayak use for guests. Adults only. (888–253–AZUL, www.azulkeylargo.com) N25°08.885′ W80°23.724′

Chart 7 and Chart 9

D2 and A4 **Marriott Key Largo Bay Resort,** MM 103.8 B/S, US 1, Key Largo. This large, premium hotel has balcony rooms and two-bedroom suites, a sandy beach on Blackwater Sound, pool, restaurant, tiki bar, kayak rentals, tennis, and miniature golf. Guests with kayaks may land and launch off the sandy area near Breezer's tiki bar. (305–453–0000, www.marriottkeylargo.com) N25°08.679′ W80°23.873′

Chart 9

B2 **Doubletree Resort Key Largo,** MM 102 B/S, US 1, Key Largo. As part of an extensive makeover, this former Howard Johnson has been rebranded as a Doubletree hotel. The large sand beach provides easy access to Tarpon Basin and mangrove tunnels off Dusenbury Creek. Kayak rentals and tours, tiki bar, pool, and restaurant. (305–451–1400, www.doubletreekeylargo.com) N25°07.340′ W80°25.090′

B2 **Largo Lodge,** MM 101.7 B/S, US 1, Key Largo. Efficiencies in quiet, wooded setting on Florida Bay. Adults only. Beach with seawall. (800–INTHESUN, www.largo lodge.com) Lodge: N25°07.098′ W80°25.260′. Concrete ramp: N25°07.098′ W80°25.260′.

B4 **Tarpon Flats Inn & Marina,** MM 103 O/S, 29 Shoreland Drive, Key Largo. A fishing camp on Largo Sound, restored in the British colonial style. Features waterfront rooms, some with kitchens. Caters to fishermen, but kayaks are available for guest use. Use the floating dock for launching. (866–546–0000, www.tarponflats.com) N25°07.974′ W80°23.964′

Chart 11

A3 **Bay Cove Motel,** MM 99.5 B/S, US 1, Key Largo. Small motel with efficiencies. Kayaks to loan. Gravel launch. (305–451–1686, www.baycovemotel.com) N25°05.583′ W80°26.667′

A3 **Sunset Cove Beach Resort,** MM 99.3 B/S, US 1, Key Largo. Cute cottages and efficiencies. Sand beach. Kayaks for guest use. (305–451–0705, www.sunsetcovebeach resort.com) N25°05.606′ W80°26.655′

A3 **The Pelican,** MM 99.3 B/S, US 1 Key Largo. Cottage efficiencies on Florida Bay. Free use of kayaks. Concrete ramp. (305–451–3576, www.thepelican-keylargo.com) N25°05.561′ W80°26.691′

B1 **Key Largo Grande Resort,** MM 97 B/S, US 1, Key Largo. Balcony rooms and suites overlooking Florida Bay. Pool, tiki bar with beach grill, nature trails through hardwood hammock, and kayak rentals. (305–852–5553, www.keylargogrande.com) N25°04.071′ W80°28.295′

B2 **Rock Reef Resort,** MM 98 B/S, US 1, Key Largo. Cottages in a shady, tropical setting on Florida Bay. Units 9 and 10 are on a small sandy beach. (305–852–2401, www.rock reefresort.com) N25°04.702′ W80°27.658′

B2 **Kona Kai Resort and Gallery,** MM 97.8 B/S, US 1, Key Largo. Luxury suites in a lush, tropical setting on Florida Bay. Pool, tennis courts, and sandy beach on premises. Adults only. (305–852–7200, www.konakairesort.com) N25°04.674′ W80°27.696′

B2 **Coconut Bay Resort,** MM 97.7 B/S, US 1, Key Largo. Modest motel with pool. 800–385–0986, www.theflorida keys.com/coconutbay) N25°04.645′ W80°27.728′

B2 **Bay Harbor Lodge,** MM 97.5 B/S, US 1, Key Largo. Waterfront cottages and efficiencies, pool, dock, beach, and free kayak use. (305–852–5695 or 800–385–0986, www.thefloridakeys.com/bayharborlodge) N25°04.645′ W80°27.728′

Chart 12

C6 **Popp's Motel,** MM 95.5 B/S, US 1, Key Largo. Modest efficiencies in a quiet "Keysie" atmosphere on Florida Bay, with hammocks and tiki huts. Beach with seawall and concrete boat ramp. (305–852–5201, www.popps.com) N25°03.181' W80°29.090'

Chart 13

A3 **Dove Creek Lodge & Marina,** MM 94.5 O/S, 139 Seaside Avenue, Tavernier. Elegant lodge catering to fishermen and paddlers. The floating dock with kayak cradle provides access to the ocean and Dove Creek. There are regular rooms, suites, and family apartments. Kayaks and ecotours available. Adjacent is the popular Snapper's Waterfront Saloon & Restaurant, which also has 4 guest rooms (305–852–5956). (305–852–6200, www.dovecreek lodge.com) N25°02.386' W80°29.535'

C2 **Island Bay Resort,** MM 92.5 B/S, US 1, Tavernier. Efficiencies and cottages, steps from sheltered beach on Florida Bay. (800–654–KEYS, www.islandbayresort.com) N25 01.004' W80 30.824'

Chart 13, Chart 14, and Chart 15

C1, C5, and A6 **Coconut Palm Inn,** MM 92 B/S, Jo Jean Way, Tavernier. Elegant inn on Tavernier's Community Harbor offers one- and two-bedroom suites, some with kitchens, screened porches, and gardens. There is a 450-foot sandy beach, 2 docks, and a pool. A two-night minimum is usually required. (800–765–5397, www.coconut palminn.com) N25°00.751' W80°31.062'

Chart 16

A4 **Smuggler's Cove Resort,** MM 85.5 B/S, US 1, Islamorada. Restaurant, motel, and marina on Snake Creek. (800–864–4363, www.smugglerscoveresortmarina.com) Concrete ramp: N25°57.158' W80°35.343'

A5 **Ragged Edge Resort & Marina,** MM 86.5 O/S, 1243 Treasure Harbor Road, Islamorada. This family resort overlooking the Atlantic Ocean offers suites, efficiencies, a laundry, heated pool, dock, and free use of bikes. (800–436–2023, www.ragged-edge.com) N24°57.231' W80°34.300'

B3 **Pelican Cove Resort,** MM 84.5 O/S, US 1, Islamorada. Three-story hotel with ocean-view rooms and suites, some with kitchens. (800–445–4690, www.pcove.com) Boat ramp: N24°56.576' W80°36.252'

B3 **Holiday Isle Resort,** MM 84.3 O/S, US 1, Islamorada. Famous party-time resort with motel efficiencies, restaurants, souvenir and dive shops, a beach, tiki bar, pool, and kayak rentals. Land at sandy kayak launch at north end of beach near Rumrunner's tiki bar. *Note:* This location has been sold for possible redevelopment; call ahead for status. (800–327–7070, www.holidayisle.com) Sandy launch: N24°56.537' W80°36.256'

B3 **Chesapeake Resort,** MM 83.4 O/S, US 1, Islamorada. Oceanfront rooms are just steps from a sandy beach launch. Pool, kayak rentals, boat ramp, and guest laundry. Next door is the Whale Harbor restaurant. (800–338–3395, www.chesapeake-resort.com) N24°56.122' W80°36.808'

B4 **Drop Anchor Resort & Marina,** MM 85 O/S, US 1, Islamorada. Colorful one- and two-bedroom suites, some right on the ocean beach. (888–664–4863, www.drop anchorresort.com) Concrete ramp: N24°56.890' W80°35.770'

B4 **Coconut Cove Resort,** MM 84.8 O/S, US 1, Islamorada. Small oceanfront resort has motel rooms and tent sites. Beach, pool, marina, and free kayak use. (305–664–0123, www.coconutcove.net) N24°56.810' W80°35.944'

Chart 16 and Chart 17

C2 and A6 **Islander Resort,** MM 82.1 O/S, US 1, Islamorada. You can't miss its landmark sign in the heart of Islamorada. Renovated 1950s villas. Large, sandy beach on the ocean ringed with riprap. Sandy opening in the riprap at fishing pier. Across US 1 is Lorelei's Restaurant. (800–753–6002. www.islanderfloridakeys.com) N24°55.108' W80°37.774'

Chart 17

B4 **La Siesta Resort,** MM 80.4 O/S, US 1, Islamorada. Cute, colorful oceanfront cottages with one, two, or three bedrooms. Beautiful ocean beach and pool. Units 101–106 are closest to beach. (800–222–1693, www.lasiesta resort.com) Sandy ramp: N24°54.163' W80°39.052'. *Note:* Slated for condo conversion. Call ahead for status.

B4 **Pines and Palms Resort,** MM 80.4 O/S, US 1, Islamorada. Caribbean-style cottages on ocean, all with kitchens. Pool, laundry, and kayak rentals. Units 1–3, 6–7

and 9–10 are closest to the beach, which has a seawall. (800–624–0964, www.pinesandpalms.com) Concrete ramp: N24°54.200' W80°38.990'

B4 **Sands of Islamorada,** MM 80.1 O/S, US 1, Islamorada. Parrots greet guests at this modest oceanfront motel with pool, hot tub, and small beach with seawall. Units 18–19 are closest to the water. (888–741–4518, www.sandsof islamorada.com) Concrete ramp: N24°54.037' W80°39.221'. *Note:* Pending condo conversion; call ahead.

B4 **Breezy Palms,** MM 80.1 O/S, US 1, Islamorada. Oceanfront rooms, efficiencies and one- or two-bedroom cottages. Pool and swimming beach (no kayaks allowed on beach). Units 110–113 and 210–213 (upper level with balconies) are closest to the beach. (305–664–2361 www.breezypalms.com) Concrete ramp: N24°54.023' W80°39.231'

B5 **Kon Tiki Resort,** MM 81.2 B/S, US 1, Islamorada. Rooms with kitchens. Resort has a beach and dock on Little Basin. (305–664–4702, www.kontiki-resort.com) N24°54.751' W80°38.658'

B6 **Cheeca Lodge & Spa,** MM 81.8 O/S, US 1, Islamorada. A luxury oceanside resort; elegant, yet very paddle-friendly. The beachside cabanas have hammocks and screened porches overlooking the ocean. Condos with multibedrooms and full kitchens also available. Pools, hot tub, full-service spa, kayaks to use, fishing pier, sunset boat tours, and outdoor and indoor dining and beach bar. Land at the south end of the beach, and register your boats with the front desk. (800–327–2888, www.cheeca.com) N24°54 936' W80°37 975'

Chart 17 and Chart 18

D1 and B4 **Matecumbe Resort,** MM 76.3 O/S, US 1, Islamorada. Water-view units on Matecumbe Bight. All 32 units have kitchens and sleep four. Boat ramp and beach with seawall. (305–664–8801) N24°52.123' W80°42.190'

D1 and B4 **White Gate Court,** MM 76.1 B/S, US 1, Islamorada. Cute yellow cottages; beach and a dock on Matecumbe Bight. Pets welcome. (800–645–GATE, www.whitegatecourt.com) N24°52.200' W80°42.545'

D1 and B4 **Coral Bay Resort,** MM 75.8 B/S, US 1, Islamorada. Water-view cottages with kitchens. Tidal pool, heated swimming pool, and fishing pier. Sandy beach and boat ramp on Matecumbe Bight. (305–664–5568, www.coralbayresort.com) N24°51.961' W80°42.833'

Chart 19

B5 **Lime Tree Bay Resort,** MM 68.5 B/S, US 1, Long Key. Pure Keys relaxation with waterfront efficiencies, hammocks, tiki huts, and pool. Beach has low seawall. (305–664–8919 or 800–723–4519, www.limetreebayresort.com) N24°49.484' W80°48.958'. *Note:* Slated for conversion to condo hotel in 2008. Call ahead for status.

Chart 20

A5 **Bayview Inn & Marina,** MM 63 B/S, US 1, Conch Key. Small, family-owned, friendly motel with pool, tiki hut, apartments and rooms, and general store. Bay and ocean access from its boat ramp. (305–289–1525, www.bayview inn.com) Concrete boat ramp: N24°47.414' W80°53.348'.   Sandy beach: N24°47.404' W80°53.309'

A5 **Conch Key Cottages,** MM 62.2 O/S, US 1, Walkers Island. Cute resort on its own small island connected to US 1 by a short causeway. Efficiency and 1–2 bedroom cottages, pool, and beach. Free use of two-person kayak during stay. (800–330–1577, www.conchkeycottages.com) N24°47.065' W80°53.810'

C1 **Yellowtail Inn,** MM 58.2 O/S, US 1, Grassy Key. Oceanfront cottages and efficiencies. Manatee Bay Restaurant is next door. Kayaks available. (800–605–7475, www.yellow-tailinn.com) N24°45.558' W80°57.238'

C1 **Bonefish Resort,** MM 58.1 O/S, US 1, Grassy Key. Modest oceanfront efficiencies. Small, sheltered beach, and tandem kayak rentals. (800–274–9949, www.bonefish resort.com) N24°45.507' W80°57.318'

C2 **Gulfview Waterfront Resort,** MM 58.5 B/S, US 1, Grassy Key. Efficiencies on the bay. Kayaks for guest use. Within walking distance of the Dolphin Research Center and the Wreck and Galley Grill. (305–289–1414, www.gulfviewwaterfrontresort.com) N24°45.955' W80°56.904'

Chart 20 and Chart 21

C1 and A6 **Seashell Beach Resort,** MM 57.5 O/S, US 1, Grassy Key. This resort features 10 efficiencies, each one mere steps from the Atlantic Ocean. Kayaks for guest use. Beach has riprap and concrete ramp. (305–289–0265, www.seashellbeachresort.com) N24°45.289' W80°57.611'

Chart 21

B5 **Valhalla Point Resort,** 56.5 O/S, Banana Boulevard, Little Crawl Key. Secluded oceanfront resort near Curry Hammock State Park. Eight rooms, some efficiencies, face the beach. (305–360–2726, www.keysresort.com) N24°44.589' W80°58.744'

Chart 22

A6 **Tropical Cottages,** MM 50.5 B/S, 243 61st Street, Marathon. Restored 1950s beach cottages. Free use of kayaks and canoes. Sandy beach. Adults only. (305–743–6048, www.tropicalcottages.com) N24 43.159' W81 04.242'

A6 **Coconut Cay Resort & Marina,** MM 50.5 B/S, US 1, Marathon. Efficiencies, beach, pool, and concrete boat ramp. (877–354–7356, www.coconutcay.com) N24°43.245' W81°03.821'

B4 **Banana Bay Resort Marathon,** MM 49.5 B/S, US 1, Marathon. 10 acres on the Gulf. Restaurant, tiki bar, pool, tennis, Jacuzzi, beach. Kayak rentals. (305–743–3500 or 800–BANANA–1, www.bananabay.com) N24°42.980' W81°05.080'

B5 **Sombrero Cay Club,** MM 50 O/S, 19 Sombrero Boulevard, Marathon. Located on a canal off Boot Key Harbor. Pool, tennis, and golf on premises. Kayak rentals. (800–433–8660, www.sombreroresort.com) Concrete ramp: N24°42.769' W81°04.801'

B5 **Sombrero Reef Inn & Fishing Lodge,** MM 51.9 O/S, 500 Sombrero Beach Road, Marathon. Efficiencies on canal a short distance from the ocean. Kayaks for rental. (305–743–4118, www.sombreroreefinn.com) Concrete ramp: N24°42.061' W81°04.769'

Chart 26 and Chart 30

C2 and B6 **Old Wooden Bridge Guest Cottages and Marina,** MM 30.5 G/S, Watson Boulevard, Big Pine Key. A 14-unit efficiency motel, store, and marina located at the foot of the bridge linking Big Pine to No Name Key. Access to Bogie Channel. (305–872–2241, www.oldwooden bridge.com) N24°41.843' W81°20.909'

Chart 27

C4 **Bahia Honda State Park,** MM 36.8 O/S, US 1, Bahia Honda Key. Cabins for rent. Information: 305-872-2353; reservations: 800-326-3521, www.reserveamerica.com. Boat ramp. N 24°39.396' W81°16.690'.

Chart 30

C3 **Parmer's Resort,** MM 28.5 G/S, 565 Barry Avenue, Little Torch Key. Five acres on Pine Channel, providing gulf and ocean access. Rooms, efficiencies, one- or two-bedroom suites, pool, and laundry. Near Parrotdise Restaurant. Boat ramp; units closest to ramp are named Snapper, Tern, Pelican, and Wahoo. (305–872–2157, www.parmers resort.com) N24°40.438' W81°23.245'

Chart 31

A2 **Looe Key Reef Resort,** MM 27.4 O/S, Ramrod Key. Outdoor tiki bar, pool, and concrete ramp on a canal. It is a 15-minute paddle out to Ramrod Channel. Launch is free if staying at the resort. (800–942–5397, www.diveflakeys .com) N24°39.695' W81°24.356'

A3 **Dolphin Resort & Marina,** 28.5 O/S, Pirates Road, Little Torch Key. Full kitchens, screened porches, and kayak rentals. Guest cottages 3 and 4 are closest to the marina's sandy beach. Access to Pine Channel. (800–553–0308, www.dolphinmarina.net) N24°39.889' W81°23.188'

C2 **Little Palm Island Resort,** 28.5 O/S, Little Munson Island in Newfound Harbor. Access by motor yacht shuttle from the resort's Shore Station on Pirates Road, Little Torch Key. Special arrangements and reservations required to land by kayak for lodging, dining, or spa. (305–872–2524, www.littlepalmisland.com) N24°37.435' W81°24.123'

B7 **Big Pine Key Fishing Lodge,** MM 32.8 O/S, US 1, Big Pine Key. Boat ramp, motel, and campground on Spanish Harbor Channel. Grocery store, laundry, recycling, and a small swimming beach. Nature trail leads along the waterfront into the Great White Heron National Wildlife Refuge. Launching for registered guests only. (305–872–2351) Concrete boat ramp: N24°38.890′ W81°19.898

Chart 39

C4 **Sugarloaf Lodge & Restaurant,** MM 17 G/S, US 1, Sugarloaf Key. Waterfront rooms, tiki bar, and a restaurant that serves breakfast, lunch, and dinner. Access to Upper Sugarloaf Sound. (800–553–6097, www.sugarloaflodge.com) N24°38.831′ W81°33.919′

Chart 47

B4 **Fairfield Inn and Suites,** MM 2, 2401 N. Roosevelt Boulevard (US 1), Key West. Studios to one-bedroom suites. One pool and a tiki bar. Kayak tours. (305–296–5700, www.fairfieldinnkeywest.com) N24°33.776′ W81°46.641′

B4 **Banana Bay Resort Key West,** MM 2, 2319 N. Roosevelt Boulevard (US 1), Key West. Adult waterfront resort. Marina has a kayak landing on a canal. Pool, sunning beach, and tiki bar. (866–566–6688, www.bananabay resortkeywest.com) N24°33.735′ W81°46.678′

Paddle-Friendly Dining

Here are a few special places where you can easily pull in a boat and get a bite to eat on your day or overnight trip. They are all "Keys casual," so customers with sandy feet and wet bottoms are welcome. Toasting the sunset is a perfect way to end a paddling adventure, so we've included some favorite watering holes as well.

Chart 7

D2 **Caribbean Club,** MM 104 B/S, US 1, Key Largo. The only food they serve is potato chips (unless Robbie is cooking up a barbecue), but this is our all-time favorite place to toast the end of a trip and the sunset. The original hotel burned down years ago, but this is where a couple of scenes of the famous Bogart and Bacall film *Key Largo* were shot. Adjacent to Florida Bay Outfitters, which has a small, sandy beach launch. N25°08.724′ W80°23.820′

B3 **Buzzard's Roost,** MM 106.5 O/S, 21 Garden Cove Drive, Key Largo. Casual, excellent seafood dining and bar. Located at the end of a home canal near Garden Cove. Channel Marker 19 is at the entrance to the canal. (305–453–3746, www.buzzroost.com) Kayak-level dock: N25°10.228′ W80°22.286′

Chart 9

B3 **John Pennekamp Coral Reef State Park,** MM 102.5 O/S, US 1, Key Largo. The snack bar has lunch selections and ice cream (we recommend the hot dog with everything). Great gift shop; aquarium next door. Land/launch on the north end of Cannon Beach, outside the swimming buoys. Pay the pedestrian entrance fee if arriving by kayak. (305–451–1202, www.floridastateparks.org/pennekamp) Cannon Beach: N25°07.564′ W80°24.329′

Chart 11

B1 **Key Largo Grande Resort,** MM 97 B/S, US 1, Key Largo. Beach grill, open to the public, serves a great grouper sandwich. Nice lunch stop for paddlers and there's a tiki bar, too. (305–852–5553, www.keylargoresort.com) N25°04.071′ W80°28.295′

B2 **Mandalay Restaurant & Marina,** MM 97.5 O/S, East Second Street, Key Largo. An open-air seafood restaurant on the ocean, frequented by sailboaters who land their dinghies on the gravel beach. Live music. (marina: 305–853–0296; restaurant: 305–852–5450; www.the mandalay.com) N25°04.381′ W80°27.631′

Chart 13

A3 **Snapper's Waterfront Saloon, Restaurant and Turtle Club Bar,** MM 94.5 O/S, Seaside Avenue, Tavernier. Eat outside on the dock for lunch or dinner. Each night features entertainment, which may be a live local radio show. Reservations suggested for evening dining. Pull up to small concrete ramp to the right of the Turtle Bar. (305–852–5956, www.dovecreeklodge.com/dining.htm) N25°02.411′ W80°29.513′

Chart 16

A4 **Island Grille,** MM 85.5 O/S, US 1, on the west side of the Snake Creek Bridge, Islamorada. Land on their gravel beach for dining dockside at this lively lunch and dinner spot. Inside is nightly entertainment; outside, a manatee is likely to swim by. (305–664–8400) N24°57.091′ W80°35.316′

B3 **Holiday Isle Resort,** MM 84 O/S, US 1, Islamorada. This famous party-time resort has several open-air restaurants and bars. Land at sandy kayak launch at the north end of the beach near Rumrunner's tiki bar. *Note:* This location has been sold for possible redevelopment; call ahead for status. (800–327–7070, www.holidayisle.com) Sandy launch: N24°56.537′ W80°36.256′.

Chart 16 and Chart 17

C2 and A5 **Lorelei's Restaurant & Cabana Bar,** MM 82 B/S, US 1, Islamorada. Famous for its sunsets, seafood, and live music at the outdoor tiki bar. Land on the gravel beach beyond the tiki bar. (305–664–4656, www.loreleiflorida keys.com) N24°55.326′ W80°38.011′

Chart 17

B5 **Worldwide Sportsman, Zane Grey Lounge and Islamorada Fish Company,** MM 81.5 B/S, US 1, Islamorada. Rest stop for shopping at Worldwide Sportsman BassPro Shop, home of the sister ship of Ernest Hemingway's fishing boat. Dine at the Islamorada Fish Company or the Zane Grey Lounge. (305–664–4615) Concrete boat ramp: N24°54.932′ W80°38.375′.

B5 **Cheeca Lodge & Spa,** MM 81.8 O/S, US 1, Islamorada. Check in with the beach hut if stopping for a casual lunch at the Beach Bar or the Ocean Terrace Grill. Land at the south end of the beach. (866–591–ROCK, www.cheeca.com) N24°54.936′ W80°37.975′

D2 **Hungry Tarpon at Robbie's Marina,** MM 77.4 B/S, US 1, Islamorada. Land at the sandy beach next to the kayak shop; go inside to see if they want you to pay the launch fee. The Hungry Tarpon is tiny, but its breakfast and lunch are legendary. Visit and feed the real tarpons next door at Robbie's. (305–664–0535, www.hungrytarpon.com) N24°52.992′ W80°41.455′

Chart 21

B2 **Island Tiki Bar & Restaurant,** MM 53.9 B/S, US 1, Marathon, next to Marathon Boat Ramp. (305–743–4191) N24°43.996′ W80°01.086′

Chart 22

B3 **Cajun's Cove at 7 Mile Marina & Grill,** MM47.5 B/S, US 1, Marathon. A favorite spot for charter boat captains, serving lunch and dinner daily. Land on a small gravel beach. (305–395–0546) N24°42.509′ W81°06.860′

Chart 34 and Chart 35

E5 and D6 **Picnic Park & Key West Fishcutters,** MM 25.1 G/S, US 1, Summerland Key. Picnic area and restaurant (take out or eat in, BYOB) on picturesque canal with working fishing boats and lobster traps. Watch them bring in the catch, then order it up inside. Small kayak landing. (305–744–3335) N24°39.688′ W81°26.396′

Chart 34

E1 **Buon Appetito Ristorante,** MM 21 O/S, Drost Road, Cudjoe Key. Land at adjacent Cudjoe Gardens Marina boat ramp. Open for dinner only. (305–745–1711) Ramp: N24°39.494′ W81°30.340′.

Chart 44

C6 **Geiger Key Marina,** MM 10.8 O/S, Geiger Road, Geiger Key. Friendly, fun tiki bar and smokehouse on the "backside of paradise." Live music on weekends. (305–296–3553, www.geigerkeymarina.com) N24°34.905′ W81°38.910′

Chart 46

C5 **Hurricane Joe's Bar & Grill,** MM 4.2 O/S, US 1, Stock Island. Lunch and dinner daily. Located next to Lazy Dog Island Outfitters. A great place to end a day of paddling the Key West salt ponds. (305–294–0200) N24°34.262′ W81°44.853′

Chart 47

C3 **Captain Runaground Harvey's Floating Pub and Grub,** Garrison Bight City Marina, N. Roosevelt Boulevard, Key West. Local hangout, serving seafood fresh from Charterboat Row. (305–296–9907, www.strandlopersport fishing.com/runagrounds.htm) N24°33.592′ W81°47.075′

D3 **Louie's Backyard,** 700 Waddell Avenue O/S, Key West. Land at adjacent Dog Beach. It's pretty fancy inside, but paddlers are welcome to a casual lunch on the Afterdeck. They serve up excellent seafood and Caribbean dishes. (305–294–1061, www.louiesbackyard.com) N24°32.829′ W81°47.571′

D2 **Cayo Hueso Cafe,** Fort Zachary Taylor Historic State Park, Key West. Take a tour of the historic fort, the have lunch or a snack. Land at east end of the beach away from swimmers; use the kayak area marked with buoys. If arriving by kayak, be sure to pay the park pedestrian entrance fee. (305–295–0037, www.fortzacharytaylor.com) N24°32.720′ W81°48.540′

C2 **Simonton Street Beach,** north end of Simonton Street, Old Town Key West. All the eating and drinking that Duval Street offers is just a block away, but only if you're comfortable leaving your boat on a city beach that is a popular hangout. Two Friends Patio Restaurant is closest, on Front Street. It's an open-air seafood sports bar and a great spot for people-watching. (305–296–3124, www.two friendskeywest.com) N24°33.721′ W81°48.338′

Go-to Points

Chart	Grid	Label	Latitude	Longitude
Chart 1	B4	1 Angelfish Ocean	25° 20.018'	80° 15.272'
	B3	2 Angelfish Bay	25° 20.092'	80° 16.656'
Chart 2	B3	1	25° 19.705'	80° 21.019'
	B4	2	25° 19.640'	80° 20.993'
	B3	3	25° 19.549'	80° 21.067'
	B3	4 Ghost Trap Lake	25° 19.577'	80° 21.548'
	B2	5 Cable Creek	25° 19.142'	80° 22.459'
	C2	6 Little Card Sound	25° 18.372'	80° 22.617'
	D5	7 Steamboat North	25° 17.166'	80° 19.782'
Chart 3	A4	1 Steamboat North	25° 17.166'	80° 19.782'
	C3	2 Steamboat South	25° 15.982'	80° 20.522'
Chart 4	B1	1	25° 15.978'	80° 26.322'
	B1	2	25° 15.855'	80° 26.164'
	B2	3	25° 15.432'	80° 25.945'
	B2	4	25° 15.284'	80° 25.962'
	B2	5	25° 15.402'	80° 25.792'
	B2	6	25° 15.676'	80° 25.626'
	B2	7	25° 15.878'	80° 25.511'
	A2	8	25° 16.031'	80° 25.357'
	A3	9	25° 16.275'	80° 24.884'
	A3	10	25° 16.322'	80° 24.756'
	A3	11	25° 16.035'	80° 24.607'
	B2	12 C111 Canal	25° 15.427'	80° 25.387'
	B2	13 Jim Smith Creek	25° 15.774'	80° 25.222'
	B3	14 Short Key Cut	25° 15.635'	80° 24.067'
Chart 5	D1	1 Jewfish Creek North	25° 11.904'	80° 23.114'
Chart 6	C6	1	25° 12.122'	80° 25.588'
	C2	2	25° 12.752'	80° 29.219'
	C2	3	25° 12.412'	80° 29.242'
	D5	4 Blackwater Pass	25° 11.941'	80° 26.080'
	B4	5 Long Sound Pass	25° 13.373'	80° 27.272'
Chart 7	B2	1	25° 10.382'	80° 23.182'
	C3	2	25° 09.051'	80° 22.099'
	C3	3	25° 09.232'	80° 22.283'
	C3	4	25° 09.299'	80° 22.319'
	D2	5	25° 08.995'	80° 23.107'
	D2	6	25° 08.504'	80° 23.014'
	D3	7	25° 08.502'	80° 22.817'
	D2	8	25° 08.610'	80° 23.256'
	B2	9 Jewfish Creek	25° 10.969'	80° 23.321'
	B4	10 Rattlesnake	25° 10.028'	80° 21.824'
Chart 8	B3	1	25° 10.835'	80° 29.376'
	B5	2 Boggies North	25° 10.527'	80° 27.177'
	B5	3 Boggies South	25° 10.337'	80° 27.032'
	D7	4 Dusenbury Creek	25° 08.600'	80° 25.453'
Chart 9	A2	1	25° 08.083'	80° 25.487'
	B2	2	25° 07.831'	80° 25.739'
	B2	3	25° 07.610'	80° 25.582'
	B2	4	25° 07.771'	80° 25.401'
	B1	5	25° 07.676'	80° 26.595'
	A4	6	25° 08.504'	80° 23.014'
	A5	7	25° 08.502'	80° 22.817'
	A4	8	25° 08.610'	80° 23.256'
	A4	9	25° 08.233'	80° 23.753'
	A3	10	25° 08.323'	80° 24.258'
	B4	11	25° 07.432'	80° 24.001'
	C3	12	25° 06.952'	80° 24.127'
	C3	13	25° 06.905'	80° 24.058'
	C3	14	25° 06.834'	80° 24.133'
	A2	15 Dusenbury Creek	25° 08.600'	80° 25.453' Map
	B4	16 S. Sound Mangroves	25° 07.282'	80° 23.897'
	C3	17 Trail Of Tears	25° 06.317'	80° 24.473'
	C3	18 S. Sound Creek	25° 06.155'	80° 24.850'
Chart 10	D5	1	25° 05.764'	80° 28.400'
	B6	2 Little Buttonwood Sound	25° 07.824'	80° 27.431'
	C4	3 Upper Swash Pass	25° 06.512'	80° 29.034'
Chart 11	B2	1	25° 04.523'	80° 27.160'
	B3	2	25° 04.756'	80° 26.982'
	C3	3	25° 03.116'	80° 26.780'
	B2	4 Rock Harbor	25° 04.277'	80° 27.263'
	B3	5 Home Canal	25° 04.978'	80° 26.169'
	A1	6 Lower Swash Pass	25° 05.397'	80° 28.520'
Chart 12	A4	1	25° 05.364'	80° 31.393'
	B5	2 Butternut Key	25° 04.827'	80° 30.605'
	B2	3 Bottle Key	25° 04.008'	80° 33.210'
Chart 13	C1	1	25° 00.915'	80° 31.146'
	B3	2	25° 01.785'	80° 29.821'
	A3	3 Dove Creek	25° 02.194'	80° 29.565'
	D2	4 Tavernier Key	24° 59.813'	80° 30.284'

Chart	Grid	Label	Latitude	Longitude
Chart 14	C5	1	25° 00.915'	80° 31.146'
	C3	2	25° 00.411'	80° 33.441'
	C3	3	25° 00.042'	80° 33.583'
	C3	4	25° 00.001'	80° 33.069'
	D4	5	24° 59.891'	80° 32.819'
	C4	6 Tavernier Cr Bay	25° 00.880'	80° 32.702'
	D5	7 Tavernier Cr Ocean	24° 59.865'	80° 31.762'
Chart 15	C2	1	24° 58.072'	80° 35.708'
	A4	2	25° 00.411'	80° 33.441'
	A4	3	25° 00.042'	80° 33.583'
	A4	4	25° 00.001'	80° 33.069'
	B5	5	24° 59.891'	80° 32.819'
	B7	6 Tavernier Key	24° 59.813'	80° 30.284'
	B6	7 Tavernier Cr Ocean	24° 59.865'	80° 31.762'
Chart 16	C1	1	24° 55.262'	80° 38.232'
	C1	2 Little Basin North	24° 55.328'	80° 38.563'
	A4	3 Snake Cr Ocean	24° 57.020'	80° 35.217'
Chart 17	A5	1	24° 55.262'	80° 38.232'
	A5	2 Little Basin North	24° 55.328'	80° 38.563'
	B5	3	24° 54.848'	80° 38.935'
	B5	4 Little Basin South	24° 54.689'	80° 38.890'
	A4	5	24° 55.675'	80° 39.993'
	D1	6	24° 52.814'	80° 42.244'
	C2	7	24° 53.127'	80° 41.463'
	C2	8 Wheel Ditch	24° 53.102'	80° 41.787'
	B2	9 Lignumvitae	24° 54.166'	80° 41.676'
	D3	10 Indian Key	24° 52.723'	80° 40.679'
Chart 18	B4	5	24° 52.810'	80° 42.448'
	B4	6	24° 52.814'	80° 42.244'
	A5	7	24° 53.127'	80° 41.463'
	A5	8 Wheel Ditch	24° 53.102'	80° 41.787'
Chart 19	B5	1	24° 49.072'	80° 48.887'
	B6	2	24° 49.582'	80° 47.447'
	B5	3 Mangrove Creeks	24° 49.423'	80° 48.475'
Chart 20	C3	1	24° 45.912'	80° 55.927'
	B2	2	24° 46.195'	80° 56.195'
	B4	3	24° 46.751'	80° 54.850'
	C4	4	24° 45.872'	80° 54.670'
	C3	5 Duck Key Channel	24° 45.911'	80° 55.393'
Chart 21	B5	1	24° 44.756'	80° 58.952'
	C3	2	24° 43.834'	81° 00.773'
	C2	3	24° 43.740'	81° 01.183'
	C3	4	24° 43.319'	81° 00.674'
	C4	5	24° 43.980'	80° 59.462'
	B5	6 Crawl Key Sound	24° 44.816'	80° 58.302'
	B4	7 Deer Key	24° 44.510'	80° 59.291'
	B3	8 Coco Plum Trail	24° 44.058'	81° 00.376'
Chart 22	C4	1	24° 41.531'	81° 05.762'
	C4	2	24° 41.604'	81° 05.924'
	C3	3	24° 41.709'	81° 06.020'
	C4	4	24° 41.781'	81° 05.841'
	C4	5	24° 41.498'	81° 05.291'
	C4	6 Sister Creek	24° 41.765'	81° 05.672'
	B3	7 Boot Key Mangrove	24° 42.116'	81° 06.157'
Chart 23	A6	1 Pigeon Key	24° 42.294'	81° 09.315'
	B4	2 Molasses Key	24° 41.158'	81° 11.328'
Chart 24	B3	1	24° 46.056'	81° 17.140'
	C2	2	24° 45.318'	81° 18.916'
	D1	3	24° 44.390'	81° 19.469'
Chart 25	C2	1	24° 42.973'	81° 18.017'
	B1	2 Little Pine Key	24° 43.732'	81° 19.590'
Chart 26	B4	1	24° 42.973'	81° 18.017'
	D4	2	24° 40.919'	81° 18.866'
	B2	3	24° 42.081'	81° 20.433'
	B1	4	24° 42.033'	81° 21.303'
	B1	5	24° 42.363'	81° 21.496'
	A3	6 Little Pine Key	24° 43.732'	81° 19.590'
	B2	7 No Name Mangrove	24° 42.137'	81° 20.583'
	D3	8 Refuge Bight	24° 40.848'	81° 19.562'
	B1	9 Doctors Point	24° 42.321'	81° 21.196'
Chart 27	C4	1	24° 39.916'	81° 16.053'
	B2	2	24° 40.919'	81° 18.866'
	B1	3 Refuge Bight	24° 40.848'	81° 19.562'
	C4	4 South Sound	24° 39.684'	81° 16.109'
Chart 28	D3	1	24° 45.689'	81° 24.335'
	D3	2	24° 45.571'	81° 24.076'
	C5	3	24° 46.407'	81° 22.406'
	B3	4	24° 47.278'	81° 24.443'
	D3	5 Cutoe	24° 45.979'	81° 24.881'
Chart 29	A2	1	24° 45.689'	81° 24.335'
	A2	2	24° 45.571'	81° 24.076'
	B2	3	24° 44.651'	81° 24.387'
	C2	4	24° 43.644'	81° 24.248'
	C5	5	24° 43.305'	81° 21.245'
	B2	6 Howe Key Creek	24° 44.501'	81° 24.198'

Chart	Grid	Label	Latitude	Longitude
Chart 30	A1	1	24° 42.127'	81° 25.187'
	C2	2	24° 40.555'	81° 24.546'
	A6	3	24° 42.081'	81° 20.433'
	A5	4	24° 42.033'	81° 21.303'
	A5	5	24° 42.363'	81° 21.496'
	A5	6 Doctors Point	24° 42.321'	81° 21.196'
	A6	7 No Name Mangrove	24° 42.137'	81° 20.583'
Chart 31	A6	1	24° 39.210'	81° 20.736'
	B5	2	24° 38.660'	81° 21.046'
	B6	3	24° 38.362'	81° 20.655'
	C5	4	24° 37.318'	81° 21.801'
	C4	5	24° 37.622'	81° 22.609'
	C3	6	24° 37.561'	81° 23.519'
	C3	7	24° 37.424'	81° 23.837'
	B6	8 Coupon Bight	24° 38.767'	81° 20.848'
	C3	9 Coral Heads	24° 37.127'	81° 22.829'
	C3	10 Mangrove Tunnel	24° 37.456'	81° 23.736'
Chart 32	C3	1	24° 47.409'	81° 28.232'
	B3	2	24° 48.016'	81° 28.411'
	C2	3	24° 47.460'	81° 29.900'
	D4	4	24° 46.281'	81° 27.474'
	C3	5 Contents East	24° 47.861'	81° 28.099'
	C3	6 Content Pass	24° 47.557'	81° 28.921'
	C2	7 Content West	24° 47.158'	81° 29.781'
Chart 33	D4	1	24° 42.881'	81° 28.777'
	D3	2	24° 42.495'	81° 29.036'
	D3	3	24° 42.848'	81° 29.822'
	C1	4	24° 43.613'	81° 31.112'
	B5	5 Big Torch Mangroves	24° 44.357'	81° 27.080'
	A5	6 Water Keys	24° 45.253'	81° 27.159'
	B3	7 Raccoon Key	24° 44.720'	81° 29.848'
Chart 34	B3	1	24° 42.881'	81° 28.777'
	B2	2	24° 42.495'	81° 29.036'
	B2	3	24° 42.848'	81° 29.822'
	B3	4	24° 42.276'	81° 28.801'
	B3	5	24° 42.001'	81° 28.772'
	C3	6	24° 41.439'	81° 28.570'
	C4	7	24° 41.408'	81° 27.956'
	D4	8	24° 40.801'	81° 27.480'
	B2	9 Knock North	24° 42.053'	81° 29.100'
	D4	10 Knock South	24° 40.617'	81° 27.596'
Chart 35	A2	1	24° 42.206'	81° 30.750'
	A2	2	24° 41.947'	81° 31.036'
	B2	3	24° 41.603'	81° 30.346'
	A4	4	24° 42.276'	81° 28.801'
	A4	5	24° 42.001'	81° 28.772'
	B4	6	24° 41.439'	81° 28.570'
	B5	7	24° 41.408'	81° 27.956'
	C5	8	24° 40.801'	81° 27.480'
	A3	9 Knock North	24° 42.053'	81° 29.100'
	C5	10 Knock South	24° 40.617'	81° 27.596'
Chart 36	C1	1	24° 37.853'	81° 31.015'
	C2	2 Tarpon Creek	24° 37.580'	81° 30.621'
	C4	3 Key Lois	24° 37.117'	81° 28.823'
Chart 37	D6	1	24° 43.882'	81° 31.289'
	C5	2	24° 44.939'	81° 32.795'
	B4	3 Sawyer South	24° 45.221'	81° 33.301'
	B4	4 Sawyer North	24° 45.530'	81° 33.893'
Chart 38	B2	1	24° 42.637'	81° 35.543'
	B6	2 Cudjoe	24° 42.117'	81° 31.233'
	A3	3 Johnston Patch	24° 43.227'	81° 34.522'
	A1	4 Barracuda East	24° 43.199'	81° 36.375'
Chart 39	B1	1	24° 39.585'	81° 36.348'
	C2	2	24° 38.965'	81° 35.749'
	C2	3	24° 38.840'	81° 35.347'
	C2	4	24° 38.656'	81° 35.367'
	B3	5	24° 39.518'	81° 34.335'
	B3	6	24° 39.154'	81° 34.252'
	C6	7	24° 38.279'	81° 31.657'
	C2	8 Fivemile Mangrove	24° 38.614'	81° 35.498'
	C2	9 Fivemile South	24° 38.811'	81° 35.125'
	B2	10 Fivemile North	24° 39.335'	81° 35.865'
	A4	11 Dreguez Cut	24° 40.144'	81° 33.587'
	C1	12 Old Finds #1	24° 38.079'	81° 36.709'
Chart 40	A4	1	24° 37.178'	81° 33.666'
	B4	2	24° 36.560'	81° 33.868'
	A2	3	24° 37.000'	81° 35.405'
	A4	4 Missle Pad Creek #1	24° 37.361'	81° 33.799'
	B4	5 Missle Pad Creek #2	24° 36.465'	81° 33.918'
	B3	6 Sugarloaf Creek Sound	24° 36.476'	81° 34.361'
	B3	7 Sugarloaf Creek Ocean	24° 36.174'	81° 34.223'
Chart 41	A6	1	24° 43.024'	81° 37.226'
	C4	2	24° 41.155'	81° 39.967'
	C3	3	24° 41.383'	81° 40.135'
	C3	4	24° 41.263'	81° 40.195'
	C3	5	24° 41.301'	81° 40.394'
	C3	6	24° 41.491'	81° 40.463'
	C3	7	24° 41.164'	81° 40.565'
	C3	8	24° 41.273'	81° 40.730'
	A7	9 Barracuda East	24° 43.199'	81° 36.375'
	B6	10 Barracuda West	24° 42.854'	81° 37.824'
	C4	11 Snipe East	24° 41.600'	81° 39.860'
	D2	12 Mud Keys North	24° 40.797'	81° 41.390'
Chart 42	B6	1	24° 40.036'	81° 37.697'
	A4	2	24° 41.155'	81° 39.967'
	A3	3	24° 41.383'	81° 40.135'
	A3	4	24° 41.263'	81° 40.195'
	A3	5	24° 41.301'	81° 40.394'
	A3	6	24° 41.491'	81° 40.463'
	A3	7	24° 41.164'	81° 40.565'
	A3	8	24° 41.273'	81° 40.730'
	B2	9	24° 40.778'	81° 41.707'
	C2	10 Mud Keys South	24° 39.200'	81° 41.665'
	B2	11 Mud Keys Middle	24° 40.097'	81° 41.608'
	B2	12 Mud Keys North	24° 40.797'	81° 41.390'
Chart 43	D4	1	24° 36.456'	81° 39.830'
	D5	2	24° 36.589'	81° 38.798'
	D4	3 Jim Pent Point	24° 36.958'	81° 39.591'
	C3	4 Duck Key	24° 37.190'	81° 40.976'
	A2	5 Mud Keys South	24° 39.200'	81° 41.665'
	B7	6 Old Finds #2	24° 38.139'	81° 36.878'
Chart 44	A6	1	24° 36.244'	81° 38.577'
	C4	2 Geiger North	24° 34.731'	81° 40.056'
	C4	3 Geiger South	24° 34.158'	81° 40.079'
Chart 45	B6	1	24° 38.165'	81° 43.531'
	B6	2	24° 38.559'	81° 43.507'
	B6	3	24° 38.948'	81° 43.939'
	B5	4	24° 38.456'	81° 44.374'
	B5	5	24° 38.003'	81° 44.721'
	C5	6	24° 37.943'	81° 44.878'
	C5	7 Cayo Agua	24° 37.768'	81° 44.649'
	B6	8 Lower Harbor Lake	24° 38.787'	81° 43.958'
Chart 46	D3	1	24° 33.871'	81° 46.944'
	D3	2	24° 33.822'	81° 46.409'
	A6	3	24° 36.230'	81° 43.445'
	A6	4	24° 36.410'	81° 43.300'
	D4	5 Riviera Canal	24° 33.876'	81° 45.010'
Chart 47	C4	1	24° 33.871'	81° 46.944'
	C4	2	24° 33.822'	81° 46.409'
	C5	3	24° 33.751'	81° 45.443'
	C5	4	24° 33.640'	81° 45.504'
	C5	5	24° 33.793'	81° 45.292'
	C5	6	24° 33.659'	81° 45.379'
	C4	7	24° 33.502'	81° 46.292'
	C5	8 Riviera Canal	24° 33.876'	81° 45.010'
Chart 48	F13	1	24° 33.871'	81° 46.944'
	F2	2 Mooney Harbor	24° 32.908'	82° 09.246'
Chart 49	B3	1	24° 35.372'	82° 08.159'
	B5	2	24° 35.176'	82° 06.977'
	D5	3	24° 33.482'	82° 06.666'
	E2	4 Mooney Harbor	24° 32.908'	82° 09.246'
Chart 50	C5	1	24° 37.848'	82° 52.218'
	C4	2	24° 37.228'	82° 53.071'
	B2	3	24° 38.087'	82° 55.255'
	C5	4 Dry Tortugas	24° 37.505'	82° 52.384'
	C2	5 Loggerhead Key	24° 37.915'	82° 55.175'
Chart 51	A11	1 Shell Creek*	25° 12.412'	80° 29.242'
	D11	2 Upper Swash Pass	25° 06.512'	80° 29.034'
	E11	3 Lower Swash Pass	25° 05.397'	80° 28.520'
	E9	4 Bottle Key	25° 04.008'	80° 33.210'
	E10	5 Butternut Key	25° 04.827'	80° 30.605'
	F8	6 Cut	25° 03.077'	80° 34.980'
	F8	7 Cut	25° 02.541'	80° 34.384'
Chart 52	G9	1	24° 58.468'	80° 49.488'
	F6	2	25° 01.804'	80° 55.379'
	D6	3	25° 04.802'	80° 55.948'
	D5	4	25° 05.322'	80° 56.577'
	C5	5	25° 06.386'	80° 56.717'
	C6	6	25° 07.462'	80° 55.115'
	C7	7	25° 07.431'	80° 53.492'
	C9	8	25° 07.866'	80° 52.380'
	C8	9	25° 07.465'	80° 51.348'
	C9	10	25° 07.380'	80° 49.558'

On Chart 6, This Go-To Point Is Labeled #3

Index

About the Authors

Mary and Bill Burnham have authored six guide-books and hundreds of articles on hiking and paddling in the southeastern United States. They lived in Key Largo and guided kayak trips throughout the Keys while researching this Atlas. They are American Canoe Association certified kayak instructors and work as guides part-time in Virginia and the Keys. What's their favorite Key? Any one that they can kayak out to and set up a tent facing the setting sun. Visit their Web site at www.BurnhamInk.com to sign in and say hello.